Up to our Knees

Books by Pat Anderson

NOVELS
The McGlinchy Code
The Crimes of Miss Jane Goldie
Torrent
A Toast to Charlie Hanrahan
Catalyst

FACTUAL
Clash of the Agnivores
Fear and Smear
Never Mind the Zombies
Yellow Peril
Rattus Agnivoricus
Up to Our Knees

FOR CHILDREN
The Skyscraper Rocket Ship
The Ceremony at Goreb Ridge
The Brain Thing
The Football Star
Mighty Pete and the
School Bully School

Up to our Knees

ANTI-CATHOLIC BIGOTRY IN SCOTLAND

Pat Anderson

Snowy Publications MMXVII

First published 2016
This edition 2017

Copyright © 2017 Pat Anderson

All rights reserved.

ISBN: 1545043418
ISBN-13: 978-1545043417

To Mick, wherever you are

Contents

Preface ix

<u>Introduction</u> xi

1. A Divided Nation 1
2. Divisions Unleashed 11
3. Fools in the Gap 17
4. Rebellious Scots 23
5. Why Don't You Go Home? 30
6. The Great White Hope 41
7. Roll of Honour 51
8. The Balancing Act 59
9. Rome on the Rates 68
10. U-Boats by Night 77
11. Glasgow Characters 86
12. Justification by Media I 95
13. Justification by Media II 106
14. Paedophile Priests 116
15. Irish Slaves 132
16. Most Oppressed People Ever..................... 143
17. Bigotry is Dead – Long Live Bigotry............ 156
18. Non-Protestant Protestants 166

Notes... 177

Preface

This is not a completely in-depth and wide-ranging study; that would take years of research and I would expect a doctorate at the end of it. I have, however, taken an approach that I believe others have avoided. Too many investigations feel the need to balance things up by looking at sectarian bigotry *towards* Scottish Protestants by Catholics. This, I believe, is a mistake and the research I have done backs this up; evidence of such bigotry simply does not exist.

I may be going against the accepted narrative here, but I am not a revisionist historian. Such an individual starts with a pre-conceived idea and then goes out to find evidence to back up their theory. I, on the other hand, went into my research cold and turned up some evidence that surprised me. My conclusions, therefore, are derived from my research. The conclusions I reached, however, would not please any anti-Catholic bigot and I would fully expect such a person to accuse me of having an agenda, even though I do not.

Hopefully, I have provided enough evidence to satisfy any non-bigoted reader. You might not agree with my conclusions but if it provides some food for thought and a different way of looking at things, then my work has been worthwhile.

A couple of points to consider. There is a major difference between not wanting to be dominated by the Catholic Church and hating Catholics and Catholicism. Often the desire can lead to fear and hatred, but not necessarily. After all, British people are welcome as tourists all over the World, although many nations long ago threw off the yoke of the British Empire and have no desire to be dominated by Britain ever again.

The Republic of Ireland fits into both my point and my allegory. There might be individuals there that still hate the English but, in general, it is all in the past. Very much in the present, however, is the reality of the great influence that the Catholic Church has had in Ireland until fairly recently. It is quite reasonable to imagine that wanting rid of this overly-pervasive influence does not mean that the Irish people are going to start burning churches or even priests.

This is an important point since it is central to my thesis of how anti-Catholic bigotry began in Scotland. It was not an immediate consequence of the Reformation; it actually came from outside the country. This might be a hard notion to swallow but, hopefully, I have provided enough evidence to support it.

I have used the convention of employing the English spelling 'Stuart' when speaking of the family ruling both England and Scotland. Much though she would have liked to have been, Mary, Queen of Scots was never Queen of England. I have, therefore, used the Scottish spelling, 'Stewart', in her case.

I hope you enjoy the book and find it informative as well as entertaining.

Introduction
A New Way:
The Reformation in Scotland

Reading any history of the Middle Ages in Europe, one thing stands out; it was all about families. You will read about nations doing such-and-such and how the papacy felt about this and that. The truth is, however, that those nations and that papacy were under the control of families; powerful families. Sometimes the same family might control the papacy as well as a nation and the situation was used to promote that family as much as possible.

Some families rose to brief power, only to disappear back into obscurity, like the Borgias. Others, though, had managed to worm their way into positions of power all over Europe. The Medici family, for example, had built a fortune from trading and banking. This allowed it to stretch its tentacles from its native Florence to all over Europe. The Medici married into royal families and entered the Church, dominating bishoprics and even producing four popes. The Medici, however, paled into insignificance next to the Habsburgs.

The Habsburgs turned dynastic marriages into a family business. Once they had secured a new territory, they made sure that no other family could do what they had done by subsequently marrying only within their own bloodline. This, of course, led to genetic problems and, even in the 16th Century, the Habsburgs were renowned for their physical disabilities and deformities. The Habsburg Jaw, or *mandibular prognathism* as it is known today, is a condition that causes the lower jaw to be longer than the upper, leading to a jutting chin and, sometimes, great difficulty in speaking, eating or even breathing.[1]

Not only were many Habsburgs hideously deformed; they were often quite feeble-minded as well. Charles II, for example, could not speak until he was four and could not walk until the age of eight.[2] Another Habsburg, a princess with a lower jaw like an open till drawer, had to be constantly attended by servants when outside.

If it were to rain, the poor woman was so simple-minded that she would stand, her mouth filling with water, and drown!

So successful were the Habsburgs that their huge chins stuck out on the coins of numerous nations and territories, including the new colonies in America. They even got a foot in the door in England; Henry VIII married Catherine of Aragon, whose sister married a Habsburg and produced Charles V, the Holy Roman Emperor. No doubt the Habsburgs already had one of their family lined up as a spouse as soon as Mary, daughter of Henry and Catherine, was born. (She eventually did marry a Habsburg.) It was hardly surprising that Henry was desperate for a son.

Of course, the Habsburgs had their rivals, chief of which was the Valois family that ruled France.[3] Other rulers took sides in this ongoing enmity, changing their allegiances as it suited their own agendas. Meanwhile, the rulers of the tiny nations of Europe wanted nothing more than to escape the attentions of these two powers. This was especially the case in Italy, which often provided the battleground for Habsburg and Valois ambitions. Into this already volatile situation came the Reformation.

Despite what many people think, the Reformation was not about overthrowing a corrupt Catholic Church and replacing it with a simpler organisation; it was about ideas. Martin Luther had discovered that there was a whole different way of looking at how one got to Heaven. There was no need to do good works or go to confession; all you needed was faith. Of course, there was a good deal more to it than that but, essentially, that was what Luther was saying.

Practically overnight, Europe was sent into turmoil as the new ideas spread and were taken up by many. It must have been an exhilarating time for ordinary people; and a frightening one for rulers. The Peasants Revolt in Germany showed that there was something dangerous in letting the lower orders read the Bible in their own language and presenting them with new ideas on religion.[4] Luther soon proved, however, that he was firmly on the side of those already in power.[5]

German rulers, therefore, had no reason to fear Luther's ideas and some of them took them up enthusiastically. Of course, there were those that genuinely believed in the new religion but it was also a convenient rallying call for opposition to the Habsburgs. Such a situation also arose in the Spanish Netherlands (Modern Holland, Belgium and Luxembourg), where the new religion became mixed up with the fight for Dutch independence; again, the Habsburgs were the enemy.

War in Germany was indecisive and led to the principle being adopted of *cuius regio, eius religio* – the ruler decides the religion – under the Peace of Augsburg in 1555.[6] This, however, only extended to Catholicism and Lutheranism. Excluded from these provisions were other Reformed religions; and there were plenty of them about.

The problem with Luther's revolution was, as he quickly discovered, that not everyone was willing to set the limits where he had. Things that Luther held dear, like transubstantiation, veneration of the Virgin Mary and even the singing of hymns in church, were tossed aside by others that considered them symbols of Catholicism. New churches sprang up all over Europe, all with different doctrines. The only things they had in common were a firm belief in Justification by Faith and hatred of the Catholic Church.

There was one other thing that all the new churches had in common, not only with each other but with the Catholic Church; that thing was intolerance. The Reformation had at first promised freedom but it soon became clear that conformity was the order of the day. What one had to conform to was determined by where one lived: Catholicism in Austria and certain parts of Germany, Lutheranism in other areas of Germany, Calvinism in Geneva. For ordinary people, it must have seemed as if they had just swapped one set of masters for another.

All over Europe, Catholics were burning Protestants, Protestants were burning Catholics, Protestants were burning Protestants and everybody was burning Anabaptists. So many people were going up in flames that probably global warming started, not with the Industrial Revolution, but in the 16th Century. Not every place in Europe, though, subscribed to this intolerance.

Mention Transylvania and everyone immediately thinks of old, black and white horror films, with the Frankenstein Monster, Dracula and the Wolfman doing battle with villagers, armed with flaming torches and pitchforks and led by the Burgomeister. This is primarily due to Bram Stoker setting his novel in the area. In reality, Transylvania, which the actual name suggests, is a beautiful place. It was also one of the most tolerant places in Europe in the 16th

Century.[7] By law, all churches had to live side by side and discrimination was completely illegal. The place has certainly been treated rather badly by history.

Equally, Scotland has been judged rather harshly by popular misconceptions of history. No matter how much you love the country, it has to be admitted that it is quite often a dark, dank, miserable place. And the public face of the Scottish Presbyterian has been of a dark, dank, miserable individual. A Scotsman was certainly not the type you would want to invite to a party! It is rather easy, therefore, to imagine the Reformation in Scotland as ushering in a period where dour, Catholic-hating Presbyterians were ready to burn anyone that inadvertently scratched his chest immediately after doing the same to his forehead. In fact, the Reformation in Scotland was a remarkably bloodless affair; certainly, when compared to England.

The number of Protestant martyrs in Scotland was actually less than two dozen, compared to about three hundred in England.[8] The contrast is even more pronounced if we look at the numbers of Catholic martyrdoms. In England, more than six hundred souls died for their Catholic faith; in Scotland, Catholic martyrs amounted to the grand total of one![9]

Of course, the obvious answer to this is that the population of England is far bigger than that of Scotland, so, proportionately, Scotland was no better than England. The fact is, however, that although the population of England is now about ten times that of Scotland,[10] the situation was completely different in the 16th Century. In 1600, there were about 800,000 people living in Scotland,[11] while the population of England and Wales combined was roughly 4 million.[12] The respective martyrdom figures, then, show that the Reformation in Scotland was nowhere near as murderous as that in England.

Unlike in practically every other country in Europe, the Reformation in Scotland was a popular mass movement, which took those in power completely by surprise.[13] It was not led or instigated by the nobility but by ordinary people learning of the new ideas coming from the continent. This fact also puts paid to another myth: that education in Scotland only started with the Reformation. How could the people find out about and discuss the new ideas of Luther and Zwingli if they were just an uneducated mass?

Bibles printed in English had made their way across the border from England, as well as translations of the ideas of Reformers from Germany and other areas. It was a heady mix and found a willing audience among a population tired of a Scottish church that was viewed as corrupt. There were other elements involved in the decision of many people to follow the new religion, not least of which was the fear of French domination.[14]

John Knox, at the time the Reformation took hold in Scotland, was in Europe, having fled England, where he had been helping to shape the Anglican Church under Edward VI, when Mary Tudor came to the throne. He then committed a huge political error by publishing a book, called, *The First Blast of the Trumpet against the Monstrous Regiment of Women'* in which he outlined his opposition to women being allowed to rule.[15] This was intended as a diatribe against Mary Tudor and Mary of Guise. Unfortunately, Mary Tudor died soon after the book was published, leaving the new Queen of England, Elizabeth, incensed at Knox's presumption.

His way back to England now blocked, by his own hand, Knox must have been completely disheartened. Then came the news from Scotland. Knox hurried back to help take charge of the Scottish Reformation. This is not as self-serving as it sounds; events had shown, time and again, that a strong hand was needed to stop things running out of control. Geneva, especially, had realised, through bitter experience, that Calvin's dictatorial ways were preferable to the anarchy that ensued when he was absent.[16] Knox obviously feared the same in-fighting happening in Scotland. And his fears were entirely justified by all the disagreements between the Reformed churches of Europe.

When Knox arrived in Scotland, it looked as if there might be civil war, with England and France being dragged in as well. Two armies faced each other, with the Scottish Regent's forces bolstered by soldiers from France. Rather considerately, however, Mary of Guise died before either side had recourse to arms. The French pulled out, the Regent's army gave in and the Protestants had won with scarcely a drop of blood spilled.

With Protestants now firmly in control of the country, it was time to consolidate their position and make sure that Roman Catholicism was removed altogether. Everywhere else in Europe this was the cue for wheeling out the chopping block and gathering firewood; not in Scotland, though. In Scotland, a rather more efficient, common-sense and humane method was found.

Instead of priests being rounded up and slaughtered wholesale, the clerics were given a choice: either continue to minister in the new church or retire with a stipend for the rest of their lives. Most monasteries and convents were left to their own devices, with the simple rule that they were not allowed to take on new recruits. Thus, the Roman Catholic Church in Scotland was just pensioned off and left to die a natural death.[17]

In fact, Catholicism did not die out in Scotland at all. Nobody seemed to be particularly bothered; so long as the Catholics worshipped in secret or in remote areas.[18] Celebrating mass was illegal but prosecutions were extremely rare and nobody lost their life for doing so. One thing, however, that was frowned upon was proselytising, trying to convert people back to Catholicism. Such was the mission of John Ogilvie, Scotland's only Catholic martyr and now a Catholic Saint.

A member of the landed gentry, Ogilvie went to Europe as a young man, where he was educated at some prestigious institutions in Germany and France. He converted to Roman Catholicism, was ordained a priest and became a member of the Society of Jesus. He felt a burning desire to go back to Scotland to minister to the few Catholics in Glasgow and also help bring others back to the faith. He was finally granted permission and returned to Scotland in 1613.

After a year, he was betrayed and arrested. He was tortured relentlessly but refused to divulge the names of his fellow Catholics. He was then tried as a traitor, because he refused to swear allegiance to James VI. After being paraded through the streets of Glasgow, he was hanged and drawn at Glasgow Cross.[19]

We were told the story of Blessed John Ogilvie, as he was known then, at school to illustrate how Catholics had suffered at the hands of the evil Protestants. I don't remember the details of the lessons but, no doubt, we finished with a rousing chorus of *Faith of Our Fathers*. It helped to ingrain in us a belief that Scotland had, since the Reformation, been a hotbed of sectarian bigotry against Catholics.

Something they never bothered to point out at school was that if some earnest, idealistic Calvinist from Scotland had gone to proselytise in France, Italy or Spain, they would have been subjected to much the same treatment that Ogilvie suffered, or worse. Anyone associated with him would have been rounded up and put to death as well. The latter, however, did not occur in Scotland.

It was probably an easy matter to find all those that had played a part in Ogilvie's ministry; there were very few Catholics in the Glasgow area, after all. Remarkably, when they were arrested, these people were imprisoned, fined and then pretty much admonished not to do it again. None of them were tortured and none were put to death.[20] Given the way Catholics and Protestants were murdering each other all over Europe, this was an astonishing act of leniency.

It appears that Catholicism in Scotland was treated in much the same way as modern Amsterdam views the buying and selling of recreational drugs. The Catholic Church might not appreciate being classed alongside drugs, but it is the attitude of the authorities that I am highlighting. The taking and trafficking of drugs are not, despite what many believe, legal in Amsterdam. It is simply the case that the authorities are prepared to turn a blind eye unless you are blatantly flouting the law openly. And that seems to have been how things operated in Scotland; as long as you were not shoving your Catholicism in people's faces, you would be left to just get on with it.

Tolerance is a word that is bandied about quite a lot these days, with nobody giving much thought to what it actually means. Folk speak of being tolerant of black people, homosexuals etc. when 'tolerant' is not what they mean at all. Tolerance is being prepared to put up with something, or someone, with which you do not agree and possibly feel downright antipathy towards. In the true sense of the word, Scotland after the Reformation could be described as a tolerant society. It was one of the few such places in the whole of Christendom.

Let us fast-forward about four hundred years to 2006. Figures were published that showed that sectarian assaults were on the increase in Scotland, with Roman Catholics bearing most of the brunt of this bigotry.[21] Some commentators viewed this as part of long-standing, anti-Catholic hatred in Scotland; something that nobody wanted to face up to.[22] As we have seen, however, this virulent, often violent, anti-Catholicism was not always a feature of Scottish society.

Essentially, the Protestants of Scotland had taken a pragmatic approach towards Catholicism after the Reformation, expecting it to just die out. There were no 'pogroms' against Catholics, as there were in other countries. And yet, here we were, four hundred years later, viewing anti-Catholic hatred and violence as something peculiarly Scottish. Not only that, but people were prepared to believe that this had been part-and-parcel of the Reformation in Scotland. What had happened over those four hundred years?

Actually, quite a lot happened, as you might expect; four centuries is a long time, after all. The most significant thing that happened during this time was Scotland coming a lot closer to England, due to the Union of Crowns in 1603 and the Union of Parliaments in 1707. To understand part of the cultural effect of this, it is worth looking at the Reformation in England.

Up to our Knees

A Never-Failing Irish Industry.

1
A Divided Nation: England under the Tudors

Henry VIII might have a (deserved) reputation as a womaniser, but he was not the gluttonous, lecherous, old sinner he comes across as. Well, perhaps he was, but he was also renowned for his intelligence and religious piety. He was a committed Catholic, who persecuted Protestants with the best of them and wrote a booklet attacking Luther, called, *Defence of the Seven Sacraments*. Pope Leo X awarded him the title *Defender of the Faith* for his efforts.[1] But everything was far from rosy in the Tudor household.

Henry's wife, Catherine of Aragon, had already been wed to his older brother, Arthur, who, Catherine swore, had died before the marriage was consummated. Even so, they had to get special permission from Pope Julius II for the marriage to go ahead. As time went on, however, Henry began to believe that the whole thing had been a mistake. The lack of a male heir, he was convinced, was a punishment from God. And Henry desperately needed a male heir.

If his daughter, Mary, inherited the throne, then there was every chance that England might descend into the type of civil war that had brought Henry's father to the throne. England had never had a queen, ruling in her own right, and the assumption was that there would be fierce competition for her hand; Habsburg chins would already be looming on the horizon. A male heir was essential to ensure the steadiness of, not only the Tudor dynasty, but England itself. With his current marriage cursed by God, Henry's only recourse was to get it annulled and find another wife.

Pope Clement VII might possibly have agreed to dissolve the marriage; in fact, it is highly likely since he was a Medici, a family to rival the Habsburgs in the pursuit of power and influence. Unfortunately, Clement had got himself embroiled in politics that were beyond his control and found himself on the wrong side of the continuing conflict between the Habsburgs and the Valois. This conflict, as usual, was occurring in Italy.

With the resources at his disposal, Charles V, of course, won the war, leaving Pope Clement at his mercy. Thereafter, Clement had to make sure he kept on the Emperor's good side. Charles, as a Habsburg, was hardly going to countenance a family link to the throne of England being severed. Consequently, Pope Clement could not even consider granting Henry's request.

Henry was left with no option but to break with Rome if he wanted his marriage annulled. That did not mean, however, that he wanted to abandon Catholicism. His dissolution of the monasteries notwithstanding, Henry proved where his sympathies lay when the Six Articles were made law in 1539.

By terms of the Six Articles, it was made illegal to deny transubstantiation, while confession and clerical celibacy were confirmed as integral doctrines of the Church of England.[2] It was clear that Henry's new church was in no way Protestant; nor was it intended that it should be. In fact, Protestants were not to be tolerated, even though England was deemed to be on the side of the Reformation.

Let us take the date of November 1534, when the Act of Supremacy made Henry VIII head of the Church in England, as the date at which England officially broke from Rome and the nation became, nominally at least, Protestant. After that date, until Henry's death in 1547, there were 53 Protestant martyrs in England, according to Foxe's famous book.[3] And those are only the ones that are recorded in the *Book of Martyrs*; there were certainly a lot more than that. In fact, it is possible, if not probable, that more Protestants died under Henry's supposed Protestant regime than under 'Bloody' Mary's Catholic one.

Although the history books record Henry's break with Rome as the being the Reformation reaching England, it was actually nothing of the sort. Essentially, the Church of England was just the Catholic Church with the King at its head instead of the Pope. Ann Boleyn was a Protestant and was instrumental in helping to keep her co-religionists from the flames. Once Ann was executed, however, Protestants found themselves persecuted just as much as they had been before the break with Rome.

Things began to look up for English Protestants when Henry died.

The young Edward VI was only nine when he came to the throne in January 1547 so, by terms of Henry's will, a council of regency ruled the kingdom until he came of age.[4] There is still debate over the legitimacy of Henry's will; whether it was a forgery or a manipulation by a powerful group of Evangelical Protestants.[5] Whatever the truth, the fact was that the figures ruling England when Edward was king were intent on taking it in a more Protestant direction. It was time for a *real* Reformation.

There were a few foreign Evangelicals on hand as well to make sure that things went in the right direction; one of those foreigners was John Knox.[6] Unfortunately, Edward died before he reached his sixteenth birthday, leaving all the Protestants to flee abroad when his half-sister, Mary, came to the throne.

The problem with the Reformation in England was that it was pretty much a top-down affair, imposed on the common people, often against their wishes. The rebellion in the North of England, known as the *Pilgrimage of Grace*, happened because of the wholesale plunder of the monasteries under Henry VIII.[7] And, as for the rest of the changes, not everyone was happy about the way things were going. People *liked* their ceremonies, their saints and their statues. The iconoclasm that came about under Edward VI caused uproar and this combined with economic suffering to bring about more rebellions.[8] Catholicism was far from dead in England.

After the brief interlude when Lady Jane Grey was placed on the throne, Mary rode to London to the sound of cheering and partying everywhere; she witnessed the same scenes in the capital.[9] Her mother, Catherine of Aragon, had always been extremely popular and Mary was greeted with the same enthusiasm. Perhaps now things could get back to normal.

Mary's popularity waned somewhat when it became clear who her choice of husband was. She was going to marry the grandson of her own mother's sister, Philip II, son of the Holy Roman Emperor, Charles V. It was hardly a match made in Heaven for Philip; he was only twenty-six and Mary was eleven years older, rapidly advancing into middle age. Being a Habsburg, though, it was a case of 'chin up', lie back and think of the family.

After a failed revolt against her in 1554, Mary became paranoid about Protestants and had many of them burned at the stake. Not everyone agrees that these actions dented her popularity,[10] but they certainly must have done, since her death was hardly mourned and the accession of Elizabeth was met with just as much celebration as Mary's had been.[11]

The problem with Mary was that she had married a Habsburg, and a Spanish one at that. Philip conjured up visions of the Spanish Inquisition and the infamous *autos-da-fé*, where, after great ceremony, heretics were executed.[12] Burning, although not rare, was not the usual means of execution in England, where hanging, drawing and quartering was the norm. The burning of heretics under Mary, therefore, was seen as her coming under the influence of her Spanish husband; something that counted against her in most people's eyes.

What Mary's reign showed was that, although most of them were not overly enamoured with Evangelical Protestantism, English people were not ready for a wholesale return to Roman Catholicism, especially if it brought foreign influences into the country. Henry's quasi-Catholic Anglicanism was looked back on with nostalgia.

With Mary dead, all the Protestants could now come back out of hiding; and there were certainly plenty of them, despite Mary's best efforts. They looked to the new queen, Elizabeth, to carry on where the government of her half-brother had left off. The majority of people, however, wanted their church the way Henry had made it. Then, of course, there were the Catholics, who were waiting to see what was going to happen next.

Elizabeth's solution was to find some sort of middle ground, which resulted in the Thirty-Nine Articles of Religion, which was made law in 1563.[13] These Articles still form the doctrine of the Anglican Church, both in England and abroad.

Some aspects of the Articles were most definitely Protestant, such as the doctrines of Predestination, Justification by Faith and the repudiation of the existence of Purgatory. Other elements, however, were left deliberately vague. It was quite possible, in fact, to believe in transubstantiation; so long as you did not call it by that particular name. Church services themselves were full of ceremony; a visiting Catholic would feel far more comfortable at a Church of England service than a Protestant would.

Of course, many Protestants in England were extremely disappointed and wanted more radical reforms. They looked to Scotland with envious eyes and wanted a Calvinist church in their own country.[14] Such people, and there were plenty of them, could easily prove to be a major problem. In these Protestants' eyes, Elizabeth was also far too tolerant of Catholics in England.

Elizabeth, like the Protestants in Scotland, saw no reason to persecute Catholics, as long as they kept out of the public eye and did not make a show of their illegal practices. Unfortunately, events, and the actions of the Catholic Church and Catholics themselves, were to change Elizabeth's mind.

As far as Catholic Europe was concerned, Elizabeth was not the legitimate monarch of England. The dissolution of Henry VIII's marriage to Catherine of Aragon had not been sanctioned by the Church and was, therefore, invalid. Edward VI had been in the fortunate position of his mother marrying Henry, and he being born, after the death of Catherine of Aragon. Elizabeth, on the other hand, was a bastard. The rightful heir to Mary Tudor was, in fact, Mary Stewart, Queen of Scots.

After her misadventures in Scotland, Mary Stewart ended up fleeing to England, where Elizabeth was at a loss about what to do with her. As a fellow monarch, and, indeed, a relative, Elizabeth felt obliged to provide asylum to Mary. Elizabeth, however, knew how much of a threat Mary posed to her crown and so she was kept prisoner, albeit in very luxurious prisons.

As well as being a Catholic and acceptable to powerful interests in Europe, Mary was a more attractive proposition as a monarch than Elizabeth. When she arrived in England in 1568, Mary was still only twenty-five. She had already buried two husbands and abandoned a third and had proven her fertility by producing a male heir. Elizabeth, on the other hand, was thirty-four, had never married and showed no sign of ever doing so. It was highly unlikely that she would ever produce an heir of either sex.

And so, there sat Mary, like a princess in a fairy tale, just waiting for a bold king, prince or nobleman to come and claim her and win a kingdom; possibly two kingdoms, since, once Mary's position in England had been consolidated she would no doubt want to retake her Scottish throne. Her marriage to the Earl of Bothwell could be discounted since it had been performed under Protestant rites; besides, she could claim that she had been coerced. All it needed was a man of ambition, with the right connections and enough power to try to realise it.

Such a prospect no doubt was in the minds of the nobles that took part in the ill-fated *Rising of the North* in 1569.[15] This enterprise was a complete failure; not least because the leaders were prepared to stab each other in the back at the drop of a hat. The rising, however, did have one, unintended, consequence.

When Pope Pius V heard about the rising of these northern nobles, he issued a Bull, condemning Elizabeth, threatening excommunication to any Catholics supporting her and virtually implying that it was every Catholic's duty to remove her.[16] Word of the Papal Bull did not arrive in England until after the uprising had been crushed, rendering it useless as far as the northern nobles were concerned. It did, though, succeed, unsurprisingly, in infuriating Elizabeth. And not only Elizabeth.

Overnight, every Catholic in England had become a potential traitor. The Pope had made it plain that the allegiance of English Catholics should be to their church, not to their country. Essentially, Pius was helping to instigate the very repression and persecution he had condemned in his Bull.

This was an enormous mistake on the part of Pius; no doubt he, and others, recognised this since such action was never again taken by the Vatican. As far as English Protestants were concerned the Bull was proof positive that Catholics could not be trusted. The English became absolutely paranoid about Catholics and anti-Catholicism became ingrained in English culture for many years. As we shall see later, it is still there.

In 1570 a second edition of John Foxe's book, *The Actes and Monuments*, popularly known as the *Book of Martyrs*, was released. After a lot of criticism of the first edition, Foxe had made extensive revisions and additions, producing a monstrous tome. Given the anti-Catholic atmosphere in England, the book was welcomed with open arms. In 1571, the Convocation of Canterbury ordered that a copy of the book be placed in every cathedral church, so that everyone could read it.[17]

The book purports to be a history of Christianity, with particular emphasis, as the title suggests, on Christian martyrs. Anyone expecting a proper, reliable history, however, would be sorely disappointed. It was a work of propaganda, nothing more. Historical accuracy was sacrificed in the cause of promoting an anti-Catholic agenda. The problem for Foxe's polemic was that, prior to the 16th Century, there was no such thing as a Protestant. That, however, was not going to stop Foxe.

Every heretic and malcontent that had been put to death by the Catholic Church was presented as a kind of *proto-Protestant*. The true nature of these individuals and sects was subsumed under a torrent of lurid accounts of their sufferings and deaths under the Catholic Church. His telling of the story of Girolamo Savonarola, for example, made the man out to be a victim of the Pope, rather than his own ambitions.[18] In fact, Savonarola's *Bonfire of the Vanities* and supposed democratic leanings would have received short shrift from Elizabeth!

When it came to more contemporary times, Foxe had far more to work with. Court records, letters and lurid eye-witness accounts of torture and death all went into his book. He took care, however, to blame the persecution of Protestants under Henry VIII on the likes of Thomas More. When it came to Mary Tudor, the persecution, of course, was all her own work, aided and abetted by her Spanish husband.

The book was highly influential and led to anti-Catholic feeling in England right up to the present time. Essentially, English Protestants were led to believe that the Catholic Church was evil and had been torturing and murdering Protestants for centuries. Torturing and murdering *by* Protestants, both on Catholics and other Protestants, were studiously ignored.

Into this already inflamed atmosphere came Huguenot refugees from France. The St. Bartholomew's Day Massacre seemed to prove Foxe right about the perfidy and treachery of Catholics. The full facts about what happened in Paris are shrouded in mystery, but there is no shortage of theories. For every historian contending that Catherine De Medici and her son, Charles IX, lured the Huguenot leaders to Paris in order to kill them, there is another ready to show that the Huguenots had been hatching a plot of their own. One thing on which everyone seems to agree is that nobody planned the mob violence and mass slaughter that started in Paris and spread throughout France. That was not the story, though, that the refugees brought with them.

Of course, the English were only too ready to believe the tales of an organised cull; after all, they knew that Catholics could not be trusted. Stories began to reach England of celebration masses in Rome and the Pope congratulating the French. Counter-claims that the Pope was celebrating what he thought was the thwarting of a Huguenot plot[19] were ignored. The arguments rumble on to this day.

While English hysteria about Catholics was gaining momentum, perhaps one of the most surprising things was that Elizabeth continued to allow Mary Stewart to live. Mary was left in her gilded cage, sitting like some star prize in a TV game show. Perhaps that is why she was allowed to live; her simple presence might encourage plots, or rumours of plots, which would unite the divided Protestant society against a common enemy.

Mary was in her forties when she was finally removed as a threat. Quite why it was decided to get rid of her at that late stage is unclear. Whether or not the case against Mary was trumped-up or not is not really an issue. She had been voicing her claim to the English throne for years and was never backward in letting everyone know that she would support any plot to make her queen. If she was plotting to assassinate Elizabeth in the 1580s, then it was hardly anything new. The real reasons for her execution lay elsewhere; perhaps Elizabeth, now in her fifties, was becoming aware of her own mortality and dreaded what might happen if she were to die before Mary.

At any rate, the aftermath of Mary's death helped feed the anti-Catholic paranoia of the English even more. Phillip II of Spain, Mary Tudor's widower, decided that the killing of Mary Stewart was his cue to invade England and restore Catholicism. It is hard to understand why he had not organised his invasion twenty years earlier, when he could have wed Mary and snatched the English throne for himself and his family. Considering that he happened to be a Habsburg, you would have thought the chance of another throne to add to the family's collection would have been irresistible.

As it was, he had actually proposed to Elizabeth before his wife was cold in her tomb, showing a true Habsburg nose (or jaw) for the main prize. He had been a good friend to Elizabeth over the years so maybe he still considered himself in with a chance. By 1587, though, he had had enough of English pirates, with Elizabeth's permission, looting his country's ships. It was time to act in order to, as he broadcast, restore England to the true religion.

It was with astonishing arrogance that the Elizabethan English considered themselves perfectly justified in indulging in piracy. That same arrogance also underlies the way English historians invariably excuse the actions of corsairs like Francis Drake. That arrogance was, and is, part of the legacy of John Foxe.

Foxe's book, you will recall, was put forward as a history of Christianity. Part of his thesis was that Christianity had been instituted in England by Joseph of Arimathea, well before the Roman church was founded.[20] According to Foxe, then, the Church of England was the restoration of Christ's original church. No mere Reformation for England; Luther, Calvin, Zwingli and the rest were reduced to an irrelevance. It was Christian England standing alone against the diabolical malevolence of the Church of Rome.

If that sounds vaguely familiar it should. It is reminiscent of England standing alone against the Nazis, 'The Few' and all that, even though there were all different nationalities involved in the Battle of Britain. Foxe's book caused more than arrogance about the Church of England and hatred of Catholics; it also affected the attitude of the English towards foreigners, especially continental Europeans.[21] The story of Francis Drake finishing his game of bowls before joining battle with Johnny Foreigner is part-and-parcel of this arrogant attitude.

Which brings us back to Phillip's planned invasion. The Spanish Armada was mostly defeated by the weather, which meant that, although Drake got a good deal of credit for his battle tactics, the real hero was God Himself. Evidently, the Almighty was on the side of England and against the Church of Rome. The English were good, godly and righteous; it was official. Meanwhile, the Roman Catholic Church was Satan's representative on Earth and something to be both feared and hated.

We have already seen how Protestantism in England was hardly what you could call homogeneous. For some, Elizabeth's church was *too* Protestant, while, for others, it was nowhere near Protestant enough. This situation, quite obviously, was going to end in trouble. The only thing holding the nation together was fear of foreign invasion and anti-Catholicism.

Notwithstanding the attempted invasion by Philip II and Pius V's Papal Bull, it is entirely possible that the anti-Catholic agenda was the result of a conscious effort by Elizabeth's government. William Cecil and, more especially, Francis Walsingham, operated a network of spies throughout England and in the courts of Europe. Walsingham was not above using *agents provocateurs* too, as can be seen from his use of one to trap Mary Stewart.[22] One wonders how many other times such agents were used.

There was no point in having all these agents unless they were going to be used, which makes one wonder *how* they were used. Some historians suggest that Walsingham was, in fact, the instigator of the plot into which Mary was drawn.[23] But what about the other Catholic plots?

It cannot be denied that such plots came in extremely useful in keeping the nation, or, at least, the Protestant majority, together. If the plots had not existed, they would have to have been invented. It is entirely reasonable, given Walsingham's way of working, to suggest that the plots *were* invented, and then brought to fruition by *agents provocateurs*. In this way, the threat from Catholicism was made to appear bigger than it actually was.

Elizabeth died in March 1603, almost making it to the age of seventy; a good innings for those days, even among the rich and powerful. Her reign was, and is, considered a 'Golden Age' of peace and prosperity. In reality, however, there were serious tensions bubbling away under the surface. It was inevitable that there would eventually be a confrontation between High-Church Anglicanism, which almost seemed a continuation of the Catholic Church, and *real* Protestantism, in the shape of Puritanism and Nonconformity.

Elizabeth's heir was obvious; Mary Stewart's son, James VI of Scotland. As he made his way south, away from the poverty of Scotland to the rich court of London, little did James suspect that he and his family were going to be deluged by all the concealed problems left behind by Gloriana.

2
Divisions Unleashed: The Stuarts

James decided, when he assumed his new role of James I of England, to continue Elizabeth's earlier policy of leaving Catholics to just get on with it; providing, of course, they kept out of the limelight. Considering he had grown up in that kind of atmosphere in Scotland, it was an easy decision to make. Coming from Scotland, however, meant that he was unfamiliar with the situation in England. There was a huge split between the Protestants, which was going to become more prominent as the years went on.

We have already seen that the only thing holding Protestantism together in England was paranoia about Catholics, especially foreign Catholics. Elizabeth's idea of making a church that suited everybody was not quite the success it was supposed to be. High-Church Anglicanism was too close to Catholicism for comfort, as far as Low-Church members and Puritans were concerned. This split was going to end up rending the country asunder during the reign of the Stuarts.

Unlike Elizabeth, James was none too keen to get involved in wars against the Habsburgs or in riling up other European nations by sending ships out on piratical missions. It was the quiet life for him; enjoying court life with his favourites and trying to run the country peacefully. Of course, less war meant less taxation, which pleased everyone no end. It meant, however, that there was no common enemy to pull the country together.

Fortunately for James, the *Gunpowder Plot*, a madcap scheme to restore Catholicism as the dominant religion in England, occurred in 1605. The plan was to kill James and his elder son, Henry, put James's nine-year-old daughter, Elizabeth on the throne as a puppet monarch and turn the country back to Catholicism. Even if they had succeeded in blowing up the Houses of Parliament and killing James and his son, there was no way the plot could have succeeded without foreign help, which was distinctly lacking.

The incident, however, gave England a pantomime villain in Guy Fawkes, whose effigy was to be burned every year on November 5th, by order of Parliament.[1] Fawkes had not been the ringleader, but his adoption of the name *Guido* as well as the fact that he had fought for Habsburg Spain in the Netherlands, probably helped conjure up visions of another Spanish Armada.

The November 5th bonfires usually had effigies of the Pope, and other Catholic hate-figures, being burned alongside those of Fawkes, giving them a distinctly anti-Catholic flavour. But, then, maybe that was what was meant to happen. Anti-Catholicism helped to hide the divisions within English Protestantism and there are those that believe that the Gunpowder Plot was deliberately manufactured.[2]

Puritans in England had been hopeful that James would institute reforms in the Anglican Church; after all, he came from a Calvinist country. James, however, preferred the current Anglican way, especially since the monarch was head of the church. Like most monarchs, James wanted to unite his separate kingdoms and decided that a uniform church was the way to go. To that end, he started to impose bishops on the Church of Scotland, as well as the celebration of feast days and services that conformed more to the Anglican confession.[3] He also made it illegal for General Assemblies to be held without royal permission.[4] In effect, he left a complete mess for his successor to contend with; disappointment among Protestants in England and anger at royal interference in religious affairs in Scotland.

Henry having died in 1612, it was James's younger son, Charles, who succeeded to the throne. He continued his father's quest to bring the church in Scotland into the Anglican fold, causing nothing but trouble for himself. The introduction of the Book of Common Prayer to Scotland led to riots when it was used at St. Giles Cathedral.[5]

In England, Puritans had even more to complain about. Charles had married a French Catholic princess, Henrietta Maria, who was not crowned Queen of England because she refused to take part in a Protestant ceremony.[6] Many in the country were outraged when she brought her French Catholic servants to court. Charles's own support for the Arminian Archbishop Laud, who opposed the

Calvinist doctrine of predestination and wanted more ceremonial in Anglican services, further angered Puritans.[7] The majority of the House of Commons happened to be Puritan or Low Church and they tried to wring religious concessions from Charles in return for allowing taxation to finance his involvement in the Thirty Years War.[8] Relations between the Crown and Parliament became so strained that civil war was inevitable.

The English Civil War is no longer seen in isolation; nowadays it is viewed as part of a wider conflict, known as the Wars of the Three Kingdoms, or the British Civil Wars, since Scotland and Ireland were involved as well.[9] It is generally considered that these wars started when the Covenanters in Scotland revolted against Charles's attempts to change the Church of Scotland. The Bishops' Wars, as these conflicts came to be called, led to complete humiliation for Charles, with the Covenanters left in control of Scotland.[10] Charles, of course, could not raise enough funds to pay for a decent-sized army, leading to even more conflict with the English Parliament.

The ins-and-outs of the Civil Wars need not concern us here, but it is interesting to look at the reasoning behind the conflicts in Scotland and England. The overriding concern in Scotland was to maintain the freedom of the Church and to keep its Presbyterian and Calvinist values intact.[11] Some of the nobility took advantage of the situation to settle old scores and get one up on their rivals; for example, the Campbells against the MacDonalds.[12] In the main, however, it was the Covenanters against the Crown. The situation in England was somewhat different.

As usual in England, anti-Catholic paranoia played its part. Suspicions of a Papist plot to take over England were rife, even among ordinary people. Pamphlets of the period reflected this attitude, showing that it was a genuine, if unfounded, fear.[13]

Despite the difference in how the Scottish and English viewed the conflict, there were some signs that the peculiarly English anti-Catholic paranoia was beginning to infect Scotland. There is a bronze stool in St. Giles Cathedral in Edinburgh, commemorating a woman named Jenny Geddes, who famously accused the Dean of 'saying a mass' when he began the new Anglican-style service.[14] It is unclear whether Jenny Geddes even existed, but the story points to the fact that the imposition of High-Church Anglican services was viewed in some quarters as a sort of creeping Catholicisation. Nevertheless, it was still the case that the main point of the Bishops' Wars was to maintain the Presbyterian nature of the Scottish Church.

In fact, this is a theme that can easily be discerned throughout the 17th Century. When Charles I was executed in 1549 there was not the great rejoicing in Scotland that one might expect. On the contrary, there was outrage at the presumption of the English Parliament in acting alone in this matter. With the trust between the two kingdoms seriously dented, the Scottish decided to take another route to secure their church's independence.

Negotiations were held between the Scottish Government and Charles's son and heir, also called Charles. Under the terms of the Treaty of Breda, Charles Junior promised to uphold the Presbyterian nature of the Church of Scotland and he was crowned King Charles II in Scotland soon afterwards.[15] This showed that the Scottish fight against the Crown was not inspired by the same anti-Catholic paranoia that existed in England, otherwise they would hardly have been ready to trust another Stuart. They were obviously prepared to go to any lengths to preserve their church.

Fearing that Charles II would raise an army in Scotland to fight for his English throne, the English Parliament sent an invasion army to forestall this. Scotland subsequently ended up with an occupying army billeted on it and was forced into being under Cromwell's military dictatorship.[16]

The Restoration, when it came, was greeted with hysterical joy in England; the English, unlike the Scots, had not been used to being under a Puritanical regime. No Christmas, no other feast days, no dancing, no drunkenness; in fact, no fun at all was the law during the Interregnum. The anti-Catholic paranoia was temporarily forgotten; they would have welcomed the Devil himself so long as they were allowed to smile again.

Almost as soon as he was comfortably ensconced on his throne, Charles II reneged on his deal with the Scottish Presbyterians. It was an easy thing for him to do since the English Parliament was all in favour of restoring High-Church Anglicanism as the dominant religion in England. Laws were even made to allow the King to remove dissidents and Nonconformists from positions of authority.[17] Nobody wanted to go back to the dark days of the Commonwealth.

The Presbyterians in Scotland soon discovered that not only was

High-Church Anglicanism back in favour in England, but that Charles was determined to follow his father's, and his grandfather's, policy of forcing the Church of Scotland to go down the same path. There then followed what has become known as the *Killing Time*; a period of nearly three decades of persecution of the Covenanters.[18]

In England, too, there was persecution of Nonconformists, although not as sustained as it was in Scotland. In fact, nobody quite knew where they stood in England. For a while the King's policy would be one of tolerance, then it would be back to repression of Nonconformists; sometimes both policies were followed at the same time![19] The biggest problem with Charles, however, was the succession.

The *Merry Monarch* lived up to his name by going through a long string of mistresses and siring many illegitimate children. When it came to his wife, Catherine of Braganza, however, his fecundity counted for nothing. With no legitimate issue, the throne would pass to Charles's brother, James. James just happened to be a practising Roman Catholic.

With such a prospect in store, it was not surprising that anti-Catholic paranoia raised its ugly head again. Many in England were prepared to believe a character called Titus Oates and his story of a 'Popish Plot'; then again, there were just as many that were not. It is testament to the fear of returning to civil war or to the Commonwealth that so many were ready to denounce Oates as a charlatan. The man ended up being thrown into prison, with the added punishment of being whipped through the streets and put in the stocks once a year.[20] It seemed that the fear of going back to the days of austerity under Cromwell trumped the paranoia about Catholics.

The accession of James went ahead remarkably smoothly, considering the opposition to a Catholic being king. Pretty much straightaway, however, things started to go wrong. James decided that a policy of tolerance was the way to go. And not only mere tolerance; he wanted rid of the Test and Corporation Acts, which restricted the civil liberties of non-Anglicans, altogether. The Anglican Establishment was outraged and Parliament refused to co-operate. James prorogued and then dissolved Parliament and got rid of the Acts on his own.[21] This not only removed legal restrictions on Roman Catholics, but on Nonconformists as well.[22] That was something that the Establishment was not going to stand for.

Rather weirdly, while he was increasing opportunities for Nonconformists in England, James continued his brother's policy in Scotland of persecuting Covenanters. Part of his policy of tolerance was extended to Scotland; namely, the lifting of restrictions on Catholics and Dissenters. The Dissenting community in Scotland consisted of nothing more than a few Quakers, essentially meaning that James's measures mainly applied to Catholics. Moderate Presbyterians were also to be tolerated, as long as they caused no trouble; Covenanters, however, were still subject to severe restrictions.[23]

Not surprisingly, there were few that mourned when William of Orange was invited to invade and take over the throne of England. James had to flee and this was considered an abdication by both the English and Scottish Parliaments. William was actually James's nephew and was also married to his daughter, Mary, which says a lot about family loyalty among royalty!

William was a staunch Calvinist, who saw his coronation ceremony as a 'popish mockery'[24] but he was no bigot. He sponsored the Toleration Act of 1688 and was disappointed when Parliament did not extend toleration as far as he had wanted.[25] His idea had been to lift restrictions on all faiths, including Roman Catholics.

In Scotland, William had to accept the rights of Parliament as well as the Presbyterian system before being accepted as King.[26] As a Calvinist himself, he was probably more than happy to acquiesce.

In England, anti-Catholic paranoia was to the fore yet again, shown not least by the fact that Titus Oates was released from prison and given a pension.[27] Rather wisely, Oates faded into the background and into obscurity. The country had come back to his way of thinking, but there was no point in taking chances!

Meanwhile, anti-Catholicism was taking root, as one might expect, in what was effectively an English colony. The whole of Ireland might be under English authority but Ulster was something special. It was a planned effort to displace Catholics and replace them with Protestants. Such an enterprise was bound to cause trouble.

3
Fools in the Gap: The Ulster Presbyterians

There is a well-documented phenomenon, noticed by psychologists, psychiatrists and anyone involved in child care, that children always seem to be more loving toward the parent that treats them badly. Whether the abuse is physical, emotional or sexual, a child will show more affection to the parent dishing out the abuse than to the one that does not. It is probably some sort of survival mechanism; hoping that a show of preference will somehow stop the abuse. Scottish Presbyterians in Ulster showed much the same traits.

The idea of placing Protestants in Ulster at the beginning of the 17th Century was supposed to bring twofold benefits: helping to pacify a notoriously rebellious area and bringing 'civilisation' to the indigenous population. The plan was helped in no small part by the *Flight of the Earls*,[1] which left vast tracts of land free for the English to appropriate. This land was leased, at modest rents, to settlers from England and Scotland; thus began the Plantations of Ulster.

If the Scots that moved to Ulster thought they were going to have an easy time of it, they could not have been more wrong. Much of Ulster had been laid to waste during the wars with England, meaning that the settlers had to work hard just to make the place habitable, let alone profitable. There was also the problem of the Catholic Irish, most of whom were, understandably, none too pleased about being thrown off their land. And then there was religion.

Many of the settlers were English and Anglican, making them more acceptable as far as the authorities in London and Dublin were concerned. The Scottish Presbyterians, on the other hand, were viewed pretty much the same as Nonconformists in England and suffered just as many restrictions. It was hardly surprising, then, that the Scottish settlers were often confused about where their loyalties lay.

During the Wars of the Three Kingdoms, the Protestants in Ulster found themselves under attack, in 1641, by a native Irish army, determined to drive out the interlopers and reclaim their country. A Covenanter army was sent from Scotland to defend the Protestants and atrocities were committed by both sides.[2] This was Scotland's first foray into a war against Catholics.

At first, the Scottish Presbyterians in Ulster supported the Parliamentarians, following the lead of their fellows in Scotland. After Presbyterians were removed from the English Parliament it became clear that the Roundheads were reneging on their promises in the Solemn League and Covenant of 1643.[3] This eventually led to the Scottish Covenanters taking the side of Charles II against the Parliamentarians, bringing the Ulster Presbyterians with them.

Now the Presbyterians in Ulster found themselves on the same side as the Irish Catholics. They were extremely lucky to escape Cromwell's genocide in Ireland; many surrendered or went over to the Parliamentarian side to escape the fate of the people of Drogheda, who were completely massacred.[4] Essentially, they were back to Square One, since Cromwell and the English Parliament had no more love for Presbyterianism than had Charles I.

Understandably, the Scottish Presbyterians in Ulster took the side of William of Orange when James Stuart tried to regain his throne. The sheer weight of English propaganda against James, coupled with the fact that he had raised an army of Irish Catholics to bolster his forces, led Ulster Protestants to believe they were facing 1641 all over again. If the Ulster Presbyterians thought they were going to benefit from William's success, however, they were to be, once more, sadly disappointed.

As we saw earlier, William's grand plans for religious tolerance were thwarted by the English Parliament. There was nothing he could do about it since the 1689 Bill of Rights severely limited the power of the monarchy.[5] Presbyterianism may have become the established mode of church government in Scotland, but Ulster came directly under the power of England, where Presbyterians, Nonconformists, and Dissenters, just like Catholics, were still excluded by the terms of the Test and Corporation Acts.

Even when Scotland united with England in 1707 it made no difference to the Presbyterians in Ulster. England and Scotland retained their separate laws and forms of church government, meaning that the Ulster Presbyterians were no better off. Daniel Defoe summed up the situation.

> It seems somewhat hard, and savours of the most scandalous ingratitude, that the very people who drank deepest of the popish fury, and were the most vigorous to show their zeal and their courage in opposing tyranny and popery, and on the foot of forwardness and valour the Church of Ireland recovered herself from her low condition, should now be requited with so injurious a treatment as to be linked with the very Papists they fought against…There will certainly be no encouragement to the Dissenters to join with their brethren the next time the Papists shall please to take arms and attempt their throats. Not but they may be fools enough as they always were to stand in the gap.[6]

The persecution of the Ulster Presbyterians by the Anglican Establishment was far more noticeable in Defoe's time, due to the fact that the number of Scots in Ulster had swollen so much that they vastly outnumbered the English in the province. Rather ironically, given future events, this influx was mostly caused by a famine in Scotland in the late 1690s.[7]

For most of the 18th Century the Presbyterians in Ulster were treated just as badly as the Catholic Irish. Not only did they have religious restrictions to contend with but the Penal Laws meant that they had to pay tithes to the Anglican Church of Ireland, while their ability to trade was severely curtailed.[8] It was hardly surprising that a distinctly anti-English feeling began to show itself in this community. Many fled to America, where they were among the first to flock to the Independence banner against the hated English.[9]

The Ulster Presbyterians that fled to America are often seen, rightly or wrongly, as at the forefront of the American 'frontier' mentality; pushing to find new lands, fighting savage Indians etc.[10] The same mentality developed in Ulster during the 18th Century, with the Presbyterians seeing themselves as frontiersmen standing against the Catholic 'savages' surrounding them.[11] And just like their counterparts in America, they could not rely on the authorities to protect them; all they could rely on was themselves. This was to lead to serious trouble at the end of the 18th Century.

Towards the end of the century, restrictions on Catholics, Nonconformists and Dissenters began to be lifted.[12] Most of these restrictions had been economic and, in the new climate, Presbyterians in Ulster found themselves suddenly facing competition for land leases and jobs. Landowners were not too fussy about to whom they leased land; they were predominantly Anglican and viewed Catholics and Presbyterians, Irish and Scots, with equal distaste. Not surprisingly, this economic competition often erupted into violence between Catholics and Presbyterians, with each side feeling it was under attack from the other.

Two gangs formed in County Armagh: the Catholic Defenders and the Protestant Peep O' Day Boys. Both groups armed themselves to the teeth and there were sectarian atrocities on both sides.[13] The Peep O' Day Boys later formed themselves into an organisation called the Orange Order, which attempted to make itself a more respectable group.[14] Orange Order histories, however, ignore completely the connection with the Peep O' Day Boys;[15] keeping up a pretence that the Order was not born out of anti-Catholic, sectarian violence. In fact, the Order positively denies any link with the Peep O' Day Boys, explaining away accusations of atrocities against Catholics by the simple expedient of claiming that such incidents took place before the Order was born.[16]

When the Irish Rebellion occurred in 1798, the Orange Order was instrumental in the fight against the United Irishmen. In fact, the military leaders at the time acknowledged their debt to the Order.[17] But the English authorities went even further than that. Stories were spread around Ulster that Protestant communities were being targeted and murdered by the Catholic United Irishmen.[18] Of course, the Orange Order was only too willing to believe such tales and disseminate them widely.

In fact, the Society of United Irishmen was a completely non-sectarian organisation, inspired by the new USA and the French Revolution, which was dedicated to the foundation of a republic in Ireland.[19] The 1798 Rebellion was an attempt, with French support, to throw the English out of Ireland and start up just such a society. It had many Protestant members and, indeed, one of the founding members of the United Irishmen and leader of the 'rebellion' was a Protestant called Wolfe Tone.[20]

On a side note, it is interesting how the American colonies breaking with Britain is called the American War of Independence, while Wars of Independence is also the phrase to describe the struggle of the Netherlands to throw off their Habsburg overlords. Why, then is the same kind of fight in Ireland called a 'rebellion'? It certainly reveals a lot about the English psyche.

On the United Irishmen side, the 'rebellion' was not a sectarian war; in fact, there were some Ulster Presbyterians that were on the side of the United Irishmen and who were slaughtered by the British forces.[21] There is evidence that the British side did not view things in the same way and there was a distinctly sectarian dimension to their actions, such as in Tullow, County Carlow. When one of the local leaders of the United Irishmen, Father John Murphy, was executed, his body was burned and local Catholics forced to open their windows to let in the 'holy smoke'.[22]

Although the British Government used Protestant paranoia about Catholics to help put down the 'Rebellion', a more long-term strategy was going to be needed. The French had supported the 'Rebellion', even though very few of their troops had landed in Ireland. Next time Britain might not be so lucky. The French army was destroying all opposition on the continent and the British Government was terrified that Ireland would provide a stepping-stone to Britain. Something drastic needed to be done.

That something was uniting Ireland with Britain to form the United Kingdom. The Dublin Parliament would be dissolved and Irish MPs would sit at Westminster instead. Many Irish Protestants were outraged, especially the Orange Order; they knew what was coming next.[23]

Lord Castlereagh, in Dublin, and William Pitt, at Westminster, both realised that the only way the Union was going to work was with further emancipation for Catholics. Although many rich Catholics had been given the vote in 1793, Catholics were still barred from sitting in Parliament, either at Dublin or Westminster. Remedying this, and giving Catholics a voice in the government of the UK, would be the only guarantee of keeping the French out of Ireland. Unfortunately, everybody else realised it as well.[24]

A great deal of bribery went into passing a bill in the Dublin Parliament to unite Ireland with Great Britain and the Catholic emancipation clauses had to be withdrawn, not least because they were opposed by King George III.[25] The bill was subsequently passed at Westminster and, on the 1st January 1801, the British Government took over the direct running of Ireland. The opposition of the Orangemen soon melted away when they realised that there would be no Catholic representation. Pitt and Castlereagh both resigned, knowing that the new situation was of no real benefit to Britain. Catholic emancipation was going to have to come sooner or later.

It eventually came in 1829, having been opposed not only by Orangemen in Ireland, but in Scotland and England as well.[26] The franchise was not extended by this Act; indeed, it was contracted, as the property qualification for voting was increased.[27] As for sitting in Parliament, it was still a rich man's game as MPs received no payment. The fears of the Orangemen were unfounded; at least for the present. The property qualification alone would guarantee the Protestant Ascendancy in Ireland.

An interesting point of note is how the Orange Order was now active in Scotland and clearly on the side of their colleagues in Ireland, especially Ulster. During the 1798 'Rebellion', many Scottish soldiers joined the Orange Order and, when the fighting was over, took the organisation back home with them. Such is the story given by the Orange Order itself and there is no reason to doubt its veracity.[28]

What is doubtful, though, is that these soldiers had some 'Road to Damascus' revelation in Ulster and suddenly became receptive to anti-Catholic prejudices. Something must have happened in Scotland to make the people readier to submit to anti-Catholic paranoia and hatred. It is time to look at how these attitudes spread from England into Scotland.

4
Rebellious Scots: Bigotry comes to Scotland

We have already seen how it was only hatred and fear of Catholics that held together the divided Protestants in England. In fact, it was probable that Mary Queen of Scots was kept alive so long in order to facilitate this paranoia. Catholic uprisings and Phillip II of Spain's attempt to invade England helped to convince English Protestants that their paranoia was well founded. Such attitudes had not yet affected Scotland but two things happened to change all that; the first was the Union of Parliaments in 1707.

The famine in Scotland in the 1690s was not just due to failed harvests; there was a serious economic crisis going on as well. William of Orange was at war with France from 1692 until 1697, part of the ongoing dynastic struggles in Europe. Although this did not directly affect Scotland, it meant that trade with the continent, especially France, was disrupted and often blocked completely by the English Navy.[1] This hardly made either William or the English Parliament very popular with the Scottish.

William was implicated in the Glencoe Massacre and the blame was laid directly at his door by most Scots.[2] And then came the Darien Scheme. This madcap operation was doomed to failure from the start but William got a lot of the blame for siding with the East India Company and imposing a ban on English people and institutions investing in the scheme.[3] He also stopped the English colonies from helping the settlers in Darien, for fear of upsetting the Spanish.[4]

The failure of the Darien Scheme practically bankrupted Scotland, but the Scottish Parliament did not immediately go cap-in-hand to the English. In fact, the Scottish Parliament was getting more and more outraged by the actions of its counterpart in England.

When Anne Stuart succeeded to the thrones of England and Scotland, the English Parliament began to ride roughshod over the wishes of the Scots. Scotland was dragged into the war against France, as part of the Spanish War of Succession, without any consultation with the Scottish Parliament.[5] The Scottish Parliament was also not consulted when it came to establishing who would succeed the childless Anne to the British thrones.[6] Scotland responded by threatening to select a different monarch and to pull its forces out of the war.[7]

After some tit-for-tat legislation by the Scottish and English parliaments, it became obvious that a union would be beneficial to both parties. Politically the English needed Scotland. The most terrifying prospect was that the Scottish Parliament might invite James Edward Stuart, son of the ousted King James, to take over the throne. The upper and middle classes in Scotland, meanwhile, needed money; and lots of it. And so, for good or ill, the Scottish Parliament voted itself out of existence and Scotland became part of Great Britain.

Of course, Scotland was now directly involved in Ireland, both as part of the British Parliament and as part of the British Army. That did not necessarily mean, however, that it was automatically infected with English anti-Catholicism; some kind of catalyst was needed for that to happen. Such a catalyst arrived in 1745.

The Jacobite Rebellion has become so shrouded in legend and sentimental nonsense that it is sometimes difficult to discern the reality. Teary-eyed renditions of *Will Ye No' Come Back Again* and *The Skye Boat Song* have led to misconceptions that the uprising was some kind of bid for Scottish independence. The whole war is often portrayed as Scotland versus England but that was not the case at all.

The very idea of James Edward Stuart on the throne was enough to send shivers up the backbones of many in Scotland, reviving memories and stories of persecution under James VII. When Charles Edward Stuart raised an army to put his father on the throne, the Presbyterians in the Scottish Lowlands were hardly going to rally to the cause.

Bonnie Prince Charlie's motivation was pretty obvious but that of others were mixed. The French had originally given Charles practical help, but the fleet they gifted had been destroyed in a storm, meaning that they were no longer going to invade England.[8] Politically, though, the French Government was right behind the Jacobite cause. That was hardly going to inspire confidence among

Charles's intended supporters in Scotland. There were, however, other factors to motivate the Highlanders.

The Campbells were raising a force to stand against Charles, which no doubt persuaded many to join the Young Pretender. It is notable, in this respect, that the first to declare support for Charles was a MacDonald; the MacDonalds were the long-standing enemies of the Campbells.[9] So, for the Scottish clans it was not just about putting a Stuart back on the throne; it was about a good, old-fashioned clan feud as well.

There is no point in going over the whole campaign; it is not relevant to what we are looking at and, if you are anything like me, you find accounts of battles extremely boring. Suffice it to say that, as you will already know, the Jacobites lost and Bonnie Prince Charlie disappeared, never to be seen in these parts again.

The English reaction to the uprising was to be expected; anti-Catholic paranoia was to the fore yet again. Even as early as February 1744, when Charles was trying to raise forces in France, action was taken against English Catholics.

> A proclamation was immediately published for putting the laws in execution against papists and nonjurors, commanding all papists, and reputed papists, to depart from the cities of London and Westminster, and from within ten miles of them; for confining papists, and reputed papists, to their habitations, (not to remove from thence above five miles) and for putting in execution the laws against riots and rioters. In another address from the parliament, his majesty was exhorted to augment his forces both by sea and land; the Habeas corpus act was suspended for six months; and several persons of distinction were apprehended on suspicion of treasonable practices. In short every precaution was taken that seemed necessary for the preservation of public tranquillity.[10]

The suspension of *Habeas Corpus*, meaning that people could be imprisoned indefinitely without trial, was the usual measure instituted by the Westminster Government when faced with a crisis. One cannot help but wonder if Charles's difficulty in attracting adherents in England was because all the possible recruits were safely locked up. At any rate, it was clear that the Government saw the uprising as a Catholic one.

And it was not only the Government that saw things in this light. Ordinary people also suspected a Catholic plot and were ready to inform on their neighbours, merely on hearsay evidence.[11] No doubt the march of the Jacobite army southwards into England was viewed with the same terror. It was hardly surprising that the huge band of 'Papists', in outlandish dress and armed to the teeth, inspired every city it approached to surrender immediately. Probably many English Catholics were frightened as well by the army of hairy-arsed savages, with their ancient, barbaric language.

Everyone knows about the aftermath of the Battle of Culloden; the destruction of Highland culture and the clans, the banning of tartan and bagpipes and the wholesale slaughter of anyone suspected of being a Jacobite. Most people in Scotland view this period as a shameful time in the history of the nation. Especially when viewed through the prism of late-Victorian Romanticism, it is seen, along with the Highland Clearances, as a brutal extermination of a people and its culture.

In modern times, the destruction of Highland culture is usually seen as being the responsibility of the brutal, chauvinistic English. We are all familiar with 'Butcher' Cumberland and the disgraceful behaviour of his troops; burning houses, slaughtering whole families and the like. It is something that modern Scots look back on with distaste. Attitudes at the time, however, were somewhat different.

The Duke of Cumberland was made Chancellor of the universities of Aberdeen and St. Andrews and given the freedom of the city of Glasgow, while the Glasgow Journal reported 'the greatest rejoicings that have been known in the city'.[12] The General Assembly of the Church of Scotland, meanwhile, sent a letter to Cumberland, thanking him for giving them the ability to meet 'in a state of peace and security exceeding our greatest hopes... owing to...your generous resolution in coming to be the deliver (sic) of this Church and Nation.'[13]

The Presbyterians in the Scottish Lowlands had received a serious shock from the Jacobite Rebellion, especially given the initial successes of Charles's army. Almost for the first time, they were aware of the threat posed by the large number of Catholics in the Scottish Highlands. Anti-Catholic hatred took root in Scotland and flourished from then on. English sectarian bigotry had thrived in an atmosphere of Catholic uprisings, Papal pronouncements and attempts at invasions. Such threats had not been a problem in Scotland; after 1745 there seemed every reason to indulge in paranoia.

We have seen how, in England, anti-Catholic paranoia served to unite Protestants in a common cause; indeed, it is possible that such an atmosphere was actively encouraged to that very end. In the second half of the 18th Century the same phenomenon occurred in Scotland. There might be a divide between Presbyterians and Episcopalians, but that paled into insignificance next to the threat from Catholicism.

Events that had occurred in Scotland were now looked at in a new light. Presbyterians and Episcopalians no longer needed to be mutually antipathetic and, indeed, could live together in harmony. The imposition of bishops on the Church of Scotland could no longer be blamed on fellow Scottish Protestants, or Anglican Protestants for that matter. It was obvious that the real enemy, as the English had always maintained, had been Catholicism.

The attempts to force episcopacy on the Church by James VI/I were simply airbrushed out of history. The main emphasis was transferred onto Charles II and, more especially, James VII/II. It had been nothing more than a plot to impose Catholicism on Scotland. This misinterpretation of history can still be found on some of the more bigoted websites.

With this anti-Catholic paranoia in their minds, it was hardly surprising that Scottish soldiers in Ulster found common cause with the Orange Order there. As we saw in the last chapter, the Presbyterians in Ulster had developed a siege mentality, with enemies all around. English Protestants had viewed themselves in the same light; surrounded by hostile Catholics in Europe and in their own country. Scotland had now been drawn into this paranoia, making the trinity complete. England, Scotland and Ulster were now united in 'defending' Protestantism against Papists. The importation of the Orange Order into Scotland was a symptom of this paranoia, not a cause.

The murder of Highlanders, the burning of their homes, the expropriation of their lands and the banning of their culture[14] mattered not at all to the Protestants of the Lowlands. Nor would the verse of *God Save the King*, which many claim as anti-Scottish, cause them any concern.

> Lord, grant that Marshal Wade,
> May by thy mighty aid,
> Victory bring.
> May he sedition hush,
> and like a torrent rush,
> Rebellious Scots to crush,
> God save the King.[15]

Unlike the Highlanders, the Lowland Protestants no longer saw themselves as Scots; they were *British*. This is evident in the insistence by many in calling Scotland 'North Britain' from the 18th Century onwards.[16] It is doubtful, though, that this was any kind of conspiracy; even intelligent men like David Hume were not averse to using the expression. (On a side note, nobody in England ever called their country 'South Britain'.)

A huge part of being British, then, was being anti-Catholic. The English had long been paranoid about Catholicism and now Scotland had been infected as well. This paranoia was defined as 'defence'; defending Protestant Britain against the Catholic hordes of Europe. Such ideas of 'defence' were already familiar to the Presbyterians of Ulster; it was only a matter of time before they were asked to join this 'Anti-Catholic League' on a more official basis.

The annexation of Ireland to create the United Kingdom was another crisis point in the development of anti-Catholic hatred and paranoia in Scotland. Ireland now appeared closer than ever, presenting the perceived threat from Catholics to be on two fronts: the Scottish Highlands and Ireland. Scottish Protestants came to associate themselves more and more with their co-religionists in Ulster; both of them threatened by Catholics in their own countries.

The Government in London cynically exploited these fears to keep a hold over its 'partners' in the United Kingdom. Not only did hatred and fear of Catholics keep religious divisions among Protestants under control in England; the same policy worked wonders in Scotland, where the Union with England was now seen as the only way to safeguard Protestantism. As for Ireland, it was the 'divide and rule' tactic that England employed throughout her empire. This way of working, however, was dropped whenever the occasion demanded it.

The granting of the vote to Irish Catholics (albeit well-off ones) and allowing them to become MPs was a kick in the teeth to the Irish Protestants, but it was necessary for the defence of England. And that is what everything was geared toward: England. The Protestants of Ireland, and, especially, Ulster could pretty much be taken for granted. As Daniel Defoe had pointed out, it did not matter how many times they were knocked down, they were always back up on their feet, ready to be used again.

Meanwhile, the spread of anti-Catholic attitudes in Scotland were brought sharply into focus when Irish Catholics came to live there in a mass migration caused by the Great Famine. Now the paranoia came into full flower. Not only did the Scots have Catholics to the North of them, Catholics to the West of them; they had Catholics right in their midst. It was a situation they hated but, unfortunately, there was not a thing they could do about it. Those Irish Catholics were citizens of the United Kingdom and could live wherever they liked within that sainted realm. No wonder the Orange Order had been opposed to the Act of Union with Ireland.[17]

Much of the antagonism towards the Irish Catholics was expressed in what could be called racist terms but was the hatred really racist? It is a kind of chicken-and-the-egg conundrum; were the Irish hated because they were Catholics, or were they hated because they were Irish?

5
Why Don't You Go Home: Racism or Sectarianism?

When I was learning Spanish at school, our teacher, as well as text books, would use Spanish magazines and even adverts that she had recorded from the radio while she was in Spain. I always remember one of the articles from the magazine, which asked ordinary Spaniards how they felt about people from other parts of Spain. One character from Madrid said of people from Andalucia, *'¡Son Gitanos!'* – 'They're Gypsies'. For some reason that has stuck in my mind all these years; maybe writing this book was in the back of my mind when I was a teenager!

Practically everywhere you go in the world, there is a kind of snobbishness among one set of people towards another. City dwellers view those that live in the countryside as 'bumpkins'; not over-endowed with grey matter. Rustic folk, meanwhile, see their urban cousins as sly, cunning and not to be trusted. Both sets of people make up derogatory names for each other.

Although this kind of thing is mostly harmless, it can turn pretty nasty, evolving into disgraceful stereotypes. Northern Europeans view those from the South of the continent as lazy and feckless. Citizens of the USA feel the same about Mexicans and other people from Latin America, while the target of the British version of this way of thinking is the Irish. Of course, not everyone is involved in this stereotyping and such prejudice is not limited to the people named. Many Americans, for example, view black people in the same manner. You will, however, notice something that most of those believed to be lazy have in common; they are Catholics.

Apologies for bringing up my schooldays again, but I remember how shocked we all were when a character in our reading book said she had never seen a Catholic woman work so hard as a local housewife.[1] The way it was presented in the book made it appear as a common perception that Catholics were lazy.

And it *was* a common perception and still is for many people. The idea has been around for a long while but was finally given a pseudo-scientific gloss with the publication, in 1905, of *The Protestant Ethic and the Spirit of Capitalism*.[2] Max Weber, the German author of this work, has gained renown as one of the 'fathers' of Sociology. Weber's *magnum opus* still incites controversy and there are still historians, sociologists and economists ready to argue his case.[3]

Sifting through the convoluted complications of copyright law is not for the faint-hearted, but it looks to me as if Weber's book is in the public domain. If anyone is interested in reading it, it is available for download at various websites.[4] Essentially, though, Weber's thesis is that radical, fundamental Protestantism, most especially Calvinism, was responsible for modern industrialisation and modern capitalism; in fact, the whole structure of Western civilisation.

Simply put, with there no longer being the need to do good works to get to Heaven, Protestants looked at their lives in a different way. Since God had predestined that only the chosen ones, the *Elect*, would be saved, the preoccupation now was to try to determine who the *Elect* actually were. One way to do so might be to look at those that were successful on Earth; maybe that was God's way of showing who His Elect were.

Luther, who had been a monk himself, developed part of the monastic ethos into everyday life, most notably the Benedictine motto, *Laborare est Orare*. Not for Luther, however, any grim asceticism; he saw nothing wrong with having a good time while on Earth.[5] John Calvin took things further. To him, the whole world was a monastery, where hard work showed one's duty to God, and perhaps even one's membership of the *Elect*.

The Calvinist philosophy embraced asceticism with a vengeance; enjoyment was a vice of the *Damned*. Since everyone should work for God's glory, idleness was condemned. Charity was viewed as a sin against God, therefore, because it encouraged dependence and was against Divine laws that everyone should work. Being unemployed, or even starving to death, was one's own fault and marked one out as one of the *Damned*. Forbidden to enjoy their riches, and barred from charitable works, radical Protestants needed something else to do with their money. Calvin had an answer ready; they were to invest the money in other capitalist ventures.[6] Thus, so Weber's argument goes, was born the modern capitalist system.

There have been countless arguments against Weber's thesis, not least of which is that capitalism, by its very nature, is a decidedly *un*-Christian system. It goes against everything that Christ taught; all the people mentioned as going to be saved in the Sermon on the Mount, the Beatitudes, for example, were, according to this version of Calvinism, destined to burn in the bowels of Hell. Then again, much of Protestantism in past years tended to focus on the 'Chosen People' stuff in the Old Testament and the Book of Revelation; skipping all the awkward bits in-between.

Weber's ideas fall down completely when one looks at the nations that prospered after the Reformation. England was not really what one would call a Protestant nation. The clinging-on to old, Catholic styles of church government and ceremonial marked the country out as unique among nations that called themselves 'Reformed'. Scotland, on the other hand, was among the most radical, Calvinist places on Earth. And yet, England thrived, building trade and empires, while Scotland trudged along as its poorer neighbour. Not until after the Union with England were numerous markets opened to Scottish trade.

Possibly the biggest argument against Weber, though, is that his whole thesis is built on fallacies. His primary sources, for example, turn out to be, awkwardly, inspired by agenda, rather than thoughts of historical empiricism.[7] A glaring example of this is Weber's use of American Puritans to illustrate his points. He visited the USA and produced an essay on his findings, called *The Protestant Sects and Spirit of Capitalism*. This work too, however, was based on a fallacy; a fallacy invented by the Americans themselves.[8]

We are all familiar with Thanksgiving Day in the USA, where everyone remembers the Puritans that came over on the Mayflower; the Founding Fathers. By their diligence and hard work, these Puritans, along with others of their ilk, built the modern United States. The American Industrial Revolution began in New England,[9] leading to the industrialisation of the Northern States, as opposed to the agricultural South. This entrepreneurial spirit eventually built the USA into an economic powerhouse, trading all over the world. This American view of US history is, however, a complete invention.

After the Civil War, there was an attempt to rewrite American history; an attempt that was largely successful. The Southern States were pretty much expunged from early Colonial history. Also expunged was the real origin of the wealth of the USA: slavery.

Think of slavery in America and you immediately imagine cotton fields and tobacco plantations, filled with hundreds of overworked slaves. So successful has been the rewriting of American history that everyone believes that slavery was limited to the likes of Virginia, Georgia and the Carolinas. In fact, slavery was endemic all over the Thirteen Colonies. New England's burgeoning economy was originally based on it.[10]

The money for the great entrepreneurial activity in the North originally came from slavery and the slave trade. Even at a most basic level, the use of slaves in New England for domestic chores freed up the householders to engage in other, more profitable ventures.[11] The USA was not built on the hard work of devout Puritans, but on the hard work of African slaves.

And what of Britain? Bristol and Liverpool were major centres for the slave trade and many grew rich from it. Even other areas were linked to the slave trade; shipbuilders built the vessels to carry the Africans across the ocean, blacksmiths made chains and shackles, while goods were produced to trade for slaves in West Africa. Glasgow's famous Tobacco Barons benefited directly from the use of slaves; some of them even owned their own plantations. Just as in America, slavery provided the cash to invest in the Industrial Revolution. Even the new factories were mostly built to produce cotton goods; using cotton picked by slaves. Most of England's, and then Britain's wealth, can be traced, directly or indirectly, to slavery.[12]

Weber mentions none of this in his works, which, in this light, can be seen as a desperate justification of empire and the capitalist system. There is also the hint of an agenda. When studying History at university, one is always cautioned to check one's sources in case of possible bias or prejudice. Max Weber's mother was descended from French Huguenots[13] and was a strict Calvinist. Weber was close to his mother's family; in fact, so much so that his father tried to counter their influence on his son.[14] Weber's aunt on his mother's side was married to historian Hermann Baumgarten, who is claimed to be a major influence on young Weber.[15] It is more than probable that Hermann was not the only member of his mother's family to influence Max.

Weber's ideas were not new but he put them into a more formal, academic format. His book and essays should, perhaps, be viewed in the context in which they were written. The German-speaking lands, in the years leading up to the First World War, were a hotbed of new political ideas and new slants on old ones. Ideas were being expounded everywhere about religion, race, philosophy and political ideologies. Weber no doubt imbibed all these ideas in much the same way as did a young man in Vienna by the name of Adolf Hitler.

Weber might well be called a 'revisionist historian', a label that most respectable historians would baulk at. The phrase conjures up visions of holocaust deniers and writers that ignore important evidence because it does not agree with their agenda or use so-called evidence from decidedly dodgy sources; in short, folk that do not know what the hell they are doing. As I said, most historians would hit the roof if you called them 'revisionist'. One historian, however, positively revels in it.

Ruth Dudley Edwards studied History at University College in Dublin and has won prizes for her biographies. I have never seen Edwards explicitly claim to be a believer in Max Weber's nonsense; her writings, however, show that she most definitely is. Much of her work declares, either implicitly or explicitly, that the English conquest and subjugation of Ireland was a good thing. Part of one of her articles in the Belfast Telegraph illustrates this point perfectly:

> The eternal whingeing (of the Irish) resembles that so brilliantly satirised in The Life of Brian: "But apart from the sanitation, the medicine, education, wine, public order, irrigation, roads, the fresh-water system and public health, what have the Romans ever done for us?"
> The British did most of that for us, along with giving us their language, democratic, legal, educational and other institutions, access to all opportunities in their country even after independence and - in the case of Northern Ireland - the right to stay in, or leave, the United Kingdom as the majority decides.[16]

Edwards appears to believe that, without the English invasion, the Irish would never have developed any kind of modern civilisation at all. Like other 'revisionists', she ignores any evidence that does not fit. The truth is that the Irish, in their own country, had no vote, no rights, no money, no land and no wherewithal to improve their situation. Edwards's arguments are complete and utter nonsense.

As we have seen, Edwards's arguments, along with their source, the theses of Max Weber, are part of an international belief in the superiority of Protestantism, with its concomitant view of Catholicism, and Catholics, as inferior. The economic success of mostly Protestant nations were seen as proof of that notion. Anti-Catholicism was perfectly acceptable in such a climate since Catholics were demonstrably lazy and shiftless.

Anti-Catholic attitudes were also apparent during the Great Famine in Ireland. The Famine has, over the years, become such an emotive subject that it is often hard to get to the truth of claims that are made about events and attitudes. What is plain, however, is that the authorities knew well in advance that such a disaster was going to happen but made no plans to alleviate the mass starvation. Also, there was more than enough food being produced in Ireland to feed the population; profits, however, came first.

Legends have grown about *Souperism*, a term coined to describe the practice of refusing aid to the hungry unless they converted to Protestantism in one form or another, or, at least, agreed to being proselytised to. There are tales of people being ostracised by their communities for 'taking the soup', even though you could hardly blame them for trying to keep themselves and their families alive. The real finger of blame should have been, and often was, pointed at those that made their charity conditional in this way.

Quite how widespread was this practice is still a source of great debate. Certainly, the condemnation of senior, Anglican churchmen at the time proves that it was not just an occasional occurrence, confined to a few areas.[17] On the other hand, the very fact that these practices were documented at the time shows that it was not happening everywhere;[18] nobody would be suggesting such a course of action, or condemning it, if everyone was involved. One also has to be careful when talking about 'Protestant' groups. Upper-class Anglicans, middle-class Nonconformists, Presbyterians and Quakers all had different ideas about charity and, as we saw earlier, some believed that charity was a sin against God. Protestantism was not a homogeneous organisation.

If charity provision in Ireland showed divisions in Protestantism, the migration of many Irish Catholics to Scotland and England created a more monolithic response; nobody wanted them. British authorities did their best to discourage this influx, usually sending any migrants they caught back to Ireland. These migrants were, in fact, UK citizens and, as such, were entitled to go wherever they liked within the British Isles. There was, however, a way round that awkward reality.

Everybody at school learns about the 1834 Poor Law Amendment Act and the introduction of workhouses but not everybody knows about how the system worked. The whole of Britain was divided up into Poor Law Unions, each of which was responsible for the poor and unemployed in its own area. If a Union took in anyone from outside its area, other than itinerant job-seekers looking for a night's lodging, then it would be unable to claim money from the parish. So, any unemployed people found in the area, who did not come from that area, were encouraged to move on. For the Irish that meant being sent back to Ireland. Unscrupulous individuals could use this situation to their own advantage.

A boat owner would charge a pittance to bring Irish families over to the British mainland; often paid by rich 'philanthropists' wanting to move the problem on. Once they had landed, he would turn them over to the authorities for a reward and then let said authorities hire his boat to take the unwanted refugees back to Ireland![19]

In Scotland, Calvinist ideas about charity dominated. The self-help philosophy could even be seen in the fact that the victims of the potato blight in the North of Scotland were sent seed potatoes by lowland charities. These were meant to be planted to produce food in the future and the starving Highlanders were castigated for eating these potatoes instead of using them for propagation.[20] The holders of such cold-hearted attitudes were hardly going to welcome starving Irish Catholics with open arms.

A myth has grown in Scotland that the refugees from famine *were* welcomed and looked after. As the disgusting Famine Song puts it:

> I often wonder where they would have been
> If we hadn't have taken them in
> Fed them and washed them
> Thousands in Glasgow alone'[21]

This is arrant nonsense. In fact, just like in other areas of Britain, 50,000 migrants were sent back to Ireland by the authorities in

Scotland.[22] Even more might well have been sent back if it were not for the fact that this influx was not the only thing going on at the time. Like other places in Britain, Glasgow and its surrounding areas were experiencing Chartist agitation, while the middle classes were caught up in the fight to introduce Free Trade legislation and to abolish the Corn Laws. As if that were not enough to contend with, the Church of Scotland had been riven in two by the Disruption Crisis. For many, the arrival of starving Irish Catholics was the least of their worries.

Besides, despite the efforts of the British authorities to send the refugees back to Ireland, there was one indisputable fact: those Irish refuges were all citizens of the United Kingdom. Another point that would have stopped many in Britain from going too far against the migrants was that, essentially, they were not worth bothering about. Like the majority of lower-class people in the United Kingdom, the Irish Catholics were completely powerless. Not only did they not have the vote, but there would be no place for them in trades unions, Chartist groups or any other political organisations. Unless their position changed they were viewed pretty much like mice or other vermin; undesirable, but there was nothing you could really do about them.

Fast-forward to 1923 and an infamous Church of Scotland report. *The Menace of the Irish Race to our Scottish Nationality* might contain the term 'race' but it was not racist in nature. Instead, the fears expressed in the document were all about how Irish Catholics and their descendants had led to the re-establishment of the Catholic Church hierarchy and a rise in Catholic church buildings.[23] The Irish were seen as helping a Roman Catholic conspiracy to take over Scotland; something that 'indigenous' Scottish Catholics, numerically, were unable to do.[24]

What had changed to foster such fears? We have seen how anti-Catholicism was deliberately fostered throughout the British Isles by the Westminster Government as a means of maintaining control, but why was the Church of Scotland so concerned at that particular point in time? The answer lies in something that had worried the Orange Order for nearly a hundred years: the franchise.

The terms of the Catholic Emancipation Act of 1829 meant that Catholics were now pretty much treated the same as everybody else. This was of serious concern to the Orange Order, not only in Ireland but in Scotland and England as well. As the 19th Century wore on, the franchise was widened to include the middle classes and then better-off members of the working classes. This meant, of course, that middle-class and working-class Catholics were getting the vote as well. Orangemen would rather go without the vote themselves than see more and more Catholics being enfranchised. For this reason, they were in the vanguard of opposition to every extension of the franchise.

The Scottish Orange Order boasts of its opposition to the 1832 Reform Bill, as if denying people the vote was somehow a virtue.[25] When the Houses of Parliament suffered extensive damage by fire in 1834, Queen Adelaide pronounced it a judgment from God for passing the Reform Bill.[26] Doubtless every Orangeman in the UK agreed with her wholeheartedly.

Extensions of the franchise had been piecemeal and hardly wide-ranging; by 1914 only 7.7 million men had the vote[27] and most of those going off to fight in the war were unable to take part in elections. That was to change once the war was over.

The Representation of the People Act was passed in 1918, enfranchising virtually every man in the UK over the age of 21.[28] Overnight all those Irish Catholics living in Scotland and England suddenly had the vote; a frightening prospect for the Protestant Establishment. From then on, Catholics were a viable threat; a threat made all the more pressing during the depression of the 1930s, when competition for jobs was fierce.

The Church of Scotland report and the emergence of political groups like the Scottish Political League and the Protestant Action Society[29] shows that it was hatred of Catholics, rather than racial hatred of the Irish that inspired sectarian divisions. Certainly, much of the hatred of the Irish was expressed in racial terms, such as the picture on the front of this book, but this stemmed from religious antagonism, not racism.

But what about those famous signs, saying, 'No Dogs, No Blacks, No Irish'; were they not racist? The answer again is no. The reason why folk did not want Irish people in their establishments was because of their reputation for violence. This reputation came about in the mid-19th Century, when gangs of labourers traversed the country, building the new railways. As always when there are large groups of men around, alcohol was never far away, along with arguments and, of course violence.

The architects and engineers planning the railways left it to foremen, gangers, to employ groups of manual labourers, navvies. The ganger would be paid and it was up to him to pay his men. Quite often he would abscond with the money, leading to violence and even murder. Meanwhile, the navvies were supplied with beer, while they were working, to quench their thirst. This was all on credit, to be deducted from the men's pay, along with food and accommodation.[30] Understandably, the men preferred to sleep in barns and the like and buy their food and drink from local villages, instead of paying the inflated prices of the Company. Local merchants and publicans would also put their prices up when the gangs arrived, leading to trouble with the locals. Huge fights would take place, often organised in advance, between rival groups of navvies and between navvies and locals. Not surprisingly, everybody dreaded the arrival of the navvies.

Many of these itinerant labourers were Irish, leading people to believe that they were responsible for all the trouble. After all, thrifty, God-fearing Protestants would not be involved in such shenanigans, would they? And so, the myth was born of the quick-tempered Irishman, ready to fight at the least imagined insult. Large groups of women followed the navvies, for obvious reasons, and often got involved in any fighting alongside the men. Again, it was assumed that these women, who followed the Irish navvies, must be Irish themselves. They could hardly be respectable, Protestant women! It was believed, therefore, that, regardless of age or gender, the Irish were nothing but trouble.

Other nationalities are perceived to be quick-tempered and violent as well. Everybody has heard of the 'Latin temperament' prevalent among those that come from Latin America, while Italians, Spaniards and even Poles are usually depicted as touchy and easily riled. And what do all these nationalities have in common? They all come from predominantly Catholic countries.

During the Troubles in Northern Ireland, many Loyalists went out of their way to argue that the Republican side was acting from sectarian motives; anti-Protestantism rather than any political agenda. Even today there are those that are still desperate to prove that this was true.[31] The media join in as well. For example, it was alleged in a BBC documentary that Dave Allen received death threats from the

IRA for lampooning the Pope on his TV show.[32] Erstwhile members of the IRA deny that any such threats were ever made.[33] Scottish newspapers, meanwhile, always report IRA graffiti as 'sectarian' and 'bigoted'.[34]

This apparent need to associate Irish Republicanism with sectarianism betrays the feelings of those that make this association. That they view things in this manner shows that it is *they* that hold these sectarian ideas; they are trying to impose their beliefs onto their perceived 'enemy'. It is more evidence that the hatred of Irish Catholics and their descendants is not racial; it springs from sectarian anti-Catholicism.

6
The Great White Hope: Rangers

The usual narrative vis-à-vis bigotry in Scotland, especially in relation to football, is that Ulster Protestants came to Glasgow to work in Harland and Wolff in 1912, followed Glasgow Rangers and the rest is history. This, however, is a blatant example of trying to pass the buck. It is easier to blame the whole problem on the Irish, Catholic and Protestant, than to admit that Scotland itself had this problem already.

In the 1980s, I read a book about sectarianism in Glasgow football by Bill Murray, called, *The Old Firm*. I actually owned the book but, as often happens, it has gone; probably stolen by somebody that borrowed it. I am relying on memory, therefore, as well as the fact that Amazon lets you see parts of the book on its website.[1]

At any rate, three things in the book have stuck in my mind. The first is a picture, a drawing, from an early 20th Century newspaper, which depicted the two captains in the centre circle at the start of an Old Firm match. The Rangers player stood tall, with neat kit, neat hair and a haughty demeanour. The Celtic player, in contrast, was dressed in a caricature of Irish dress, the buckled shoes, the bashed tall hat, tattered coat etc. This character also had a long, unkempt beard, rickety legs, a bent back and was smoking a clay pipe.

(This familiar depiction of an Irishman no doubt derives from the clothes that Irish people wore in the middle of the 19th Century. Most lower-class people could not afford new clothes and wore the cast-offs of the middle and upper classes. This meant that they wore clothes that richer people had worn back in the 1820s and 1830s. Being at the bottom of the heap, as they were, Irish folk probably wore old-fashioned clothes for longer than most.)

The second thing I remember from the book leads directly from the first. The picture was not just there for decoration; it was part of Murray's argument that anti-Catholic and anti-Irish bigotry against

Celtic was well in evidence long before anybody arrived at the shipyards from Belfast. The third point I remember from the book actually ties in extremely well with the theme of this work.

We have already seen how Irish Catholics were not seen as any kind of threat until they had access to power, through gaining the vote. Bill Murray argues the exact same point about Celtic. Having a Glasgow team that the Irish Catholics could support probably seemed like a good idea at first; it would keep them off the streets, after all. The problem was that Celtic became far too successful for comfort, creating resentment against Irish Catholics and their team.

By the time of the First World War, Celtic had won a record 11 League titles, as well as 9 Scottish Cups. In 1910 Celtic won their sixth league title in a row; another record. In 1907 Celtic became the first Scottish team to achieve 'The Double', winning both the League and the Scottish Cup. They repeated this feat in the following season. All-in-all, in Edwardian times, Celtic was, arguably, the most successful team in Scotland. This, albeit vicarious, glory obviously made the Irish Catholic community in Glasgow far more confident about its place in society. That was not something that was going to please the Protestant Establishment.

Rangers became the 'Great White Hope' of Scottish Protestantism and, consequently, the 'Establishment Club'. Probably those with no interest in Association football cheered on Rangers, hoping that those uppity Catholics would be put in their place.

So closely did Rangers become entangled with this notion of Protestant one-upmanship that it was inevitable that the club would become closely aligned with the Orange Order, which, for many years, owned shares in Rangers.[2] This, of course, brought the politics of Ireland to Ibrox; it also brought a specific ideology to the Rangers support.

The Liberal Party in the 19th Century, just like Labour in the 20th, relied on what was called the 'Celtic Fringe', Scotland, Wales and Cornwall, as its power base. The Irish Nationalists were also pretty much on the Liberal side; they were hardly going to get Home Rule from the Tories! Things changed for the Liberal Party, however, in 1886.

William Gladstone, when he first became Prime Minister in 1868, announced that his 'Mission is to pacify Ireland'.[3] After disestablishing the Church of Ireland and introducing various land reforms, Gladstone finally decided that Home Rule was the only answer. He consequently, in 1886, introduced a bill to this effect in the House of Commons.[4] The bill was defeated without even reaching the Lords, not least because a large chunk of the Liberal Party voted against it. Effectively, Gladstone had succeeded in splitting the party in two.

The MPs that left the Liberal Party re-styled themselves as Liberal Unionists and crossed the House to the Conservative side. The Liberal Unionist Party, later to become simply the Unionist Party, joined in coalition with the Tories in Scotland to effectively wipe out the Liberal majority there. Even at a local level the Liberal Party was split. One prominent Glasgow Liberal was quick to join the breakaway party; his name was John Ure Primrose.

Primrose was Lord Provost of Glasgow between 1902 and 1905. He became Honorary President of Rangers from 1888 and then Chairman from 1912 to 1923.[5] He was also a notorious anti-Catholic bigot with links to the Orange Order.[6] At some point while he was Honorary President, Primrose publicly linked Rangers with Freemasonry.[7] Quite what this entailed I have been unable to determine but Freemasonry in Scotland has a distinctly anti-Catholic reputation.

Being anti-Catholic is something that Freemasonry tries hard to repudiate, often claiming that people are getting it confused with the Orange Order. One Masonic writer that goes down this particular path rather lets himself down with part of the quote he gives about Freemasonry in Northern Ireland:

> Sometimes lodges with predominantly Protestant memberships either forced Catholic members out or prevented Catholics from joining in the first place. For example, during the 1820s Lodge No. 424, in County Antrim, instituted a rule requiring members and candidates to swear they had never "professed the Roman Catholic religion.[8]

But that was at the start of the 19th Century, it could be argued; it is doubtful, though, that things had changed very much by the start of the 20th. Besides, why would Primrose, a confirmed bigot, choose to link himself with an organisation that was a model of tolerance?

So, not only was Rangers being viewed as the 'Great White Hope' of Scottish Protestantism against the Catholic-Irish team; it was also being dragged into notions of Protestant supremacy. And that was not all; Liberal Unionists were concerned with far more than just Ireland.

Back in the early-to-mid 19th Century, Britain was the biggest trading nation in the World. All over the planet people sailed in British ships, rode on British trains, wore British clothes and fought with British arms and ammunition. The great dogma at this time among industrialists and merchants was Free Trade; opening ports everywhere, even in other countries' colonies. Of course, this meant opening British ports to foreign merchants. Since Britain had more ships and more industrial goods to trade than everyone else, this would hardly be a hardship. It was arguments over Free Trade that first led to the formation of the Liberal Party.

During the second half of the century, however, things started to go wrong. For a variety of reasons British trade took a dramatic turn for the worse. Other nations, like the USA, France and Germany started to catch up and, in some cases, even overtake Britain in terms of industrial output and trade.[9] Rather than invest in more modern techniques, industrialists looked to the Government to come up with a solution. Free Trade did not look such a great idea anymore.

Running an empire is an expensive business: civil servants, police and the army in each colony do not come cheap. The Ancient Romans had farmed out the administration of client states to private enterprise and only colonised areas when it became completely necessary. The British Government, no matter which party was in charge, felt exactly the same way. With cheaper products and food being exported from the USA, Germany and even Russia, Britain became more reliant on captive markets outside of Europe and America.[10] A captive market meant a formal empire, with all the expensive trappings that Britain had been trying to avoid.

Just as the Romans had done, the British Establishment made a virtue out of a necessity and the myth grew of British destiny in the World, bringing civilisation to every part of the Globe. The reality was that British trade had come to depend on the Empire and that trade now relied on gunboats and troops rather than competitive prices.

As British Governments clung stubbornly to the old shibboleth of Free Trade, more and more politicians were coming to realise that it was no longer an advantage. Liberal Unionists were in the forefront of wanting to re-introduce tariffs and many, like Joseph Chamberlain, promoted the idea of turning the Empire into some kind of customs union. In fact, it was this that made many in the party oppose Home Rule for Ireland; it would be the thin end of the wedge leading to the break-up of the Empire.

Of course, the ordinary man in the street could not be expected to understand all these high-minded, economic ideologies. That was why Liberal Unionists were in the vanguard of all the flag-waving, 'sun never sets', 'rule the waves' worship of the British Empire. With John Ure Primrose's influence at Ibrox, it was inevitable that Rangers and its supporters got caught up in all this as well.

Over the years, the flag-waving chauvinism of the Rangers support has made it a target for recruitment by extremist, far-right organisations. Whenever such organisations, such as the National Front, British Nationalist Part, Scottish Defence League and even the English Defence League are in the news, a Rangers top or scarf is invariably visible among the crowd. That does not mean, however, that everyone that supports Rangers runs to sign up for these groups. In fact, attempts at recruitment at Ibrox have often been an abject failure.

The problem with right-wing groups trying to recruit Rangers supporters is that they already have, and have had for many years, their own right-wing organisations, particularly the Orange Order.[11] From the British Union of Fascists to the Scottish Defence League, all these groups failed miserably to elicit any enthusiasm among Rangers fans for their targets of hatred. For the Rangers supporters, nothing else would, or will, do but hatred of Catholics and the Irish, as this comment on the afore-referenced article shows:

> I notice the author's name is "Liam"…interesting. I won't take a THING from his mouth as even being uttered by a human, lol. I would like to see his views on the IRA & Scottish independence. I bet we can all guess.
> Just another anti-British bigoted hit-piece from a far-left radical socialist Celtic fan and Scottish Nationalist.[12]

Anyway, back to Primrose and 1912 was an important year for the man. Not only did he become chairman of Rangers, he also shared a stage with Edward Carson, welcoming him to Glasgow.[13] Carson would be preaching to the converted when he came to Scotland; after all, Scottish Presbyterians had long felt an affinity with their co-religionists in Ulster. Obviously, they would be on Carson's side against the Government's Irish Home Rule plans. Many, if not all, of those ready to give their backing to Carson's cause would be Rangers supporters. From then on, supporting Rangers became almost synonymous with support for Ulster Unionists in Scotland. Rangers supporters became indistinguishable from Orangemen.

On its website, the Grand Orange Lodge of Scotland says:

> The Protestant ethic is one of tolerance of other faiths and ideals. It is this tolerance and liberty that the Orange Order promotes and defends.[14]

Now *there* was something that William of Orange would have agreed with. Unfortunately, the Orange Order itself does not. The history that the Order gives out about itself is full of references to fights against any extension of the franchise to Catholics. They even claim that Gladstone's efforts at Home Rule for Ireland were part of a 'measure to appease Catholic opinion'. Meanwhile, the Anglo-Irish settlement of 1921 'was seen as a betrayal of Southern Protestants'.[15] Not great fans of democracy, then, and so much for that defence of 'liberty'!

Looking at what the Orange Order has campaigned for in the past and what it campaigns for now, like closing Catholic schools, it is doubtful that William of Orange would have had anything to do with this organisation. You may remember that William, a strict Calvinist, called his coronation a 'popish mockery';[16] it makes you wonder how he would view the Orange Order, with all its pomp, rituals and ceremonies. When you look at it, the Orange Order is a distinctly *un*-Protestant organisation.

Most of the Orange Lodges and bands call themselves things like 'True Defenders' and often claim that they are defending the Protestant faith. Quite from whom they are 'defending' Protestantism they never say. The biggest threat nowadays to Protestantism, and, indeed, to all Christian faiths, is apathy and secularism. In this atmosphere one would imagine that the best way to save Protestantism would be just to turn up at church. And yet, many ministers stand at the pulpit, pretty much talking to themselves, while their potential congregation is out somewhere banging Lambeg drums. It would appear that hating Catholics comes before saving Protestantism!

In fact, following the Church of Scotland's lead, it was Irish Catholics that the Orange Order was meant to hate. Unfortunately, however, those sneaky, untrustworthy Irish had pulled a fast one. By the 1920s, most 'Irish' Catholics in Scotland were second, third and even fourth-generation. They grew up speaking with Scottish accents and it was hard to tell them apart from 'indigenous' Scots. Just to be on the safe side, it meant that Orangemen were forced to hate *all* Catholics. In Glasgow, of course, there was always the Irish Catholics' football team to hate.

At Old Firm matches, then, many Rangers supporters did not sing about their football team, or even their hatred of Celtic, but songs and chants of an anti-Catholic and anti-Irish flavour, as well as Orange staples like 'The Sash'. So wrapped up in this bile did Rangers become that its support became almost indistinguishable from the Orange Order. In fact, in modern times many supporters think that 'The Sash' and 'Derry's Walls' are Rangers songs and some do not even consider themselves in any way connected with the Orange Order while singing them. Of course, the opposite applies as well.

A boy in one of my P6 classes walked along the school corridor one day, singing at the top of his voice, 'Ay's bald, ay's fat, ay's gonny get the sack – Advocaat. Advocaat.' The weird thing was that this lad came to school every day wearing a Rangers jacket and equipped with a Rangers pencil case. It turned out that he had no idea who Advocaat was; he had heard somebody else singing the song and liked the tune. I explained who Dick Advocaat was and told him not to go about singing in the corridors again.

Near the end of the school year, he came in one Monday and told us, as part of his news, that he had watched Rangers beating Celtic on Sunday. While we all tried to explain to him that the season was long since over, he was adamant that he had seen the game on television. Further investigation led to me discovering that his dad's friend had brought round a video of an old Rangers v Celtic match.

The boy actually had no interest in football whatsoever; a fact I learned when he was in P7. So why did he always bring Rangers items to school? I found out that he and his whole family were involved in the local Orange Lodge. His immediate family had as little interest in football as he had. All the Rangers stuff was about being Orange and nothing to do with the team. With a lack of products advertising the Orange Order, Rangers items were the next-best thing.

For many years, the media and the authorities in Scotland ignored the bigoted singing of the Rangers supporters, as well as the sectarian signing policy of the club itself. As such, those in power in Scotland were colluding with all this anti-Catholic bigotry. Even nowadays, the media and the authorities seldom mention it; if they do, they always feel the need to claim that the 'other side' is just as bad.

Nil By Mouth is a charity that claims to be fighting sectarian bigotry in Scotland, mainly through education. While its aims are laudable, its definitions of what constitute such bigotry leave much to be desired. On their website, it says:

> Offensive sectarian language is still used in Scotland on a daily basis, with abusive terms such as "Hun" and "Orange bastard" being used negatively against Protestants (or those perceived to be) and others such as "Fenian" and "Tim" used negatively against Catholics (or those perceived to be). This reinforces religious and racial stereotypes as well as fuelling the divisions and conflict between the denominations and people of no religious denomination.[17]

'Tim' is hardly what anyone would call a negative, sectarian stereotype; it is a word that usually signifies a Celtic supporter and one that nobody feels the least bit offended by. It shows that Nil By Mouth do not really know what they are talking about. The word 'Hun' is a negative one but refers to somebody associated with Rangers, whether players or supporters; nothing else. There are those that point to its use in Northern Ireland as some kind of sectarian slur. The simple answer to that, though, is that this is Scotland, not Northern Ireland. As for 'Orange bastard', it can easily be argued that this term is not sectarian either.

The simple fact is that if Rangers supporters are going to sing songs that align them, whether consciously or unconsciously, with the Orange Order, then they can hardly complain if they are given the epithet 'Orange'. The term is in no way a slur against Protestants; after all, Celtic has always fielded Protestant players, had Protestant managers and many Protestant supporters. And this is the problem that organisations like Nil By Mouth have to confront.

Whether it is through fear or an inability to face up to the facts, nobody seems willing to put the blame for sectarian bigotry where it belongs. The truth is that Celtic and its support are not, and never have been, guilty of sectarian bigotry. It is impossible to find any examples of Celtic supporters singing or chanting their hatred of Protestants; hatred of the Orange Order is quite another matter.

In the version of the movie 'Shaft' that came out in 2000, there is a scene where a group of friends go into a restaurant. One of these friends happens to be black, which prompts another, white, customer to start shouting racist comments over at him. The black man gets his own back by tearing holes in a napkin and placing it over the offensive customer's face, like a Ku Klux Klan hood. I will not spoil the rest of the film by revealing what happens next.

If we were to apply the way of thinking of Nil By Mouth, the Scottish media and the Scottish authorities, then that black man is just as racist as the white one. He used no racist language, like 'cracker' or anything similar, but implying that the man was a member of the KKK was a slur against his whiteness. It sounds stupid, but that is exactly the argument that Nil By Mouth is putting forward by claiming that calling Rangers supporters 'Orange' is somehow sectarian bigotry against Protestants. Those Rangers supporters, remember, are not singing Protestant hymns, but Orange anthems.

But surely all that is in the past? After all, many Catholics have played for Rangers in the past few decades. More than a few of those players, however, have mentioned that they were advised not to bless themselves when running onto the pitch, as many players around the world do. Even in the second decade of the 21st Century such practices were still being reported.[18]

The philosophy expounded by the Orange Order and by the supporters at Ibrox Stadium, who often seem like the same thing, is not Protestant at all; it is anti-Catholic in general and anti-Irish

Catholic in particular. Any argument to the contrary is easily countered with the ridiculous furore over the song *The Hokey-Cokey*.

It was in December 2008 that the news first broke about this innocuous song. Apparently, the whole row started when the disgusting *Famine Song* was banned. Some angry Rangers supporters, upset at this, discussed on their forums what songs they *were* allowed to sing. Among the anodyne ditties suggested, somebody mentioned *The Hokey-Cokey*.[19] It is unclear whether the idea that the song was anti-Catholic was brought up on the Rangers forums or if some journalist thought it up but the story was soon in the press.[20]

People close to Cardinal O'Brien later denied that the Cardinal, or anyone associated with his office, had brought the subject up at all. It was believed to have been a story trumped up by some journalist, quoting the Cardinal's press office out of context, to make the Catholic Church look ridiculous.[21]

Be that as it may, there was another element to this that nobody bothered to comment upon. No sooner had the story broken than *The Hokey-Cokey* suddenly became a favourite for Rangers supporters and Orangemen.[22] This murky little episode helped to prove, once and for all, that, despite what they might say, Rangers supporters were guilty of singing anti-Catholic songs. Even when it was fairly obvious that a song was *not* anti-Catholic, Rangers supporters only needed to *believe* that Catholics were offended by a song for it to become part of their repertoire.

It is against this bigotry that Celtic supporters sing and chant; not against Protestantism, which has nothing to do with this bile nowadays. Until that fact is recognised, then those trying to stamp out sectarian bigotry in Scotland are fighting a losing battle.

7
Roll of Honour: Bigotry or Politics?

We saw in the last chapter how, rather than face up to the problem of anti-Catholic bigotry, the media and organisations supposedly fighting sectarian hatred always try to 'balance things out' by claiming that sectarian bigotry is a two-way process. Rather desperately, they say that Celtic supporters shouting support for the IRA constitutes religious bigotry.

Not many Celtic supporters chant 'IRA' or 'Up the RA' these days, but songs like *Roll of Honour* and *The Boys of the Old Brigade* can be heard quite frequently. Are such songs bigoted? They contain no anti-Protestant lyrics so it is quite a stretch to condemn them as songs of sectarian hatred. Most would argue that they are, in fact, political and nothing whatsoever to do with religious bigotry. The IRA is a proscribed organisation in Britain, which means supporting it is, effectively, illegal. That, however, does not, in any way, turn it into sectarian bigotry.

This presents us with a bit of a dilemma. Does support for Ulster Unionism constitute anti-Catholic bigotry? Certainly, it might well be inspired by such bigotry, but is it bigotry in and of itself? The Scottish media usually portray it as such, as they similarly portray support for Irish Republican Nationalism. It is something that we really need to look at with an open mind.

We have already seen how the Presbyterians of Scottish descent had been used and abused by the Government in England ever since they had arrived in Ulster. They had faced the same discrimination as Catholics at the hands of the Anglican authorities and had come to rely on themselves, rather than England or Britain, to protect them. And, as far as they were concerned, they definitely needed protection. Memories tend to be long in Ireland and stories of Irish Catholics trying to drive the Protestants out in order to reclaim their land seemed as relevant as ever.

During the 19th Century, although factories sprang up in other areas, Ulster became the most industrialised and prosperous part of Ireland. Not everyone benefited from this prosperity, though, as Ulster Protestants ensured that Catholics were excluded from the best jobs. This, of course, seems grossly unfair, which it was, but it has to be seen in the context of the times.

Well into the 20th Century it was considered a truism that the white man had brought civilisation to barbarous areas. In America, Africa and Asia, Europeans found lands infested with half-naked savages and built great cities, transport links, ports and factories. Of course, there had already been great cities in Mexico, India, Persia, Egypt and even Great Zimbabwe in Southern Africa, but it was believed that these were like primitive mud huts next to what the Europeans built. And since the white man had built these places, then they were theirs alone and they were not giving them up for anybody.

As late as the 1990s, Ian Smith, who had led the UDI government of Rhodesia, could be heard on television detailing how white people were responsible for building hospitals and other amenities and great cities like Bulawayo. If that was how some people felt towards the end of the 20th Century, it is easy to imagine that such attitudes were much more prevalent a hundred years previously.

The Ulster Protestants felt much the same about their situation in the province. We have already encountered the myth of the Protestant Work Ethic and how radical Protestantism, like that followed by the Presbyterians in Ulster, was supposedly responsible for industrialisation and world trade. It was remarkably easy, then, for Ulster Protestants to convince themselves, and others, that the industry in the province was *their* industry and that the prosperity was *their* prosperity. Why should it be handed over to a bunch of feckless Catholics?

It is easy to dismiss these fears as nonsense but, at the time, they were genuine, no matter how unfounded they might be. Just as white Europeans in Africa saw majority rule as handing over everything they had built to a bunch of ignorant savages, the Ulster Protestants saw Home Rule in completely the same light.

'Home Rule is Rome Rule' was the cry of many of the Ulster Unionists, which reflected the deep-seated fears that they had. What would happen to them in a Catholic-controlled Ireland? They saw the way Irish Catholics were treated in Scotland and England and, indeed, the way they treated Irish Catholics. If Home Rule came about, they imagined that the tables would be turned and they would have to be the underdogs; something they had already experienced under the Anglicans. As already mentioned, memories are long in Ireland.

Unfortunately, not all the fears of the Ulster Protestants were unfounded. In the years leading up to the First World War, the struggle of working-class people in Dublin to unionise led to the 'Lock-Out' of 1913. The working classes, under the leadership of James Larkin and James Connolly, found themselves opposed by the Catholic Church, Parliamentary Irish Nationalists, the Ancient Order of Hibernians and even Sinn Fein, who all took the side of the employers.[1] When the TUC in England organised families to take in the starving children of the Dublin workers, the overriding concern of Irish Nationalists was that the children would be going to *Protestant* families.[2] These events must have frightened working-class Protestants in Ulster half to death.

(Those wishing to find out more about this shameful episode in Irish history could do worse than get a hold of RTE's brilliant TV serial *Strumpet City*.)

As we have already seen, the Ulster Protestants, while needing Ireland to be part of the UK to maintain their privileged position, did not trust the UK Government to protect them. As they had always done, they looked to themselves, forming the Ulster Volunteer Force to fight against the imposition of Home Rule. They were prepared to even fight against the British Army if need be. Fortunately, the First World War came along before their resolve could be put to the test.

Let us bypass what came after the Great War, when Ireland finally gained independence, only to be embroiled in a civil war. For once, the Westminster Government had done the Ulster Presbyterians a favour, keeping within the UK a small enclave of the six counties of Ulster which contained mostly Protestants. The other three counties contained Protestants as well but their inclusion into the new entity of Northern Ireland would have meant a Catholic majority.

Although the six counties remaining in the UK had a Protestant majority, there was still a sizeable number of Catholics living there as well. Now that everybody had the vote, the Protestants lived with the terror that Catholics might eventually outnumber them and elect to leave the UK. To stop this happening, various impediments were placed in the way of the civil life of Catholics, especially with the allocation of council houses.[3]

There have been some revisionist attempts to deny that the system under the Stormont regime was in any way unfair to Catholics in Northern Ireland. One such individual, Graham Gudgin, an economist based at Cambridge University,[4] starts one paper by saying of power-sharing in Northern Ireland, 'almost uniquely in the western world, Northern Ireland Protestants are not trusted to form a government in circumstances in which they gain a clear majority of votes in democratic elections'.[5] Hypocritically, later in his paper, he sees nothing wrong with allocating houses in terms of an equal division between Catholics and Protestants, even though, as he says, Catholics tended to have a 'larger family size'.[6]

Gudgin's arguments about Catholics 'proportionately' getting more council houses is just playing with statistics. This is obviously to disguise the fact that, in plain figures, Catholics fared less well on the lists for council houses than Protestants. In Northern Ireland, only householders were allowed to vote so a council house was more than just a question of having a place to live.

In the 1960s, taking their cue from black Americans, Catholics in Northern Ireland began to agitate for civil rights, including sit-ins and marches.[7] Unfortunately, most Northern Ireland Protestants did not see things the same way; all they saw was another 1798, or even 1641, and reacted accordingly. The Protestant Ascendancy had to be preserved at all costs.

Given the intransigence of the Northern Ireland Protestants, it was not long before things developed into a struggle between those supporting a United Ireland and those wishing to maintain the status quo. The UVF was resurrected and the IRA broke away from its leaders in Dublin, who were in favour of a cautious approach. Two diametrically opposed ideologies faced each other, with neither side being able to understand what the other was fighting for. Republicans could not comprehend the exclusivist, almost fascist standpoint of the Loyalists, while the Loyalists were terrified by the old maxim, 'Home Rule is Rome Rule'. Unfortunately, it looked as if the Loyalists might have a point.

The Protestants that had led the Home Rule movement throughout the 19th Century and into the 20th had never countenanced breaking away from Britain completely. Their idea was of a devolved parliament, like the modern Scottish and Welsh ones, with Ireland still remaining part of the United Kingdom. Even this was anathema to the Ulster Protestants and their friends among the Conservative and Liberal unionist parties. Time and time again the Home Rule leaders' hopes were dashed as the Westminster Parliament used the Ulster Protestants as a way of keeping direct control over Ireland.

The English tactic of 'divide and rule' caused no end of problems in Ireland. The Ulster Protestants were encouraged to believe that the Protestant Ascendancy was the only way to safeguard their position and even their very lives. Irish Catholics, meanwhile, came to realise that the only way they were ever going to be able to govern themselves would be to break away completely from Britain.

Since most of the restrictions faced by Irish Catholics down through the years had been imposed precisely because they *were* Catholics, it was inevitable that Irish independence would be intertwined with the Catholic faith. Despite the franchise being extended to Catholics and Catholics being legally equal to their Protestant neighbours, the truth was that the Protestant Ascendancy was still very much in place throughout Ireland in the first decade of the 20th Century. Ordinary Catholics were still at the mercy of Protestant landlords, many of them absentee Englishmen and Irish representation at Westminster was still predominantly Protestant. It was understandable that any struggle for Irish freedom was going to involve the Catholic Church in Ireland.

Despite many of the leaders of Sinn Fein and other political organisations being Socialists, the reality of an independent Ireland was going to give a lot of influence to the Church. And so it turned out. Divorce only became legal in Ireland in 1996,[8] and the buying and selling of condoms was against the law until 1985.[9] The Church was extremely clever in the way it handled any criticism. In 1971, a feminist group made a publicity stunt out of bringing a stack of johnnies from Belfast to Dublin to show how ridiculous the law was. A bishop had this to say about the stunt:

> never before, and certainly not since penal times was the Catholic heritage of Ireland subjected to so many insidious onslaughts on the pretext of conscience, civil rights and women's liberation.[10]

With the Catholic Church having such a hold over Irish society it was unsurprising that the Protestants in Northern Ireland viewed the very idea of being part of the Republic of Ireland with terror. Strangely, the Stormont Government was hardly what one could call libertarian and many facets of Northern Ireland society were just like those in the South. Abortion, for example, was, and still is, illegal in both Northern Ireland and the Republic, while Divorce, while not illegal, was extremely difficult to obtain in the North, as, indeed, it was in the whole of the UK.[11] Contraception might have been legal in the North but there were, and are, many cultural taboos affecting its use.[12] But those were *Protestant* laws and taboos and, as such, seen as completely distinct from being dictated to by the Catholic Church.

The conflict in Northern Ireland, then, was, at its most fundamental level, born of misunderstanding. Protestants in Northern Ireland believed that giving social and political parity to Catholics would result in them losing everything. Northern Irish Catholics, on the other hand, came to believe that only in a united Ireland could they ever hope to have their freedom. Neither side spoke to the other and neither side understood the attitude of the other.

Things are beginning to change in Northern Ireland and, although there is a long way to go, at least both sides are speaking and willing to make compromises. Loyalist politicians are coming to realise that the best way to maintain their separateness from Ireland is to get Northern Ireland Catholics onside by making the place more attractive to live in. Sinn Fein, meanwhile, has shown willingness to be involved in the Government at Stormont. Northern Ireland is becoming a different place. When a leading ex-member of the UDA calls on Orange parades to stop marching in Catholic neighbourhoods, calling such marches 'triumphalist',[13] then you know society there is beginning to move forward.

The Republic of Ireland, too, has changed considerably. With each passing year, the country becomes more and more secular. Church attendance has fallen dramatically and the power of the Church is dwindling to an irrelevance. In fact, the Republic actually proved itself far more modern and progressive than Northern Ireland in 2015 when it passed a law legalising same-sex marriage.[14] Northern Ireland, meanwhile, is the only place in the whole of the British Isles where same-sex marriage is still against the law, due to the efforts of the Protestant Democratic Unionist Party.[15] All the divisive lines in Ireland are increasingly becoming blurred.

There are already signs that people in Northern Ireland are becoming much more pragmatic and practical rather than being bound by ideology. For example, tuition fees at Scottish universities are free for Scottish students and those from other EU countries; students from other areas in the UK, however, have to pay, just as they do in England, Wales and Northern Ireland. This has led to an increase in applications for Republic of Ireland passports in Northern Ireland.[16] There has recently been another reason for an even bigger increase in such applications.

In June 2016, the UK held a referendum to decide upon its continuing membership of the European Union. To everyone's surprise the result was a narrow victory for those wanting to leave the EU. Quite when this break is going to happen has not yet been determined but it is going to have a major effect on people's lives. Retiring to Spain will no longer be as easy as it was and even going on holiday to mainland Europe will require a visa. Folk in Britain are already searching for Irish grandparents to acquire a Republic of Ireland passport, which will ensure easy movement in the EU. People in Northern Ireland have always had the option of obtaining Irish passports; they are now doing so in droves.

Northern Ireland Protestants are seeing the advantage of having an Irish passport and even die-hard Loyalists in Derry are applying. The Irish Government, for its part, is soothing Loyalist sensibilities by allowing them to have 'Londonderry' as their birthplace instead of 'Derry'.[17] Even fairly recently, neither course of action would have been conceivable. And only a few years ago, the Republic of Ireland President helped a UDA chief to get an Irish passport so that he could easily get to a Rangers match in Europe.[18] Barriers are being broken down on both sides.

But what has this got to do with Scotland? Well, just as the conflict in Northern Ireland was born out of ignorance and misunderstanding, so support in Scotland for either side sprouted from the same attitudes. Orangemen could only see their comrades in Northern Ireland being threatened, while many of Irish descent in Scotland naturally took the side of the downtrodden Catholics; something that they had been used to doing for well over a century. Does this side-taking constitute sectarian bigotry?

Certainly, supporting either side of the conflict might have been inspired by sectarian bigotry, but that support is not bigoted *per se*. It was entirely possible to be on the side of the UVF or the UDA without hating Catholics, or even being a Protestant for that matter. Meanwhile, the IRA received support from many Socialist and Communist groups, most of which hated every church equally, no matter what the denomination. Yes, these Northern Ireland organisations were proscribed by the British Government and it was illegal to support them, but that does not make them either sectarian or bigoted.

Fundamentally, the argument can be reduced to the level of what is sauce for the goose etc. If one sees it as okay to sing about supporting the IRA, then one can hardly complain about others singing of the UDA or UVF and vice-versa. As for the authorities, they really should be treating this as an entirely separate matter from religious bigotry.

The problem with separating this support for proscribed organisations from the scourge of sectarian bigotry, as far as the Scottish media and football and legal authorities are concerned, is that such a course would force them to face the fact that Celtic supporters have very rarely exhibited any religious bigotry. As we saw earlier, nobody has the guts to put the blame where it belongs and there always seems to be the need to say that 'one side is as bad as the other'.

Vocal support for the IRA, UDA, UVF and associated organisations is dying out as their importance in Northern Ireland diminishes. It is, consequently, becoming more difficult to maintain the fallacy that Celtic supporters are just as bigoted as those of Rangers. Our police and courts, however, seem determined to cling to it. In fact, they go further than that, exposing their own anti-Catholic bigotry in the way they deal differently with those supporting Irish Republicanism and those supporting Loyalist organisations.

8
The Balancing Act: Dealing with Bigotry

The Offensive Behaviour at Football and Threatening Communications (Scotland) Act 2012, Section 1, Subsection (2)(a)(ii) says that offensive behaviour at a football match is defined by 'expressing hatred of, or stirring up hatred against, a group of persons based on their membership (or presumed membership) of a social or cultural group with a perceived religious affiliation'.[1]

The act already mentions 'a religious group', so this part is obviously referring to something different. This special little subsection betrays everything that is wrong with supposed efforts to tackle religious bigotry in Scotland; it is a refusal to face up to what the true problem actually is. Anti-Catholic bigotry is so ingrained in our society that nobody can see it anymore. Instead, everyone sees two sides, each as bad as the other, hating each other and expressing that hatred at football matches.

The difficulty with taking this approach is that it is just not true. As mentioned earlier, Celtic supporters do not sing or chant about hating Protestants. What they do express hatred of is the Orange Order, chanting things like, 'Dirty Orange bastards'. That wee subsection in the 2012 Act is directly related to this. The Orange Order describes itself, and the media describes it, as being exactly that: 'a social or cultural group with a perceived religious affiliation'. Celtic supporters do not sing songs about hating Protestants, so this subsection is simply there to 'even up the score', so to speak.

The support of proscribed organisations is not, in itself, sectarian and should be treated separately. That subsection, however, comes into play yet again. Technically, singing or chanting about hating the UDA or the IRA could come under this law, since both organisations can be perceived as having a 'religious affiliation'. This aspect presents its own problems.

During the Troubles in Northern Ireland, there was a distinct difference in the way proscribed organisations were presented in the media. The IRA was portrayed as a terrorist group, while the UDA and the UVF were 'Loyalist paramilitaries'. This made them sound as if they were something to do with the British Army; as if they were officially sanctioned. There was also a certain feeling in Britain that these Loyalist organisations were 'on our side'; the very term 'Loyalist' itself suggested it. The fact that there was a regiment of the British Army called the UDR (Ulster Defence Regiment) further complicated matters, making it easy to get mixed up with who was official and who was outlawed.

This confusion is still evident when it comes to policing football matches. A Celtic supporter was arrested after a match against Hamilton, charged, under the Act, with behaviour likely to incite public disorder. His crime was to sing *Roll of Honour*, a song about the IRA Hunger Strikers, along with a large section of the crowd. The police had filmed this happening and, for some reason, picked this particular man to arrest.

When it came to court, however, the case was thrown out by the sheriff, due to the lack of evidence, or even understanding what the evidence should have been, by the prosecution.[2] It is notable that in this comedy of errors, with the police acting as if they were in *Carry On Constable*, nothing was said about *Roll of Honour* being legal; in fact the sheriff made it plain that if proper evidence had been presented, then the man would have been convicted.

The exact same thing happened when two men were arrested for singing about the UVF; or rather, its youth wing. Again, there was a lack of concrete evidence but the sheriff made sure to blame the legislation, saying it was 'flawed'.[3] Strangely, nobody said anything about the legislation at the other court case. Whatever the reason for this difference in approach, it certainly sends out a weird message.

The Act itself does not explicitly mention anything about proscribed organisations, but it does contain a catch-all term, calling offensive 'other behaviour that a reasonable person would be likely to consider offensive'.[4] That, however, all depends on the definition of a 'reasonable person'.

In reality, the only people that would be offended by songs about the IRA are those that support Loyalist organisations and vice-versa. Could any of those be called 'reasonable persons'? It is something that the police would be better advised to leave well alone, since these songs and chants are bound to die out sooner rather than later.

The police concentrating on this kind of thing shifts the focus away from what the real problem is. One cannot help wondering if that is the point. It helps to cover up the anti-Catholicism endemic in Scotland and to replace it with something that can more easily be viewed as 'two sides; each as bad as the other'. Removing the smokescreen of support for proscribed organisations exposes a different picture altogether.

The Scottish media likes to portray our country as a model of tolerance and inclusivity; a place that other nations could learn from. Whenever racism raises its ugly head, the media is there to condemn it. For example, the Scottish Defence League is described as 'sickening', 'poisonous' and 'extremist'.[5] Meanwhile, a counter-demonstration being held by anti-racists at an SDL rally in Glasgow was described as out to 'thwart' the bigots.[6] The whole anti-racist movement was portrayed in nothing but a positive light. As usual with the Scottish media, there is a huge amount of hypocrisy involved here.

The Daily Record points to the links between the SDL and 'Rangers-supporting casuals the Inter City Firm'.[7] It is quite reasonable to infer, then, that there are members of the SDL among the crowd at Ibrox. So, when these characters are shouting about hating Muslims and sending immigrants and asylum seekers 'home' they deserve condemnation. On the other hand, when they are at Ibrox, or any other football ground for that matter, it is perfectly acceptable to sing about hating Catholics and sending those of Irish descent 'home'.

Of course, the media would argue that they *do* condemn such behaviour but that is on very rare occasions. When they do deign to even mention these songs of hate they also have to mention that Celtic supporters were singing IRA songs; putting up the usual smokescreen. If it is not IRA songs they mention, then it is chants about 'Dirty Orange bastards', which they try to equate with hatred of Protestants.

The anti-racist demonstrators that turn up at SDL rallies will have a few choice words to say to the peddlers of hate; they will not be shouting things like, 'Go away, you uncouth fellows!' Responding to fascists by shouting 'Nazi bastards!' is more than acceptable since it is simply stating the truth. Why, then, are folk not allowed to respond in a similar fashion when Orange songs of hatred and bigotry are being thrown at them?

Sometimes the media decide that it is the victims of these hate crimes that are at fault instead of the perpetrators. I have used James Traynor's tirade before in my books but I make no apology for using it again. It is one of the most disgusting things ever to disgrace a newspaper. He published the article in answer to those that were condemning *The Famine Song*, so beloved by the Ibrox faithful. To those that complained, Traynor had this to say:

> So, to all those, of any religion or race, who think Scotland is such a bad, twisted place full of bigots and racists there is only one thing to say.
> Go.
> Go on, just gather up your prejudices, take your suspicions and pack your loathing of Scotland.
> Go find a better place to live and leave us to get on with the job of making something good of this country.[8]

In this vile, little rant Traynor makes it plain that he considers the victims of a hate crime to be the ones guilty of prejudice. It was a shameful article and a complete disgrace that a newspaper editor would allow it into his paper. The fact that it was permitted showed that this particular paper agreed with everything Traynor said. And the fact that no other media commentator saw fit to condemn this article showed that Traynor was just voicing what everyone else thought.

The most obvious point to raise about this rant, apart from its support of bigotry, is how Traynor, or the rest of his media cronies, hope to make 'something good of this country'. The starting point for any improvement is criticism of the status-quo. Since that is not to be countenanced, then there is no way that any improvement can come. Unless, of course, that 'improvement' is to be realised by removing anyone that happens to be 'different'. In this light, Traynor's little diatribe echoes the anti-Catholic sentiments expressed in that Church of Scotland report of 1923.

Of course, Traynor would completely deny espousing bigoted ideas, just as the Orange Order, its members and followers often do. Their response is that they are 'defending their culture and traditions', which is exactly the same thing said by the Scottish Defence League and the English Defence League. This kind of rhetoric is not new, having been used by the British National Party, the National Front before that and all the way back to the fascist movements of the 1920s and 1930s. The Scottish media are good at condemning such right-wing bigots, while ignoring the more obvious ones.

While the likes of the BNP, the NF, the SDL etc. have been ranting about Muslims 'coming over here', taking over and instituting Sharia Law, it is Catholics that the bigots have been obsessing over in Scotland. Tales of only getting a job with Glasgow Council, or the council in North Lanarkshire if you are a Catholic have become so ingrained that some people believe that it is a fact. This is often portrayed as a deliberate campaign by Catholics to take over bases of power; a bit like the film *Invasion of the Body Snatchers*. The reality, as always, is totally different.

Nepotism may be frowned upon but it has to be accepted that it is a reality in practically every organisation and business. If you have an auntie or uncle, or, even better, a parent, in a particular workplace, then your chances of getting a job there are significantly improved. In fact, at one time, in the mining industry it was obligatory for your sons to join you at the pit, even if they were capable of better things. If your son did not report at the colliery as soon as he left school, then you could lose your job and your family be thrown out of its home.[9]

One advantage of practising nepotism in the workplace was that it dispensed with the need for those embarrassing 'RCs need not apply' notices. Recruitment could be kept strictly Protestant without having to advertise the fact. Heavy industry in Scotland was infested with this practice and was practically a no-go area as far as Catholics were concerned. In the shipyards, all the workforce was laid off as soon as a job was completed; men had to re-apply to the foremen when a new order was secured. A family connection was indispensable in this respect; as was knowing the right handshake.

With the better-paid jobs in the shipyards and the locomotive industry closed to them, working for the council offered decent opportunities for Catholics. So, while a Protestant school-leaver could rely on his dad to get him a job at Fairfields or the Cowlairs works, a Catholic lad could rely on his old man getting him into the council.

Nobody was particularly bothered about changing this situation until the unthinkable happened. Heavy industry in Scotland went into rapid decline, shed its workforce, stopped taking on new workers and then closed altogether. Suddenly, those council jobs were no longer a poor alternative; but nepotism was still going on there, as it had been in the heavy industries, right up to the end. But now that nepotism only benefited one section of the community it was viewed as grossly unfair.

In modern industry, in every sector, whether public or private, nepotism is still a major part of employment procedure. No matter where you go you will find fathers, mothers, brothers, sisters etc. all working in the same place.[10] As in the old days, nobody seems to bother; except, of course, when those families happen to be Catholic.

The standard belief about Scottish councils in general, and Glasgow Council in particular, agrees with the following assessment: 'Getting a job with the council is easy...........if you're called Patrick Joseph Aloysius O'Brien and you have a certain lineage.'[11] And it is not only council employees that such people have a problem with. It is the elected representatives as well.

Some people have made it their business to investigate the religion of Glasgow councillors, as well as which football matches they have attended. From this they compile lists of Catholic and Celtic-supporting officials, from which they extrapolate that there is some kind of conspiracy going on. Only 31% of the Glasgow population is Catholic, so there must be something dodgy happening.[12]

This, of course, takes no account of the fact that these characters have to stand for election and could be voted out at any time. If 31% of the population have repeatedly managed to elect the people they want, then what the hell have the other 69% been doing? The truth is that the days of Protestants and Catholics voting *qua* Protestants and Catholics are long gone; if they ever even existed in the first place.

There is an accepted narrative about Glasgow Corporation/Council that says:

> In Glasgow, in addition to the one-party political domination, we have the added dimension that the one-party domination

originated in the city's real-politic agreement in the early 20th century. The city had a peculiar (unique?) understanding between the emergent progressive left-wing political party (the Labour Party) and a sizeable and discriminated-against religion/cultural grouping (the Irish Catholic interest). Their understanding was that in return for favours they would both co-operate to deliver the working-class vote.[13]

This supposed clique, it seems, has worked to help Catholics and Celtic Football Club, to the detriment of Protestants and Rangers. They have even conspired to get the number of Orange Walks reduced and perhaps, eventually, banned altogether.[14] Looking more deeply, however, reveals that the Labour councillors in Glasgow are cynical politicians first and Catholics a distant second.

In 2012 it appeared that the leader of Glasgow Council was changing his mind, and the party changing its perceived policy, vis-à-vis Orange Walks. It seemed that perhaps they were a bit hasty in wanting to cut the number of such parades.[15] It looked as if Labour were doing a deal with the Orange Order: votes for marches. This assumption was made all the more realistic when Glasgow's George Square hosted 'Orangefest' in 2016, despite a petition, with more than 28,000 signatures, opposing it.[16] So much for that great, Catholic conspiracy!

Cutting back on Orange Walks, however, pales into insignificance next to the accusations that Glasgow Council was involved in dodgy land deals with Celtic FC.[17] These charges were thrown out,[18] but that has not stopped the claims from still being made. This nonsense, of course, has been a reaction to what happened at Rangers.

We have seen earlier how Protestantism throughout the UK defined itself in terms of a backs-to-the-wall mentality of defence against a perceived threat from Catholicism. Even when there was no threat, one was invented; like the ridiculous claims made by Titus Oates in England. Covenanters in Scotland came to view their persecution not as a continuous move by the Stuarts, and even Cromwell, to bring the Church of Scotland under English control, but as an attempt at Catholicisation by James VII/II. Meanwhile, the Scots Presbyterians in Ulster had had to contend with centuries of being persecuted by the English and the Anglican Church. Eventually, they were granted civil liberties but, to their consternation, so were Irish Catholics. In competition now for jobs and land, the Ulster Presbyterians clung to the idea of the Protestant Ascendancy and paranoia about Catholicism.

With Rangers Football Club seen in Scotland as the great Protestant bulwark against the success of the Irish Catholic team, Celtic, it was inevitable that it became a focus, not just for anti-Catholic elements in Scotland, but for those in Ulster and England as well. Even when religious adherence died away, Rangers was still viewed as the 'Protestant' club; even though the very word 'Protestant' had lost its meaning.

When Rangers hit serious financial trouble, then ended up being liquidated and having to start over again in 2012, it was obvious who the supporters were going to blame. We have already encountered the paranoia about Catholics on, and working for, Scottish councils, particularly Glasgow, but it seemed that those pesky RCs had been taking over everything.

A new code-name for 'Catholic', as an adjective, has come to be utilised whenever this anti-Catholic paranoia surfaces; that phrase is 'anti-Rangers'. It is a not-so-subtle attempt to disguise the sectarian hatred inherent in this paranoia and to accuse others of that hatred instead. Sinister implications were made about HMRC,[19] while everyone, from the football authorities to the media, was said to be working to an 'anti-Rangers' agenda.[20]

This was sheer fantasy. In fact, the football authorities bent over backwards to accommodate the phoenix club; hardly surprising since the President of the SFA had been the recipient of a Rangers EBT himself! Meanwhile, the media played along with the ridiculous story that Rangers had 'come through' liquidation and was still the same club. Some went even further, accusing others of being guilty for Rangers' demise.

> Yes, 2012 will be remembered fondly by some. They will cherish the memories of how Rangers were savaged by a foaming-mouthed pack and then ripped limb from limb.
> These bloodthirsty ghouls would gladly watch it all happen again tomorrow, such is the depth of their hatred but it is time now for the more gentle, civilised and decent minded among us to rise up and to quietly take our ball back.[21]

In other words, Rangers supporters were quite right in their paranoia; everybody *was* out to get them. This, of course, provided ample justification for an upsurge in bigoted singing and chanting among the Ibrox support. Not that anyone would admit to providing such justification. Then again, nobody in the Scottish media ever mentioned the anti-Catholic chorus, even though everyone could hear it plainly. It was left to English commentators to point out how vile and offensive this singing was.

The fact that a blind eye and a deaf ear is always turned to this disgraceful choir shows that, essentially, it is being condoned. The Orange Order and the Rangers support are only the outward manifestations of anti-Catholic bigotry in Scotland; the problem goes much deeper than that.

9
Rome on the Rates: Catholic Schools

The Act of Settlement of 1701 stipulated that no Roman Catholic could become monarch of the United Kingdom. Even marrying a Roman Catholic would disqualify one from inheriting the throne. This is still law and, although there have been some calls to remove the marriage disqualification, no Catholic can become king or queen.

The knee-jerk reaction to this would be to call it out-and-out bigotry; there is, however, another way of looking at it. The king or queen of the United Kingdom is, as part of the deal, monarch of England, which is pretty obvious. The monarch of England, however, is also the titular head of the Church of England, which pretty much rules out their being of any other religion. It is a bit stupid to think of a Catholic, or someone of any other denomination or religion, being head of the Anglican Church and pledging to uphold its tenets. In that sense the bar on Catholics seems perfectly reasonable. Unfortunately, many people are not prepared to make the same concessions in the other direction.

Roman Catholic schools, as the name suggests, are schools where the pupils are brought up in the religion and ethos of the Roman Catholic Church. The main problem, as far as the Orange Order and others are concerned, is that these schools are state-run. 'Religious apartheid' the Orange Order calls it,[1] while other, supposedly non-aligned, groups see it as completely unnecessary.

When the state took over the funding of Catholic schools in 1918 there was uproar. Catholics were viewed as 'undesirable aliens' and in thrall to a foreign power, i.e. the Pope; why should Scottish Protestants metaphorically be cutting their own throats by paying rates to fund this enemy in their midst?[2] Nowadays the argument has changed and Catholic schools are often blamed for engendering the very sectarian hatred that already existed long before these schools did.[3]

Nil By Mouth, for example, argues that Catholic schools actively discriminate against Protestant employees, as I was informed in an e-mail from a senior member of the organisation:

> Probably the most relevant area of employment for you to look into for whatever piece of research you are doing is the area of education and the consistent practice of non-Catholics being overlooked and excluded from holding senior teaching and leadership posts at publicly funded schools.

This is exactly the kind of hypocrisy I was talking about at the start of this chapter. If we are to accept that the monarch in this country cannot be a Catholic since he or she is head of the Church of England, then, equally, how can anyone run a Catholic school if he or she is a non-Catholic? The answer to that would be that Catholics should not have their own state schools; there is no need for them. But is that really a reasonable argument?

As a supply teacher, I worked in various primary schools in Glasgow. In one particular school, where I worked for nearly a year, we had an assembly one week where a P7 class compared Lent to Ramadan to show how religions were not that much different. The class teacher was quite upset when the unofficial school chaplain, a Free Church minister, gave her a good talking to, angrily pointing out that the 'Reformed Church does not observe Lent'. Being a Muslim, the poor woman did not even know what the 'Reformed Church' was and had to ask me to explain.

Effectively, what this minister, a rather overbearing type as I remember, with his beard and Sherlock Holmes-style pipe, was pointing out to the teacher was that the school in which she was working was not, in fact, a non-denominational one; it was a *Protestant* school. And therein lies the problem that most, if not all, critics of Catholic schools refuse to face up to.

As many people are shocked to discover when they attend teacher-training college, Religious Education is compulsory in Scottish primary schools. Yes, part of the curriculum involves studying other world religions, but it is made clear that there is to be religious observance as well; observance which is to be of a Christian nature. Christmas, Easter, Harvest Thanksgiving etc. are all to be observed with Christian-themed assemblies or church services and schools are expected to make links with a local church. It is not explicitly stated but it is understood by all that the local church in question should be a Protestant one. This can lead to some awkward situations.

In America, the state-school system operates in the completely opposite way; religion is banned from schools altogether. American Christian groups, therefore, can usually hardly wait to get over here and get into primary schools. One lot, which were affiliated to the local church, were frequent visitors to assemblies at one of my schools. They had to be practically thrown out when parents complained about the children hearing stories of 'prophecies' telling of 'fires burning all over Scotland'. (No, I have no idea what that was about either!)

In East Kilbride, a fundamentalist American group managed to get a foot in the door at a local primary and even got involved in helping out in the classrooms. Parents were shocked when their children came home with books explaining how evolution was nonsense and showing pictures of people using domesticated dinosaurs as beasts of burden![4] And this was an ordinary, supposedly non-denominational, primary school.

Technically, even if a school's pupil population is almost, or completely, composed of Muslim children, that school is still obliged to follow a mainly Christian way of religious observance. Whether this actually happens in real life I am not sure; but the law is clear on the matter. It is hardly surprising that some Muslim parents do not want their children attending these 'Protestant' schools and there have been calls for separate, Muslim schools. It is fairly obvious why Catholic parents might not want their offspring going to such schools either, and why the Catholic Church is so determined to retain RC schools.

When the Education (Scotland) Act was passed in 1872 it was stipulated that the schools would be of a non-denominational nature. It was felt, though, that religious education should still continue:

> Whereas it has been the custom in the public schools of Scotland to give instruction in religion to children whose parents did not object to the instruction so given, but with

liberty to parents, without forfeiting any of the other advantages of the schools, to elect that their children should not receive such instruction, and it is expedient that the managers of public schools shall be at liberty to continue the said custom.[5]

Effectively, this part of the Act was allowing schools to just carry on as if they were still under the auspices of the Church of Scotland. Provision was made for withdrawing children from religious instruction, but it would have been a brave parent indeed that dared to exercise this right in Nineteenth-Century Scotland. Conformity was everything in Victorian times; nobody would want to stand out as possibly an atheist or, worse, a Catholic. In certain respects, therefore, the new schools were a continuation of the old Church schools.

Scotland has long patted itself on the back about the quality of educational opportunities in the country. The story has been that schools were set up all over Scotland after the Reformation so that people could learn to read the Bible. Even those from a humble background could, with sponsorship and grants, make it all the way to university. The 'Lad O' Pairts', working his way up from poverty to the very top became an abiding image in Scotland. So ingrained has this story become that even Moray House Teacher-Training College, now part of Edinburgh University, feels secure in repeating it.[6] The Reformation, according to this version of history, raised Scotland out of ignorance and produced a highly-educated, democratic nation. This story is, however, just that; a story.

The historian T.C. Smout and others have shown that this version of the history of education in Scotland is a complete lie.[7] In fact, education in Scotland changed little after the Reformation; real education was for the sons of the well-to-do, while lower-class children went to school to have the catechism, quite literally, beaten into them. The universities in Scotland, just as before the Reformation, rarely saw a 'Lad O' Pairts' pass their portals.

The most obvious way to judge whether the Church schools were any good or not is to look at how many scions of wealthy families attended them. The answer is, very few if any at all. The sons of the well-to-do were sent to fee-paying schools in England or to schools set up for their use in Scotland. In Edinburgh, the wealthy practically stole charitable schools, set up for the education of the indigent, and used them for their own children.[8] Meanwhile, there was the Royal High School, which, although run by Edinburgh Council since the time of Mary, Queen of Scots, was a fee-paying establishment for the sons of the wealthy. When the comprehensive system was being introduced in the late 1960s, the Royal High School stayed true to its principles and followed the money out to Barnton.

Evidently, Scottish education after the Reformation did not become the great, democratic institution that is often portrayed. The 'Lad O' Pairts' was a complete myth and all of the renowned Scottish academics, writers, artists, engineers, industrialists, politicians and entrepreneurs came from the well-to-do classes, as they always had done. This was the situation well into the 20th Century and, in many respects, it still is.

The middle classes in Scotland, as city and town dwellers, bore the brunt of the rates system, since most working-class people lived in houses that barely merited a rateable value. These wealthy individuals were no doubt extremely unhappy at having to pay for the education of the lower orders. Probably, though, they reasoned that it was worth it to keep the 'scum' off the streets. The same logic probably applied when it came to bringing Catholic schools into the state system, even though they viewed such schools with disgust.

As well as sectarian bigots, there are many that are opposed to faith schools on principle, since they profess to be atheists and see religion in schools as nothing more than indoctrination. You would think that their main concern would be to follow the American model and to call for the removal of religion from all schools. In that way, Catholics, or any other religious groups for that matter, could have no argument for having their own schools since state schools would no longer be 'Protestant'. That, however, does not seem to be the priority.

Looking at the website of the Humanist Society Scotland, for example, shows that the main concern is 'Denominational faith schools'. Mention is made of religious teaching and observance in so-called non-denominational schools but, time and again, the argument reverts to being against Catholic schools.[9]

The majority of children in Scotland attend non-denominational schools, which, for the most part, are actually Protestant schools in disguise. Surely this should be of far more concern to a supposedly secular organisation. But, instead, they want to focus on the minority, the Catholic schools. It seems that anti-Catholic prejudice is so pervasive and ingrained in Scotland that even secular groups succumb to its influence.

In the interests of fairness, however, I should point out that the Scottish Secular Society make no distinctions between Catholic and Protestant schools. They want all religion removed from schools and challenge the whole idea of *Christianity* on the rates, rather than *Catholicism* on the rates.[10] Their idea of removing religion from schools altogether, as in the USA, seems much the best way of removing the perceived idea of schools causing sectarianism in Scotland. As things stand now, it is nothing more than hypocrisy for those fighting against sectarianism to blame Catholic schools when most Scottish schools are actually Protestant.

The Protestants, especially in the Orange Order, that want rid of Catholic schools are, of course, following their own agenda. It is all part of that 'Protestant Ascendancy' thing again; something that they all miss desperately. They might well change their minds, however, and sign up for the Scottish Secular Society's plan if they knew how religious education is often conducted in 'Protestant' schools.

Although religion is compulsory in all Scottish schools, no real provision is made for preparing teachers to implement such education. And the sad fact is that many teachers have no interest in the subject whatsoever. When I was at Moray House, the head of the course had to be constantly on hand to stop people from skiving off Religious Education classes. Even those that everyone attended were quite general and tended to focus on the 'Other World Religions' element, rather than what Christianity was all about. Not that anyone was particularly bothered; in my experience, most teachers do not want to teach religion at all.

When there are subjects that many primary-school teachers find difficult, the council education department tries to make provision. Computing changed massively in the first years of the 21st Century, which meant teachers having to go to courses to keep up with new technology. Sometimes, though, the easiest way to sort things out is to provide some ready-made materials, which the teacher just needs to follow. This is what often happens with Religious Education.

The council I worked for struck the jackpot; a whole course for each stage, with lessons already planned from August to July. This came in the form of seven folders, for Primaries 1 to 7, containing papers with explicit instructions on how to teach the lessons. This was duly purchased and sent out to all the primary schools. Unfortunately, this course was produced by the Catholic Church for use in Catholic schools; but, hey! Who cared? Just remove the bits about First Confession, First Communion and Confirmation and no one would be any the wiser.

Just like the teacher I knew in Glasgow, my problems arose in the March, when it came time to do the lesson on Lent. I explained the problems to the head teacher but she, although a church-going Protestant herself, was about as keen as everyone else in teaching religion in schools; i.e. not at all. Her attitude was that if the council wanted us to use this material, then use it we would. After getting myself off the hook, I went ahead and did the lesson.

I found that I had to do a supplementary lesson straight after the first, as pupils excitedly discussed what they were going to give up for Lent. Chocolate, sweets, cakes and biscuits were all mentioned, while one self-sacrificing soul vowed to give up broccoli. They were actually disappointed when I explained the reality of the situation. Luckily, no angry parents came storming down to the school.

It has been a while, over seven years, since I have been a teacher, so I do not know if they are still using this material in schools. It might well be that it has been replaced by now. Certainly, there have been no outraged utterances from the Orange Order; but, then, maybe it is still being used and they just have not discovered yet. Then again, maybe they do not care. Probably they are of the opinion that councils can use whatever teaching materials they like; just so long as they shut down Catholic schools!

The media in Scotland pretend to be impartial in this debate but rarely do you find a TV programme or newspaper article that presents a positive case for denominational schools. Scottish media personalities, meanwhile, are free to condemn Catholic schools without any apparent need for that 'balance' the media usually deem necessary.

Kirsty Wark, for example, as well as being a news presenter, is a staple of those late-night, arty-farty programmes for the middle classes, which discuss books, plays and films that most of us have never heard of and have no interest in. Like most middle-class, arty-farty types, Wark professes to be left-wing politically; 'soft left' she describes herself as being.[11]

Her left-wing credentials were confirmed in 1990, when she gave Margaret Thatcher a torrid time of it during an interview.[12] More recently, she ended *Newsnight* by apparently acceding to the demands of a Tory MP for *God Save the Queen* to be played each night at the end of BBC broadcasting. To the fury of right-wingers all over the UK, it was *God Save the Queen* by the Sex Pistols that was played.[13] Essentially, when Ms Wark speaks nobody expects her to be bigoted in any way.

So, when Wark chipped in her tuppence-worth about Catholic schools, it was in a liberal-minded, why-don't-we-think-of-the-children way. She spoke of being separated from her best friend every day, when she went to one school, while her friend went to the Catholic school.[14] She claimed to be 'uncomfortable' with children being separated according to religion and called for a rethink of state funding of Catholic schools.[15]

What, exactly, was Wark uncomfortable with; was it the fact that children were being separated, or was it the religious aspect? It is a valid question since, when it came to high school, Wark's friend was shown the finger as Our Kirsty went off to a fee-paying school in Ayr.[16] The only conclusion to be drawn from that is that although Wark thinks it is wrong to separate children because of their religion, separating them according to class or finances is perfectly fine. It appears that Wark's discomfort, then, has nothing to do with separating children and everything to do with Catholic schools. In other words, she is nothing more than a sectarian bigot!

Strangely, or, perhaps, not so, Wark has not been called out on this hypocrisy by anyone in the media. This shows how much they all agree with her and, indeed, it constantly seems to be assumed that it is Catholic schools that are the cause of religious bigotry in Scotland.[17] This, of course, ignores the fact that sectarian bigotry is directed *at* Catholics, instead of being instigated by them. Arguments that going to a Catholic school points up one's 'differentness', making one a target are absolute nonsense. By that reasoning, anyone that is black is responsible for any racism directed at him.

Basically, the whole debate around Catholic schools is a smokescreen to help cover up the real causes of bigotry in Scotland; causes that nobody wants to tackle. Much easier to point the finger and blame Catholic schools, even though such institutions exist throughout the World without any controversy surrounding them whatsoever.

While on the subject of education, there is another anti-Catholic element that has crept into not just the collective consciousness in Scotland, but in the whole UK and other countries as well; re-writing history.

10
U-Boats by Night: Rewriting History

Probably the most pervasive rewrite of history has been the presentation of William of Orange as the great figurehead of Protestantism, sitting astride his white steed, roundly defeating the evil Catholics at the Battle of the Boyne. Part of this twisting of historical fact is that William came to Britain with the sole intention of saving Protestantism.

Of course, the Orange Order of Ireland expound this false view of history,[1] ignoring completely the fact that Pope Alexander VIII held a celebratory Mass in Rome when he heard of William's victory at the Boyne.[2] In reality, William's acceptance of the thrones of England, Ireland and Scotland, and his subsequent refusal to accept anything other than complete parity as monarch with his wife, was inspired mostly by his desperation for money and men for the fight against Louis XIV of France.[3]

Louis XIV was probably the most powerful monarch France ever had, before or after. So secure was he in his position that he revoked the Edict of Nantes in 1685, leading to persecution of the Huguenots and their subsequent flight from France.[4] As if that were not enough to rile up half of Europe, Louis also had territorial ambitions. These ambitions took him East, where he used legal pretexts to invade the Rhineland.[5]

The princes and electors of Southern Germany decided to fight, under the leadership of the Holy Roman Emperor and ruler of Austria, the Habsburg Leopold I. Of course, the Habsburgs rallied to the cause, with Charles II of Spain joining his relative against Louis of France. The Duke of Savoy joined the anti-French alliance; his family being long-time enemies of Louis XIV. Also throwing their lot in with Leopold were the Dutch, who were no friends of the Habsburgs but Louis was the biggest threat to their territory now. The Dutch *Stadtholder*, William of Orange was in the fortunate position of gaining the thrones of England and Scotland, who were duly brought into the war as well. And so, the Grand Alliance was born and Europe was plunged into another of those dynastic wars that had plagued the continent since the Middle Ages.

None of this registers with most Orangemen, or even with many Protestants, in Scotland, Ireland and beyond. One major American Calvinist organisation even insists that Louis XIV was trying to impose Catholicism on Europe. They mention that one of William's allies was the Emperor Leopold I, while airbrushing out the fact that Leopold was a Catholic Habsburg and Emperor of the Holy Roman Empire.[6]

It is easy to laugh off this ridiculous nonsense but the truth is that there are millions out there that honestly believe this garbage; not least in Scotland. That makes it far more dangerous than comical.

Surprisingly, the Scottish Orange Order's website gives a remarkably accurate and unbiased account of the Battle of the Boyne and the war in Ireland.[7] One mistake, however, that the site perpetuates is that James Stuart was intolerant. This mistake is, perhaps, understandable since many other history sites claim this as absolute fact. A reputable historian, J.P. Sommerville of the University of Wisconsin-Madison, for example, teaches this assumption as truth in his undergraduate courses.[8]

There is no real evidence of James Stuart attempting to convert Britain back to Catholicism. He removed civil restraints on, and helped promote to power, Nonconformists and Dissenters as well as Catholics. His policies in Scotland, meanwhile, were simply a continuation of what his family had been doing since his grandfather's days; trying to make the Church uniform in both his realms. He might well have been intending to impose Catholicism throughout the British Isles but the evidence is, at best, inconclusive. There is certainly nowhere near enough proof to justify stating this opinion as a fact.

The implication of support for this unhistorical view of history on the Scottish Orange Order website rather negates the rest of their accurate representation. Accepting that James was trying to make Britain Catholic again is to accept that William of Orange was the great defender of Protestantism. It also helps to perpetuate the myth that Catholics were, and are, the 'enemy within'.

This kind of thinking informs some of the ridiculous stories that have arisen about Celtic FC during the Second World War. Such tales crop up on online newspaper forums from time to time, as well as on Rangers websites, showing that there are still plenty of idiots that believe them. The most enduring one is that Celtic left their lights on to guide German bombers. If that were true, then the ARP were not doing much of a job! Some idiots even maintain that the floodlights were left on; even though floodlights were not installed at Celtic Park until the 1950s.

Apparently, there was some kind of fight among supporters at Ibrox in 1941. The newspaper clips, enthusiastically sought out and provided by members of the 'Follow Follow' website, do not really give very much in the way of detail.[9] It seems that the SFA blamed Celtic and closed Celtic Park for a month; a punishment that not everyone agreed with. That, however, does not stop the website's contributors from drawing inferences that are simply not there, including that Celtic supporters waved a Nazi flag and sang Nazi songs. Somehow, it seems highly unlikely that the denizens of Glasgow's East End were familiar with the *'Horst Wessel Song'*.

This is all part of a general attempt to paint Catholics as at best untrustworthy and at worst traitors. In the 1930s many Protestants in Scotland flirted with fascism, just like people in almost every country in Europe. What put them off, however, was that Hitler had been born a Catholic, while Mussolini was viewed as being linked with the Vatican.[10] Some Scottish Protestant organisations acted like fascists but avoided using the name; Fascism and Nazism were viewed as Catholic organisations. Some folk still see it like that.

Yes, Hitler was born in a Catholic area, to a Catholic family and was brought up a Catholic; that, however, proves nothing. Josef Stalin was brought up Eastern Orthodox but nobody has tried to relate his policies to that church. Efforts at trying to prove that Hitler was following policies sanctioned and approved by the Catholic Church are, however, still ongoing.[11] Much of this kind of thing is propagated by atheists and anti-theists, but the blatant anti-Catholicism evident in these theses are meat and drink to the sectarian bigot. For example, one site had an anti-Christian take on Hitler,[12] which a bigot regurgitated, leaving in only the anti-Catholic parts.[13]

In the real world, Hitler was supported by both Catholics and Lutherans and by many of the authorities of both churches. Those that opposed him were disposed of and, in later years, both churches faced savage persecution.[14] It is utter nonsense to link Nazism with Catholicism, Protestantism or any other religious group. And yet, still they try.

A favourite topic, especially, it seems, among British historians, is the claim that Pope Pius XII turned his back on all the Jews being systematically murdered in Nazi Germany and did nothing whatsoever to help them.[15] Quite what they hope to achieve by these accusations is unclear; the only explanation is that they are influenced by anti-Catholic bigotry. After all, Churchill was well aware of the Holocaust; what did he do to stop it? Even apologists for Churchill find it difficult to give any evidence of him helping the Jews.[16] His official biographer, it seems, could provide no evidence either.[17]

The obvious question to the doubts about Winston Churchill is, what could he have done? Bombing the railway lines to Auschwitz and other death camps would probably not have made a lot of difference. It might have delayed things for a while, but the camps would just have been moved further east, out of range of the bombers. Since, however, we are making excuses for Churchill, the same question must be asked of Pius XII; what could *he* have done?

Certainly, the Vatican had no fleet of bombers at its disposal, but the main criticism of Pius is that he should have spoken out more.[18] In fact, Pius did speak out; a lot. Critics, however, point out that he was too general in his condemnation; he should have been more specific in his attacks.[19] Protestants in England can point to the Archbishop of Canterbury, who explicitly condemned Nazi persecution of the Jews.[20] It might sound churlish, but there were no, or very few, Anglicans in Germany on whom the Nazis could exact revenge. This cannot be said for Roman Catholics.

You may remember how, in the 16th Century, the Pope's condemnation of Elizabeth I led to persecution of Catholics in England, as they were now seen as an enemy. The Vatican certainly remembered this and it helps to explain the attitude of the Catholic Church toward the Nazi persecution of Jews. To come out and explicitly condemn Nazi atrocities would put Catholics in the position they had been in England 400 years before; enemies of the state. Catholic clerics, and the faithful in the Catholic laity, would have been rounded up and murdered along with the Jews.[21] Such an outcome would hardly have been helpful. Also, as a Nazi defendant said at the Nuremberg Trials, The Pope probably thought, 'If I protest, Hitler will be driven to madness; not only will that not help the Jews, but we must expect that they will be killed all the more.'[22]

Basically, there is no evidence whatsoever that Pius XII could have done more; and most certainly there is ample evidence to show that he did no less than people in more powerful positions than his. Nobody seems to be bothered about investigating what Churchill or Roosevelt could, or could not, have done to save the Jews from the Holocaust. Then again, neither of them were Roman Catholics.

But it was not just the Vatican that stayed neutral during the Second World War, several countries took no part at all in the conflict. The neutral country that everyone is probably most familiar with is Switzerland; that is where all the prisoners of war head for in the movies. It seems a beautiful, peaceful place, where the people spend their days yodelling, eating Toblerone and playing with army knives. The reality, however, is somewhat different.

Most Swiss people do not live in the Alps in simple, wooden houses, herding goats and breeding grandchildren called Heidi. Instead, they live in large cities, like Zurich and Geneva, working just like people anywhere else in the world. The economy of Switzerland has, for hundreds of years, been based on banking and it is the home of many global financial institutions. Unfortunately, Swiss banks have a rather unsavoury past.

As the Nazis confiscated the property of German Jews and plundered the countries they invaded, their ill-gotten gains were sent to private bank vaults and private bank accounts in Switzerland. Much of this loot was in the form of gold bullion, some of which was composed of the melted-down fillings from the mouths of people that had died in the gas chambers.[23] This gold was then laundered through the banks of other nations by the Swiss banks.[24] These banks, and the Swiss economy, are still profiting from this.

As if that were not bad enough, those self-same banks, in the 1930s, were happy to receive money, gold and anything else of value from German Jews as they prepared to flee from the Nazis. The Swiss authorities refused to admit these refugees and even suggested to the Nazis that they mark the passports of all Jews with a large 'J' so that they could be easily identified.[25] Of course, the Nazis were more than happy to oblige. Any Jews that did manage to make it into Switzerland were herded into camps, where, it is alleged, they were maltreated and often made to sign over their bank details and passwords so that their accounts could be plundered.[26] Anyone caught helping Jewish refuges could lose their job, be arrested and end up destitute and disgraced.[27]

Survivors of the Nazi death camps found, after the war, that they could not retrieve their money from Swiss banks without proper documentation; something that was hardly going to make it through Auschwitz. The heirs of those that perished found their way to their parents' or grandparents' money and valuables blocked too. The banks demanded death certificates, which, of course, were not issued by the death camps.[28] Meanwhile, the Swiss banks were able to keep making money on these 'stolen' accounts.

You would imagine that there would be an international outcry about this, with people in every nation angry at this disgusting state of affairs. That, however, has not happened. Now and again the story surfaces when a new book on the subject is published, the Israeli Government makes a claim against the Swiss or the Simon Wiesenthal Centre discovers something new. In the main, the actions of the Swiss is forgotten and ignored, especially in the UK.

This can partly be explained by the fact that the Swiss banks paid what was called 'compensation' to the British and the Americans, presumably to be distributed to the victims. Effectively, though, this was tantamount to 'hush money' and the gold bullion that was handed over still languishes in the vaults of the U.S. Reserve Bank and the Bank of England.[29] And there are suspicions of far more sinister involvement by the Bank of England in helping the Nazis, including overseeing the transfer of Czechoslovakian gold to the Germans.[30]

During the war, the residents of countries that were invaded had to, of necessity, be collaborators. Not everyone was brave enough to join resistance groups and face possible torture and death at the hands of the Gestapo. People needed to eat, the buses and trains had to keep running to transport food and take commuters to work, the streets had to be kept clean and important infrastructure, like electricity, gas, water and sewage still had to be maintained. It was a question of survival. Whether you resided in the Channel Islands, occupied France or under the Vichy regime, life had to go on.

Once the war was over, the guilt kicked in. Nobody wanted to admit to helping the Nazis, no matter in how minor a way. As the crowds cheered the invading Allies and welcomed Charles De Gaulle back to France, many decided to somehow purge their guilt by pointing the finger of blame at an easy target. Women that had slept with German soldiers were dragged into the streets, where they were stripped, their heads shaved and then turned over to the baying mob, which spat at them, verbally abused them and rained blows on them. It was quite a shameful display.

Nations, of course, acted the same. Nobody really wants to point fingers at Switzerland; everybody has been fed the story of a plucky nation staying neutral in the face of Nazi aggression and Red Cross officials making sure POWs were not maltreated. How could anyone accuse these people of benefiting from Nazi atrocities? What was needed was a scapegoat. Pointing fingers at the Pope was all very well but a better one was needed. This was provided by another nation that stayed neutral during the war: Ireland.

The main reason given for Switzerland being neutral is that it was a small, vulnerable country of only about 4 million people. As one apologist says, 'One can imagine the Swiss assault on Berlin.'[31] The exact same thing could be said about Ireland, which had a similarly small population. But, one could argue, Ireland would have been fighting as part of a larger, Allied force. That would, however, apply to Switzerland just as much.

In fact, Irish neutrality was most probably in Britain's best interests. Even before the war started, there were concerns that Ireland might be invaded by Nazi Germany, leading to Britain having to fight a war on two fronts. After the rapid defeats of Poland, France and the Low Countries, as well as the rout of the British forces, the fear of an invasion of Ireland became more urgent. A plan was drawn up, called 'Plan W', whereby British forces would come to the aid of Ireland, with the British and Irish fighting together.[32]

These fears were proven to be well-founded. The Nazis *did* draw up plans for an invasion of Ireland, hoping to use it as a jump-off to invade Britain.[33] Apparently, Hitler was quite keen on the idea, but the German High Command were lukewarm and the plans never came to fruition.[34] No doubt they would have been much more interested if Ireland had been fighting alongside the Allies.

It is notable that the only online references to 'Plan W' that I could find were one Irish website and Wikipedia. Doubtless the critics of Irish neutrality would see this as evidence that the whole thing is a lie. It is far more likely, however, that it is something that the British do not like to talk about too much. Sadly, it would not be the first time that the British Establishment, media and even academia have closed ranks to pervert the truth about Ireland.

Much more easy to find are the views of your average bigot, who is determined to prove that the Irish were actually on the side of the Nazis, but were too cowardly to come straight out and join them in the war. Tales of U-boats being refuelled on the west coast of Ireland, anti-Semitic views being expressed by Irish politicians and the government allowing the IRA to contact the Nazis and invite them to come and invade are all there at the click of a button.[35]

The stories about U-boats refuelling in Ireland are just that; stories. There is not a shred of evidence to support this nonsense but plenty to disprove it.[36] Anti-Semitism in Ireland, meanwhile, was not a big problem[37] and certainly nowhere near as prevalent as it was in pre-war London, with British Union of Fascists thugs running riot. And as for the IRA, most of them were rounded up and interned for the duration;[38] the Irish Government believed as much as anyone that the IRA might seek to link up with Nazi Germany.

As for any condemnation of the IRA, claiming that they were on the side of the Nazis, one has to remember the old adage, 'my enemy's enemy is my friend'. Churchill felt exactly the same way in 1942 when Germany invaded the Soviet Union. I cannot find a direct quote, but it has been frequently reported that Churchill said he would ally with the Devil himself to defeat Nazi Germany.[39] It was a similar outlook that prompted the IRA to look for some kind of rapprochement with Nazi Germany.

One point, which happens to be true, that is often used to criticise Ireland is that they only took in around thirty German Jewish refugees.[40] But, then, one cannot help but wonder how many actually applied for visas to go to Ireland; it was hardly the 'Land of Opportunity', after all. In fact, it would hardly be a surprise to discover, if anyone ever did the research, that the Jews applying to stay in Ireland saw it as a back door to Britain.

Ireland also imposed rather strict conditions on the Jews that it did take in. They were not allowed to work and had to prove that they already had the means to support themselves independently.[41] This appears uniquely shameful until you consider what happened in the UK.

Certainly, the UK took in a lot more refugees than Ireland but the conditions they had to face were no less strict. Jewish refugees in the UK also had to prove that they had independent means and were not allowed to work, unless it was as a domestic servant. They were also rounded up and interned as enemy aliens as soon as the war started.[42] This, however, scarcely merits a mention anywhere, while references to what happened in Ireland crop up time and time again.

So, especially in Scotland, the emphasis is always on what the Pope and Ireland did during the war; never on Britain or Switzerland. There is a powerful reason why this covering-up for Switzerland and deflection of blame onto Ireland takes place; the strong connection between Scotland, and Northern Ireland for that matter, and Switzerland. Both areas are strongly Calvinist and Calvinism started in Geneva. In fact, Geneva was often called the 'Protestant Rome'.[43] Scottish, or even English, Protestants would hardly want to paint the spiritual home of their religion in a bad light. Much easier to deflect attention onto a Catholic country.

Ireland never profited from the Second World War in the way that Switzerland did and yet the campaign to impose guilt on Ireland and somehow make them apologise has been unrelenting. In some respects, this agenda appears to have worked and there are those in Ireland that *do* feel guilty and feel the need to apologise.[44] Meanwhile the Swiss sit on their filthy, ill-gotten profits and nobody seems to care.

While Ireland remained neutral during the war, it must be said that the country did provide help to the UK and the Allies. Even if one were to argue against this, it would have to be admitted that, at the very least, Ireland did nothing to hinder the fight against the Axis powers. Meanwhile, the staunch Presbyterians of the *Ossewabrandwag* carried out terrorist activities in South Africa to try to stop the country's participation in the war.[45] Not that you will ever hear very much about *that*.

But it is not only history that is perverted in the cause of anti-Catholicism; modern-day bigotry in Scotland is overlooked and seldom condemned. In fact, the peddlers of sectarian bigotry in Scotland are often portrayed as harmless eccentrics.

11
Glasgow Characters: The Downplaying of Bigotry

Haddington is the very epitome of a market town. Narrow lanes lead off narrow streets with shops displaying the corpses of hares and grouse to let you know you are in a country area. It might be the administrative centre of East Lothian Council but it is hardly what one would call a bustling area. Except when the schools come out and the council workers finish for the day, it is a sleepy place, lost in time. Even the local *Boots* looks ancient and blends in with the whole aura of the town.

Two of the most highly-influential people in history were born in Haddington, although you would hardly know it if you visit the place. Practically every second building is named after the naturalist and conservationist, John Muir, who was actually born in Dunbar. The two sons of Haddington that are all but ignored are John Knox, who needs no introduction, and Samuel Smiles, whose book, *Self Help*, influenced the whole of Victorian Britain and beyond.[1]

Haddington's St. Mary's Church is the largest church in Scotland. Building began over 700 years ago, and, although it was completed a hundred years later, there have been various additions and renovations since. It belongs to the Church of Scotland and, like other churches, it reaches out to other denominations in a spirit of ecumenism. Every Easter, other churches, including the local Catholic church, join inter-faith services at St. Mary's. Most people see this as a positive thing, but not everyone agrees.

For years, there was an unwelcome sight outside the church as these ecumenical services took place; a crowd of Protestant extremists, demonstrating against allowing Roman Catholics into God's house. This bunch of bigots was led by a well-known personality in Scotland: Pastor Jack Glass.[2]

And personality is the only way to describe the way he was treated by the Scottish media and by Scottish society at large. He looked like the original Master from *Doctor Who*, with his wee beard, bulging eyes and 'You will obey me!' approach to everyone. Like all Protestant extremists in Scotland and Northern Ireland, Glass was obsessed with three things: sex, Ulster Unionism and Catholicism. And, like all Protestant extremists everywhere, he knew, without a shadow of a doubt, that he was right about everything. He was probably confirmed in this attitude by the fact that nobody in Scotland ever condemned him for his out-and-out bigotry.

It has long been accepted that peddlers of hate are just as much to blame for violence as the actual perpetrators. Abu Hamza, for example, has never personally killed anyone but that did not stop him from being tried, convicted and sentenced to seven years' imprisonment in 2004.[3] Jack Glass could have, and should have, been arrested under the same legislation.

In 1995, a thug, who described himself as a 'Loyalist', called Jason Campbell, murdered Mark Scott, a sixteen-year-old boy, who was on his way home from Celtic Park, by slashing his throat. This shocked everyone, for all of a few days; as did all the other attacks on Celtic supporters and Catholics, usually accompanied by the cry of 'Fenian bastard!'[4] Such attacks are shockingly commonplace and are dismissed by the media as part-and-parcel of the 'Old Firm' rivalry.

Rather disgustingly, the media in Scotland makes far more of a fuss when some junior Rangers supporter is inadvertently hit by a bottle. There is no excusing the throwing of bottles but it is generally an action inspired by drunken stupidity, rather than violent hatred. In the cases highlighted by the Scottish press, a bottle has been thrown into a crowd, only to hit a young boy.[5] The papers use words like 'bottled' and 'attacked', even though the police say that the boy was 'not specifically targeted'.[6] It is probably distressing for a young boy and his family for this to happen, but it hardly compares to the pain and suffering inflicted by a schoolboy having his throat cut and being left for dead.

This disgraceful 'whatabootery' is constantly employed by the Scottish media in its quest to argue that 'one side is as bad as the other'. Even though the evidence suggests otherwise, nobody wants to point the finger at anti-Catholicism in Scotland as the main source of bigotry in this country. It appears that the Scottish media would rather see young people being murdered than admit the truth.

Invariably, when bigoted murderers appear in court, they are all 'thumbs up' to their family and friends, as if they have done something praiseworthy.[7] Obviously, they feel that they have done nothing wrong and you never hear their families apologising for what happened. Essentially, the murderers, their families and their friends behave as if these vile killings are entirely justified. That justification, of course, comes from the likes of Jack Glass, who preach hatred against the Catholic Church and Catholics.

Glass died at the beginning of 2004 and the media obituaries painted him as a passionate and caring, if misguided, individual.[8] Others talked of him being a 'Glasgow character' in a long line of 'Glasgow characters' and even compared him to Tommy Sheridan![9] It was also reported that he was a friendly, 'affable' person when you steered him away from religion.[10] No doubt Abu Hamza has always been the life-and-soul when his family and friends are celebrating *Eid*, but that did not stop anybody from locking him up.

Of course, the usual excuse given for Glass is that he hated *Catholicism*, not individual *Catholics*.[11] This, however, is a complete cop-out. Demonstrating against the visit of the Pope to Scotland, shouting, 'No Antichrist Here'[12] and trying to disrupt the visit itself, along with his hero, Ian Paisley, yelling, 'The Beast is Coming'[13] were actions that spoke volumes. Also telling was the name of Glass's campaign when he stood for office in the 1982 Hillhead by-election: 'Protestant Crusade against the Papal Visit'.[14] In all of these circumstances it is difficult to see where the line between hating Catholicism and hating Catholics is. Hypocritically, this line disappears when it comes to criticism of Israel.

There is plenty of evidence of Palestinians being forcibly evicted from their homes, as well as being continually abused and even killed. Nobody, however, is supposed to say anything about it. Unlike when they are discussing anti-Catholicism, the Scottish media are quite happy to conclude that condemning Israel means condemning the Israeli people. This is, of course, true, since it is the Israeli people that are throwing the Palestinians off their land and benefiting from this process. The media, however, goes a great deal further than that. Any criticism of Israel is portrayed as hatred of Jews in general.

This ploy has been used for a long time by Israel and its apologists to clamp down on any opposition, especially from those on the Left. There is no denying that Operation Entebbe was a heroic endeavour but film-makers could not help themselves when it came to portraying the hijackers. In the film, *Raid on Entebbe*, one passenger explains to the hijackers that she might be Jewish but she was not Israeli. One of the hijackers yells, '*Jude!*' and pushes her at gunpoint towards the separated group of Israelis. The implication is obvious: these characters hate all Jews and are no better than Nazis.[15] This is still the tactic that is used nowadays.

Ever since Jeremy Corbyn became leader of the Labour Party, there have been numerous attempts to smear him and his supporters by the party's right wing. Since the nominally Labour-supporting newspapers in the UK are on the side of the Blairites in the party, they join in the condemnation of Labour's left wing. This has taken the form of accusing Corbyn and his supporters of being anti-Semitic, due to their opposition to the state of Israel.[16] In fact, there have been constant reports of anti-Semitism in the UK, even though most of the antipathy evident is actually against Muslims.

While the Israelis are quite prepared to use the horrors of the Holocaust for their own ends, they also cannot be unaware of the underlying reason why there is so much support for Israel: Protestant obsession with the End of Days. This obsession goes all the way back to the very beginnings of the Reformation, when practically anybody with a grudge against the Catholic Church flocked to the Protestant banner. Among these malcontents were numerous groups that had been expecting the end of the World at any moment; groups that the Catholic Church had successfully suppressed. Such folk found a natural home in the new churches, who believed in the literal truth of the whole Bible. Most Protestant churches, and especially the more extremist ones, still retain elements of these beliefs. Jack Glass's congregation was no exception.

As part of his crusade, Glass founded a newspaper, called the *Scottish Protestant View*. The newspaper was continued by his congregation after Glass's death. One issue condemns Pope Francis for reaching out to Muslims, especially since he pointed out that Muslims and Christians worship the same God. 'How can that be,' the paper argues, 'when Muslims deny the divinity of Christ and His atoning sacrifice?'[17] No such Christ-denying condemnation of the Jews, however, as the paper goes all-out to show its support for Israel and Zionism.[18] But, then, the Jews in Israel are going to all convert to Christianity; after all, the Bible says so.

Fundamentalist Protestants tend not to be prepared to just sit about awaiting the End of Days; they see it as their Christian duty to actively bring it about. To this end, they have been aggressively proselytising to the Jews for years.[19] God help us all if they ever succeed, since they will then see it as their duty to bring about the end of the world!

To get back to the subject, it shows the rampant hypocrisy in our society that criticising Israel is portrayed as hatred of Jews, while professing hatred for the Catholic Church is always held to be separate from hatred of Catholics. Of course, such a position is possible to hold but it is extremely difficult to see how this applies to the likes of Pastor Jack Glass.

Another Scottish cleric that the media always presents as a reasonable man, while ignoring his anti-Catholicism, is the Reverend Stuart McQuarrie. Unlike Jack Glass, McQuarrie seems all in favour of ecumenism and, indeed, is in charge of the Interfaith Chaplaincy at Glasgow University.[20] He is also the unofficial chaplain at Ibrox, taking charge at many Rangers players' weddings and funerals, as well as commemorative services for the victims of the Ibrox disaster. He is also something of a bigot.

McQuarrie has accused Catholics of 'wallowing in their victim status'[21] and has shown himself as an apologist for the sectarian bigotry of the Rangers support. He claimed to be 'embarrassed' by *The Famine Song* but also said,

> I wanted to put forward a view that sectarianism is not just one way with one group being victimised and the other being the oppressors. Many Rangers fans feel that the Fields of Athenry is a dreadful song and equate it in the same way that Dr Reid equates the Famine Song.[22]

Condemning something with qualification is no condemnation at all. Essentially, what McQuarrie was doing was employing the usual 'whatabootery' to justify the bigotry of his fellow Rangers supporters. He continued, explaining why he found *The Fields of Athenry* offensive.

> I regard the Fields of Athenry, with other Rangers supporters, as vile, viscous (sic) and racist. The song with reference to

rebelling against the Crown is anti-British and if you consider the British people a race, it is, in that context, racist.[23] (I do not know if the good Reverend actually said 'viscous' or if nobody at the Daily Record knows how to spell 'vicious'.)

It is worth looking at the verse that McQuarrie finds so 'offensive'.

> By a lonely prison wall
> I heard a young man calling
> Nothing matters, Mary when you're free
> Against the famine and the Crown
> I rebelled, they cut me down
> Now you must raise our child with dignity[24]

So, some individual steals food for his family and describes it as 'rebelling against the Crown', which obviously refers to the law. Only a nit-picking clown with a nefarious agenda could possibly equate those few words with a call-to-arms to overthrow the British monarchy. No doubt McQuarrie would find the following lines equally anti-British and abhorrent:

> Stand ye calm and resolute,
> Like a forest close and mute,
> With folded arms and looks which are
> Weapons of unvanquished war.
> And if then the tyrants dare,
> Let them ride among you there;
> Slash, and stab, and maim and hew;
> What they like, that let them do.
> With folded arms and steady eyes,
> And little fear, and less surprise,
> Look upon them as they slay,
> Till their rage has died away:
> Then they will return with shame,
> To the place from which they came,
> And the blood thus shed will speak
> In hot blushes on their cheek:[25]

But, wait. Those lines are not about Ireland, but about the Peterloo

Massacre of 1819 and were written by English Romantic poet, Percy Bysshe Shelley. Maybe we should try to find out how many wallowing-in-their-victim-status Catholics were at St. Peter's Field on that day before asking the Reverend to give an opinion!

Compare what the Reverend found offensive in *The Fields of Athenry* with this charming little verse from *The Famine Song*:

> Now they raped and fondled their kids
> That's what those perverts from the darkside did
> And they swept it under the carpet
> and Large John he hid
> Their evil seeds have been sown
> Cause they're not of our own
> Well the famine is over
> Why don't you go home?[26]

Any reasonable person can see that *The Famine Song* and *The Fields of Athenry* are hardly in the same league when it comes to offensiveness. Reverend McQuarrie, however, is not a reasonable person and is disingenuously, and rather desperately, trying to justify anti-Catholic bigotry. He also appears to have surprisingly little to say about whether defrauding the Crown of tax revenue is 'anti-British'.

Obviously, McQuarrie was having some influence, not just on the Scottish media, but on the UK media as well. When Tommy Sheridan sang *The Fields of Athenry* on Celebrity Big Brother, *The Times* described the song as a 'sectarian anthem'.[27] No prizes for guessing where they got that idea! The problem is that it seems quite natural to accept the word of a 'man of God' before that of anyone else. If Sheridan had come out to argue his case, he would barely have been listened to. Who is going to trust a politician over a church minister? But, wait…whose name is it that keeps cropping up in newspaper articles about Glasgow Council in the 1990s? Why, it is Reverend Stuart McQuarrie, Labour Councillor for Toryglen.

McQuarrie was a councillor during Pat Lally's regime in Glasgow; a time remembered for the Garden Festival and Glasgow as the European City of Culture and not much else. It was a period when Glasgow overtook Edinburgh in the 'fur coat and no knickers' stakes. While tourists paid inflated prices at the Garden Festival and were charged a fortune to enter 'cultural' exhibitions, ordinary

Glaswegians were left out in the cold. Working-class areas were left to rot and it was near the end of the decade before attempts were made at refurbishment of Glasgow's huge council schemes. At the time, many Glaswegians felt marginalised and things like the City of Culture were happening around them, not involving them.[28]

And then came McQuarrie's proudest moment; the visit of Nelson Mandela in 1993. McQuarrie was instrumental in helping to bring the legendary South African leader to Glasgow; something he still boasts about.[29] The Scottish media reported at the time, and still do, that it was a great occasion when ordinary Glaswegians gathered in George Square and Mandela walked among them.[30] The reality, as those that were there on the day will testify, was somewhat different.

The crowd was carefully monitored by the police and some found themselves the victims of harassment because they did not fit in with the image the City Fathers wanted to portray. Mandela's 'walk among the crowd' was carefully orchestrated so that he would meet the 'right sort'. Even people that were supposed to be involved in the event were unceremoniously excluded. My brother, and other *National Union of Students* officials, had been given passes to allow them access into the City Chambers. When it came to it, however, they were refused admittance and had their passes taken off them by an MI5 officer. It was only those, and such as those, that were allowed anywhere near Mandela. Essentially, that meant the Labour clique, their hangers-on and anyone they had deigned to invite. It was nothing more than a PR exercise, typical of Lally's Glasgow.

McQuarrie himself, as part of the ruling Labour Council, was a figure of hate among the left wingers of Glasgow. In one magazine, he was labelled 'oleaginous', 'oily', 'greasy', 'slick' and 'the immoderator of the Church of Scotland'.[31] Not a popular man, then. But, then, McQuarrie will hardly bother himself over the thoughts of a bunch of Trots; not with all the friends he has made from different churches, due to his commitment to ecumenism.[32] Perhaps it is time some of his clerical chums in the Catholic Church questioned him on being an apologist for Orange bigotry; but that might be construed as not being part of the ecumenical spirit. Then again, maybe McQuarrie makes a mean Scotch broth!

The acceptance of the anti-Catholic bigotry of these two 'men of God' shows how acceptable such bigotry is in Scotland. Pastor Jack Glass is still viewed as a Glasgow 'character', who had no real harm in him, while Reverend McQuarrie is permitted to employ the old 'whatabootery' card to excuse the bigotry of his fellow Rangers supporters. But, despite what is often said about anti-Catholic bigotry, it is not merely a West-of-Scotland problem; nor is it simply a Scottish phenomenon. The whole UK still takes such bigotry completely for granted, while pretending that it does not exist.

12
Justification by Media I: The U.K.

There used to be a programme on TV, in the late 1960s and early 1970s, called *Me Mammy*. Milo O'Shea played a hapless character, completely overawed by his mother, who was forever trying to have sex with Yootha Joyce. It was a long time ago; I was a child and I was not an avid viewer of the programme. My abiding memory of it was of a maniacal woman, surrounded by statues, crucifixes, candles and holy water. It almost seemed as if she was casting spells with her collection of relics. It was all a 'Ha! Ha! Look at the funny Catholic!' kind of thing.

Then there was *Never Mind the Quality, Feel the Width*, about two tailors; one Irish Catholic, the other Jewish. This show provided double the laughs; you could laugh at the funny Catholic and then laugh at the funny Jew being confused about the funny Catholic. And the best of it was that you could pretend not to be a bigot; you were simply laughing at the Jewish character not understanding Catholicism.

These two programmes were extremely popular in their day but have to be put in context. There are some great comedy shows from the 1960s and 1970s but, as repeats on satellite channels have shown, most of them were pretty dire. Everyone seems to consider *Love Thy Neighbour* as racist, but I do not remember it like that. It tried to highlight the ridiculousness of racism and Eddie, the white bigot, always came off worst. It taught me to confront my own racism as a young teenager and the sight of the beautiful Nina Baden-Semper in a bikini certainly gave me food for thought. At school, though, all anybody seemed interested in was repeating the racist terms, like 'nig-nog'; that was what they found funny. Reading comments about the programme nowadays shows that opinion is still divided about the show. There were good intentions behind it but, for many, the programme simply reinforced their prejudices.

Other comedies had no pretentions of highlighting anything; all they provided was cheap laughs. *Mind Your Language* was all about laughing at the funny foreigners; every one of them a pretty offensive stereotype. Then there was *On the Buses*, where two middle-aged men chased after women young enough to be their daughters. The offensive, and rather unbelievable, aspect of the programme was that the young women were delighted at the attention and only too willing to shed their clothes for the old reprobates.

Essentially, much of the comedy was all about laughing at people that were *different*: black people, Pakistanis, gay people, foreigners in general, young, sexually active women and, of course, Catholics. The sad thing is that there are still people around that would find such subjects funny. That was television, but what about the movies?

The most frequent depiction of Catholicism, even obliquely, in the movies was in vampire films. A crucifix or, even better, a good shower of holy water, was enough to see off, or destroy, the most powerful of bloodsuckers. Catholic symbols were the only things that worked, apart from garlic or a sharp stick between the ribs. If you were a Protestant, you might as well just bare your neck and hope that the creature would be happy with a pint. Ostensibly, Catholicism was shown in a favourable light; but was it?

It cannot have escaped anyone's notice that vampires, along with other creatures of the night, do not, in fact, exist. They are part of a supernatural folklore, involving magic and symbols and signs to ward off evil. In this light, it is obvious that Catholicism is being portrayed in the same way, as part of superstitious mythology. Van Helsing throwing holy water at Dracula is treated the same as Harry Potter producing a patronus to fend off the Dementors. Basically, Catholicism is presented as part-and-parcel of ancient superstition. It is hardly the positive portrayal it first appears to be.

Old Hammer films involving Satan treat Catholicism in exactly the same way. In the film *The Devil Rides Out*, for example, Catholic symbols, like crucifixes and holy water, are used alongside pentagrams and magic charms and spells. Again, Catholicism is shown as being a part of centuries-old superstition.

But that was decades ago; surely things have changed? Well, not really. Just a few years ago, there was a series on Channel 4 called *Star Stories*, which lampooned the lives of various celebrities. One episode was all about Tom Cruise and in one scene he was explaining his religion, Scientology, to Penelope Cruz. The Carpenters' song *Calling Occupants of Interplanetary Craft* played in the background, Tom Cruise showed the Spanish actress models of flying saucers and the like. Cruz watched with incredulity showing on her face and then, once Cruise was finished, came out with the punchline. She said it was the craziest religion she had ever heard of, 'and I'm a Catholic, innit!' The implication was obvious; Catholicism is just as nuts as a cult that believes in a religion concocted by a science-fiction writer.

In an episode of *Red Dwarf*, one of the newer ones on the channel *Dave*, Kryten used a simile to characterise two opposite, antipathetic views. The audience laughter came right on cue as he said 'like science and the Catholic Church'. This might seem like petty nit-picking but this joke, if you can call it that, shows what the view of the Catholic Church is in the UK: a medieval, anti-scientific organisation.

In fact, the Catholic Church has had no problem in accepting new scientific discoveries; it has come a long way since the Middle Ages. The church sees no reason why evolution and Catholicism should be incompatible; after all, God must have used some method of creating life. Indeed, Pope Francis, following normal church doctrine, spoke against viewing God as 'a magician, with a magic wand'.[1] This has been pretty much the Catholic Church's position since Darwin first proposed his theory and Catholic schools have no difficulty about teaching evolution.

As for the creation of the Universe, again, there are no restrictions on Catholic schools about the theory of the Big Bang. In fact, it was a Jesuit priest that first formulated the theory of the Universe beginning at a single point[2] and the church has had no difficulty in accepting this as fact.

The reason why the Catholic Church has been able to be so flexible in dealing with scientific discoveries is that it has never accepted the word of the Bible as unchallengeable fact. The church's position has always been that many parts of the Bible are open to interpretation and are allegorical. This was one of the main differences expressed during the Reformation; the new Protestant churches were adamant that every single part of the Bible was the absolute Word of God and should be taken literally.

This has caused no end of problems for such churches when it comes to science. The solution for many Protestant churches has been simply to deny the scientific evidence and to propose alternative theories like Intelligent Design.[3] This is usually presented as a specifically American phenomenon and we have already seen how one such group infiltrated a Scottish school to spread its stories about domesticated dinosaurs and the like. These ideas, however, also have their adherents on this side of the Atlantic.

In Plymouth, there is a Creationist museum, called *Genesis Expo*, which is there to spread the 'truth' that God created the World in six days.[4] Obviously, the creators (if you will pardon the pun) of this museum, the Creation Science Movement, believe that there is an audience in the UK for this sort of thing. And there are, indeed, believers in Creationism in the UK, some of whom are in high positions.

The Caleb Foundation in Northern Ireland, which advocates the teaching of Creationism in all schools, among other right-wing, Evangelical projects, has found itself in a position of power due to its influence among politicians like Gregory Campbell.[5] One of its recent successes has been to force the Giant's Causeway visitor centre to give equal space to Creationist ideas that the World was made 6,000 years ago alongside the scientific truth of how the geological phenomenon came about.[6] This is seen as a minor triumph on the road to eliminating evolutionary ideas from Northern Ireland.

And, yet, the myth that the Catholic Church is the arch-enemy of science still persists, as if scientists are being dragged before the Inquisition like Galileo was. It would be bad enough if this opinion was held by the general population and newspaper hacks but supposedly intelligent people, even scientists, expound this nonsense.

Richard Dawkins is more famous for his anti-religious diatribes than for the fact that he is a well-qualified biologist and zoologist. He is a firm devotee of Darwin's Natural Selection theory of evolution, writing several books on the subject. It is for his stance against religion, however, that he is best known. His sneering attitude of superiority on numerous Sunday debate programmes on radio and television has probably turned more people *towards* religion, rather than away from it. He also happens to be extremely selective in his targets.

His current *bête noire* is Islam, about which he is exceedingly vocal and condemnatory, bordering on out-and-out bigotry. Like most bigots, he quite often trips himself up with his own supposed logic. For example, he sees it as his mission to convince people that Islam is a religion, not a race, so it is not racist to say anything against it. Fair enough, you might say, but then he blasts Muslims for 'forcing' women to wear the hijab. 'To hell with their culture!' he says,[7] showing complete ignorance about the whole matter.

It was not all that long ago that the majority of women in Scotland would not be seen dead going outside with their head uncovered. Anyone of my age will remember the massed rows of head-scarves (known as 'heid-squares') nodding away at each other on the bus, all decorated with pictures of Rothesay and other holiday destinations, including, in later years, Spain. Religion had nothing whatsoever to do with it; this was Scottish culture. In the same way, Muslim countries all have their own, unique, cultures. Women might not be allowed to vote, or even drive, in Saudi Arabia but they most certainly are in Pakistan, which can boast of having had a female prime minister. There is no such thing as 'Muslim' culture.

Why does Dawkins, as an atheist and supposed hater of all religion, feel the need to pick on Islam? The answer is simple; it is an easy target. You will never, ever hear Dawkins speak out against Judaism or against the various Protestant churches; they tend to speak back and mount their own challenges, which might see his popularity wane. Much easier to pick on religions that people in Britain and America already see as viable targets. One is Islam; the other is the Roman Catholic Church.

Dawkins probably talks more about Catholicism to his British audience; after all, the Catholics have quite a large lobby in America. He constantly bangs on about 'faith schools' being a force for evil in society; both in terms of indoctrinating children and helping to foster divisiveness.[8] The term 'faith schools' invariably means 'Catholic schools', especially in Scotland. Either Dawkins is completely ignorant about what he is doing or he is being disingenuous. Then again, perhaps he just does not care.

If you read my blog or have read any of my books, then you will have heard of Bill McMurdo, the son of the famous football agent. He used to host a blog, now deleted, about Rangers. Of course, the subject matter of his blog, and the various comments on it, usually had nothing at all to do with football and everything to do with sectarian bigotry. Many of the comments were of a distinctly anti-Catholic nature; often offensively so. Quite a lot of quotes were used from Dawkins's website (not always from the man himself but sometimes from other contributors) to show the 'truth' about Catholics, Catholicism and Catholic schools. It did not matter to these folk that Dawkins and his followers are atheists; as they freely admitted, all they were interested in was the anti-Catholic utterances.

I clicked on the sources given on McMurdo's website, which obviously took me to that of Dawkins and his disciples. I saw some familiar names in the comments section, as well as some familiar opinions being expressed. I made a comment myself about how the articles on the site were being used by bigots in Scotland. I received some replies of the 'Fenian bastard' and 'WATP' variety, but one of Dawkins's fanatical followers answered me as well. This individual said that it did not matter where condemnation of the Catholic Church came from; all that mattered was that it was condemned!

There did not seem to be a lot of difference, then, between the beliefs, vis-à-vis the Catholic Church, of Scottish anti-Catholic bigots and the apostles of Richard Dawkins. Of course, this stuff did not come straight from the horse's mouth, so to speak, but Dawkins has shown, on many occasions, that he hates the Catholic Church with a fury deserving of a better cause.

Dawkins did say one thing that caused a massed intake of breath, even among his followers. In an astonishing outburst, he claimed that raising a child as a Catholic was worse abuse than sexual molestation.[9] He quoted, in a completely unscientific way, an unnamed woman, who, apparently, felt that being groped by a priest as a child was nowhere near as mentally damaging as being told that her dead Protestant friend would be 'roasting in Hell forever'.[10]

This, of course, is complete nonsense. Even back in the unenlightened days of the 1960s, we were told at school that a good Protestant had far more chance of getting into Heaven than a bad Catholic. Yes, there were problems about being in the wrong religion etc. but, essentially, we learned that, for the majority of Protestants, none of that was their fault. Their baptism would probably count as viable because it was done, even if incorrectly, in God's name. In other words, Dawkins was talking rubbish.

Dawkins has displayed other signs of ignorance of Catholic and Protestant doctrine; always to the detriment of the Catholic Church.

For example, he spoke about Original Sin, saying,

> These people believe – and they teach this to tiny children, at the same time as they teach them the terrifying falsehood of hell – that every baby is "born in sin"...Original sin means that, from the moment we are born, we are wicked, corrupt, damned.[11]

Er...maybe he does not realise it, but that describes perfectly the whole, underlying doctrine of Protestantism. The Reformation was not, as many believe, about corruption in the Catholic Church; it was more fundamental than that. Whereas the Catholic Church's doctrine was that you earned your way into Heaven, with the necessary help of the grace of Christ, Protestants believed that so demeaned had man become after 'The Fall' that only God's grace could save him; any efforts on his own behalf were futile. Basically, the whole of Protestantism was, and is, based on Original Sin. Dawkins fails completely to acknowledge this fact.

Although Dawkins displays these signs of ignorance, the fact is that he is being completely disingenuous. How could anybody as intelligent as he is go through life not knowing something about simple religious doctrines? Unless he has deliberately avoided investigating religious matters, he is being extremely manipulative. He is using fear, paranoia and ignorance to engender hatred against the Catholic Church. Quite what his endgame is, only he knows; but he is playing a rather dangerous game. Most anti-Catholics, as we have seen, see themselves as 'defenders' of Protestantism. How Dawkins expects to use this mob to expunge religion from society is a mystery. Then again, perhaps he is not as clever as he thinks he is.

I began to read one of Dawkins's books, *The Blind Watchmaker* in the 1980s and his prose is just as sneering and condescending as his speeches. The book was not difficult reading; it used straightforward language without bamboozling one with over-scientific terms. What was hard to stomach, though, was Dawkins assumption that nobody was anywhere near as clever as he was, even to the extent of explaining what a big number a million is! Needless to say, I never finished reading the thing. I had no idea who the man was at the time but seeing him and hearing him over the past couple of decades has convinced me that my impression of him was correct.

Part of Dawkins's problem, however, is that not only does he see himself as the acme of intelligence; others see him in that way too. And if he sees all the World's problems as being directly attributable to Islam and the Catholic Church, then who are they to argue? It often seems as if he believes that other organised religions are not organised religions at all. Either that or Dawkins is nothing more than a bigot. But he has been to Oxford and has qualifications up to his oxters; obviously, he knows better than the rest of us mere mortals. Unfortunately, he is not the only one that has been put up on that pedestal.

There is some debate over who first said it, and it seems that it was not an original quote anyway,[12] but it has become quite common to refer to Stephen Fry as 'The stupid person's idea of a clever person.' Now, that might sound a bit snooty but, if you really think about it, it happens to be true.

Fry has nowhere near the qualifications that Dawkins has but studying at Oxbridge always makes one seem hyper-intelligent. It also helps that he has a plummy voice and is from a fee-paying school background. He presents the programme QI, where it always looks as if he actually knows all the answers, rather than reading them from a card. Everyone had the same perception of Bamber Gascoigne, who presented University Challenge for many years. Then again, Gascoigne *looked* like everybody's idea of an intellectual.

Normally such folk are pretty harmless and just get on with their lives and careers without bothering anyone; in fact, they can actually enrich people's lives. Gascoigne's TV series, *The Christians*, was a fantastic, non-judgmental, informative history, as was his book of the same name. Reading the credits in Gascoigne's book it is clear that he sees it, and the TV series, as very much a team effort and not all his own work.

Fry has proven himself to be, if not a versatile actor, at least an entertaining one. Unlike Gascoigne, however, Fry has come to see himself in the role of the all-knowing intellectual. He also happens to be a religious bigot.

On *QI*, Fry quite often spoke with utter disdain about what he called the 'Romish Church'. He never seemed to be castigated for this, even though religious bigotry should have no place in a prime-time television show. His reasons for hating the Catholic Church came pouring out when he took part in a debate at the Methodist

Central Hall in Westminster. This was the brainchild of an organisation called, *Intelligence Squared*, which is in the business of putting on such debates. The topic was, *The Catholic Church is a force for good in the World*.[13] As you might expect, Fry was arguing against the motion. Most observers claim that Fry, and his debating partner, 'destroyed the Catholic Church'.[14] In truth, Fry came across as nothing more than a hypocrite.

While blaming the Catholic Church, seemingly exclusively, for executing people, for failing to eliminate AIDS in Africa and for being anti-gay, Fry also says, 'there is nothing, sadly, that the Catholic Church and its hierarchs like to do more than to attack the Enlightenment'[15] Where the hell does he get that nonsense from? He cites the cases of Galileo and the Church's opposition to vernacular Bibles, even though that happened five hundred years ago. Closer to our own time, one of the great thinkers of the Enlightenment, David Hume, was denied a chair at both Edinburgh and Glasgow Universities because of his atheism. These were not the actions of the Catholic Church, but of Scottish Protestants.[16]

Fry saves his main attack, however, for near the end of his speech. He says,

> The Pope could decide that all this power, all this wealth, this hierarchy of princes and bishops and archbishops and priests and monks and nuns could be sent out in the world with money and art treasures, to put them back in the countries that they once raped and violated, they could give that money away, and they could concentrate on the apparent essence of their belief, and then, I would stand here and say the Catholic Church may well be a force for good in the world, but until that day, it is not.[17]

This is a man that hob-nobs with British royalty and attends their parties and dinners. You never hear him criticise *their* money and art treasures, or where it all came from. Nor does he criticise the Church of England for all *its* wealth. It is obvious that Fry is a hypocritical, sectarian bigot, for all his claims of being an atheist.

Not that he cares. His answer to any critics calling him offensive is clear. He says,

It's now very common to hear people say, "I'm rather offended by that", as if that gives them certain rights. It's no more than a whine. It has no meaning, it has no purpose, it has no reason to be respected as a phrase. "I'm offended by that." Well, so fucking what?[18]

One wonders what his reaction would be if some old-fashioned comedian, a Bernard Manning type, came on TV making jokes about 'poofs'. Or what about ridiculing mental health problems? What Fry really means is that people have no right to be offended by anything *he*, or anyone he agrees with, says. In other words, he is setting himself up as the arbiter of what is offensive and what is not. Unfortunately, there are plenty of people out there that think he is perfectly justified in his presumption.

On a side note, the audience at the *Intelligence Squared* debate was mostly comprised of students, which makes one wonder about the choice of debaters. Against the motion, along with Stephen Fry, was Christopher Hitchens, the darling of the nominally left-wing, self-appointed intelligentsia. In later years, Hitchens blotted his copybook somewhat by supporting the invasion of middle-east countries and seemingly being on the side of American Neo-Conservatism.[19] He had built up enough *kudos* over the years, however, for many to forgive him this little *faux-pas*.

The great contribution of Hitchens to the debate was the tired, old cliché of the Catholic Church being responsible for Hitler and the Nazis.[20] Perhaps he should take a look at William L Shirer's book, *The Rise and Fall of the Third Reich*. Shirer places the blame for German anti-Semitism squarely at Luther's door.[21]

Up against these two beloved individuals were placed Ann Widdecombe, who, as a Tory MP, was hardly going to be Miss Popular to an audience of students. The other speaker for the motion was Archbishop John Onaiyekan, the Roman Catholic Archbishop of Abuja, Nigeria.[22] The general opinion of the Archbishop is that he did not contribute a lot to the debate, being, as one commentator put it, 'out of his depth'.[23] This was probably more to do with the fact that his English, as one might expect, was not as good as that of the other three. Anyone of a sceptical nature might suspect that the whole exhibition was set up for the motion to be defeated.

The reaction of many people to this debate has been one of elation; celebrating the fact that Fry and Hitchens had 'demolished' the Catholic Church. Of course, everyone will have different motivations for this outpouring of glee, but it is clear that they are in party mood over the verbal destruction of the Catholic Church, *not* Christianity in general.

The anti-Catholicism of the likes of Dawkins, Fry and Hutchens, who are perceived to be intellectual heavyweights, helps to provide a rationalisation for the baseless hatred of the Catholic Church harboured by many in this country. 'Look, they're saying that about the Catholic Church and they're geniuses. I must be right, then!' is a logical, if irrational, justification for one's bigotry. Unfortunately, such people do not realise that those 'geniuses' are inspired by the same ignorance and fear in which their own bigotry is grounded. One response to the *Intelligence Squared* debate sums this up:

> Give the money back into the countries that they once raped and violated." THIS. They've taken everything from my people in Africa. It's disgusting. They took our original bible (a hebrew book) and twisted it with the King James Version. Took many of our practices and customs of Ancient Egypt and demonized our culture which they stole from. And they helped fund Adolf Hitler with his experiment in the concentration camps to help kill off the Jews and blacks. Roman Catholic Churches are pure evil.[24]

This rather confused young man unwittingly displays how anti-Catholic bigotry is fed by the media. People need rationalisations for their prejudices and the UK media are quite prepared to provide them. But it is not just in the UK that the media do such things; the media of the USA is just as guilty. Given the cultural dominance of the USA over practically the whole world, justifications for anti-Catholic hatred are spread all over the Globe.

13
Justification by Media II: The U.S.A.

The Godfather is generally considered to be the greatest movie ever made; it also displays a good deal of anti-Catholicism. If you have not seen the film, look away now.

One of the most memorable parts of the film, among many, is when Michael gets his revenge while standing as godfather for his nephew's baptism. Scenes of the Christening ceremony are intercut with violent images of enemies of Michael and the Corleone family being killed. It shows the moral bankruptcy of Michael Corleone as he 'renounces Satan and all his works'. It also, however, shows the moral bankruptcy of the Catholic Church, which is prepared to accept known criminals and killers into its arms.

This theme continues in *The Godfather, Part II*, when you can spot the priest mingling with gangsters at the First Communion party, while a Church representative accepts a cheque from the Corleone family, probably knowing full well where the money came from. Then we get onto Part III, where Michael gets involved with the Vatican Bank and receives one of the Church's highest awards. The movies are not exactly subtle in hammering home the message that the Catholic Church is a corrupt entity. There is also the underlying theme that Catholics, in the shape of the Mafia, are undermining the democratic institutions of the USA. It is almost as if it is some kind of conspiracy.

The idea of conspiracies has a long history in the USA; paranoia has been a guiding political consideration right from the foundation of the country. From Benedict Arnold to the Irish, from Freemasons to Communists, from Trades Unions to business cartels, from Skull and Bones to the Illuminati; there has always been a feeling among Americans that there is some puppet master behind the scenes, secretly running everything. This comes through in many American movies, even if just played on a small scale.

We are all familiar with the science-fiction and horror stories of the 1950s, like *Invasion of the Body Snatchers*, but, even fairly recently, American movies have shown an obsession with conspiracies and secrets. They have also, unfortunately shown a distinctly anti-Catholic flavour.

A horror film that almost everybody has probably seen is 1981's *Deadly Blessing*; it has certainly been on television often enough. A sinister-looking religious sect, who act like Amish, terrorise a young woman with their obsession with evil spirits, especially incubi. One scene in the movie shows a group of these Mennonite monsters walking through a field, one of their number swinging a censer with incense smoke pouring out.[1] It is hardly something you would expect to see the Amish, or any other Anabaptists, doing. The censer immediately makes one think of the Catholic Church, which, supposedly, helps to make the religious sect in the film much more sinister.

If you watch any movies at all, even today, which involve some kind of Protestant sect, you will notice, if you look closely, something to link the group with Catholicism. A crucifix, a statue of the Virgin Mary, holy water or even just somebody chanting in Latin is usually enough to install the connection in people's minds. It was obviously some Catholic influence that drove these individuals down the path of wickedness.

More up-to-date movies also tend to show Catholicism in a bad light. Arnold Schwarzenegger's film *End of Days*, as the name suggests, is all about Satan looking to take over the World by producing a child, who would, presumably, be The Beast of the *Book of Revelation*. This plot obviously presented the movie's makers with a problem; most Protestants would be dancing in the street at these events, seeing the awaited End of Days coming at last. The only recourse was to have the Catholic Church fight Satan; they could not, however, be the good guys. The Vatican's solution to the whole Satan problem was to kill the poor woman destined to become the mother of Satan's child. The Church in the film seemed almost as evil as Lucifer himself.

Then there are the conspiracies so beloved by Americans. *Primal Fear* had a Catholic Archbishop involved in political and financial chicanery, as well as sexual abuse. *Stigmata* showed the Catholic Church suppressing the very words of Christ because they would undermine the Church's power, while *The Da Vinci Code* goes further and accuses the Catholic Church of corrupting the whole Christian religion; an accusation close to the hearts of fundamentalist Protestants.

In 2007, New Line Cinema released *The Golden Compass*, the film adaptation of the first book in Philip Pullman's *His Dark Materials* trilogy. The movie was bound to cause controversy since Pullman's books were, essentially, rants against Christianity. Surprisingly, not much of an issue was made about the film; in America, everyone was too busy being angry about Harry Potter. Critics, however, were none too kind about the film and it, apparently, did not make enough money to justify a sequel. That did not stop the Catholic Church from being blamed for the second book not making it to the big screen.

Sam Elliott, famous for playing grizzled-old-cowboy characters, played, unsurprisingly, a grizzled-old-cowboy character in *The Golden Compass*. His take on why there was no sequel made was pretty unequivocal:

> The Catholic Church happened to The Golden Compass, as far as I'm concerned. It did incredible at the box office, taking $380million. Incredible. It took $85million in the States. The Catholic Church ... lambasted them, and I think it scared New Line off.[2]

Mr Elliott, however, is either incredibly naïve or is being disingenuous; the fact is that the film actually made very little money at all for New Line Cinema. The movie cost $180m to produce, which makes the $85m it took at the US box office pale into nothingness. It made a lot more money in overseas sales but, unfortunately, the overseas rights were sold to provide funding before the film was finished.[3] Sam Elliott's little outburst, therefore, is nothing but a pack of lies. That, however, does not stop a lot of people from agreeing with him.[4]

Rather ironically, one group that agrees with Elliott is the Catholic League for Religious and Civil Rights, which appears to think that its call for a boycott was what caused the film to bomb in the US. But, as someone in the comments section points out, Catholic pressure groups failed miserably in trying to stop the making of *Life of Brian* and *The Da Vinci Code*.[5] Film production is all about money; nothing else matters, and certainly not minority pressure groups.

The Catholic League for Religious and Civil Rights is only one pressure group among many in the USA. These groups can often have a massive impact on politics, especially at a local level but sometimes even nationally. The Moral Majority, for example, was instrumental in getting Ronald Reagan elected in 1980.[6] When it came to film and TV, however, it was not as successful as it, and others thought it was. When the TV comedy series *Soap* was cancelled, it was not due solely to the efforts of the Moral Majority; it was the show's sponsors, the money men, who got cold feet and pulled out.[7] But all the pressure groups still try their best.

James Martin, in *America* magazine, outlines some of the worst examples of anti-Catholicism in the US media,[8] although it is highly debatable whether or not sexy nuns count as such. Prurient speculation over what goes on in convents probably pre-dates the Reformation and is part of a long tradition of male fantasies about women living, or meeting, together. Even back in Ancient Rome the festival of the Good Goddess excited many a male libido.[9]

Nowadays, such fantasies are served by pornographic films set in Sixth-Form colleges, sororities, women's prisons and anywhere with an all-female population, including convents. (So I'm told!) Before the invention of the internet, videos, films or even photography, books detailing the confessions of supposed runaway nuns were all that were available. They might have been released in the name of anti-Catholicism but it is doubtful that is the reason why they were bought, or even the real reason why they were published!

Much more worrying is the advert for student loans, saying, alongside a picture of a nun, 'If you're a nun, then you're probably not a student.'[10] That will come as a surprise to all the nuns, throughout the world, working as teachers, doctors and nurses. Unlike the sexy nun portrayals, this is anti-Catholic; implying that if you are a nun then you must be a bit thick.

Strangely, James Martin argues that the likes of The Catholic League for Religious and Civil Rights are too belligerent and that a more conciliatory approach would reap more results. He should take a look at how black people were treated when they attempted a moderate course, as they did for decades. It took the founding of the Black Panthers and athletes making 'Black Power' salutes at the

Mexico City Olympics to scare the bejeesus out of the White Establishment in America and actually get changes implemented. If anti-Catholicism is to be eradicated, then there is no point in asking politely!

The entertainment and advertising media are not the only ones to display anti-Catholic traits; even the news media are infected. There was a long-standing belief among Americans that Catholics cannot be trusted; their first allegiance would always be to the Vatican.[11] Even though Kennedy's presidency proved this theory to be wrong, there are, unfortunately, those that still subscribe to it.

Part of The Patient Protection and Affordable Care Act, popularly known as Obamacare, means that employers have to help with their employees' medical insurance. This covers preventive care too, which includes contraception. Such a measure was bound to cause problems with religious organisations, such as Catholic universities, so special regulations were put in place allowing religious, non-profit employers to opt out, with a separate insurer picking up this part of the cover. Even with these safeguard, however, there were still problems.

In 2014, the owners of two companies, the arts-and-crafts chain Hobby Lobby and Conestoga Wood Specialties, a wholesale supplier of wooden doors, kitchen components and furniture, sued the US Government over certain parts of the contraceptive element of Obamacare. Both companies are owned by Christian families (the owners of Conestoga Wood Specialties are Mennonites) who objected to being involved in the provision of contraception. The US Supreme Court upheld their complaints, judging that closely-held firms should not be forced to choose between fulfilling corporate requirements and religious beliefs. The decision was a majority one, with five judges in favour, four against.[12]

One of those against the decision was Justice Sonia Sotomayor, who agreed with her colleague, Justice Ruth Bader Ginsburg, that the 'exercise of religion is characteristic of natural persons, not artificial legal entities'.[13] To stop an unwelcome precedent being set, those in favour made sure to specify that the decision only applied to the contraception element of Obamacare. That, however, could be argued to discriminate against women. The whole thing was turning out to be more complex than first thought.

Justice Sonia Sotomayor, earlier in 2014, had a legal decision to make on her own. The Little Sisters of the Poor in Colorado run centres for the care of the elderly, which means that they have employees to pay. Under the Act, the nuns could fill in a form to exempt themselves from the contraception element. The nuns argued, however, that even by filling in the form to allow an outside insurer to take over the contraception element they are, if only by proxy, providing contraception to their employees.[14]

The Supreme Court was going to have to make a decision about the nuns' argument; in the meantime, the Little Sisters applied for a stay, a temporary exemption from the contraception element of Obamacare until a permanent ruling was made. This stay was granted by Justice Sonia Sotomayor. This move made complete sense legally, since it was highly possible that the nuns' complaint would be upheld. That, however, was not the way journalist Jamie Stiehm saw things.

In the US News and World Report, an online publication best known for its 'ranking' guides to education, hospitals and cars, among other things,[15] Stiehm ranted against Sotomayor for putting 'her religion ahead of her jurisprudence'.[16] According to Stiehm, Sotomayor had completely betrayed her sex and had proven herself to be nothing but a 'good Catholic girl'.[17] Stiehm then launches into a scattergun attack on the Catholic Church, claiming that the Vatican is seeking to dominate America; all the 'good Catholics' are acting under orders from Rome. In league with all these reactionaries she mentions Rush Limbaugh but, strangely, feels no need to say how his professed religion of Methodism informs his world view.[18]

The fact that Stiehm refuses to see any correlation between Limbaugh being, nominally at least, a Methodist and his extreme right-wing opinions shows that she is nothing more than a bigot. Her obvious prejudice makes her no better than Limbaugh himself. And the fact that the US News and World Report thought this article worth publishing shows that there is an audience for this bigotry in the US.

The media do not operate in a vacuum and anti-Catholicism has deep roots in the USA; as might be expected, given the Protestant, English nature of the American elites. This was especially prevalent in the southern states, which paved the way for the Ku Klux Klan after the Civil War. It is an aspect of the Klan that is often overlooked; its members hate Catholics as much as they hate blacks.

In 1928, when Al Smith stood for the presidency, the first Roman Catholic to do so, he was vilified in the press, had numerous anti-Catholic pamphlets directed against him and was greeted in Oklahoma by burning crosses lining the railway tracks.[19]

Throughout the Nineteenth Century, and well into the Twentieth, politics was extremely divisive in the USA. It was not just slavery that caused this rift; anti-Catholicism played its part too. In the 1840s, a new political party emerged. It was officially called *The American Party* but became known as the *Know-Nothing Party*, since most of its support came from secret societies, whose members professed to 'know nothing' when asked about their clubs. It stood for what were, rather laughably, called 'Nativist' policies, including calling a halt to immigration and wanting recent immigrants to be resident in America for twenty-five years before being allowed to vote.[20]

Party politics often descended into gang warfare and this was the case in New York City in the 1840s and 1850s. William 'Bill the Butcher' Poole, the leader of the *Bowery Boys* gang, was also a prominent figure in the Know-Nothings.[21] At that time most of the immigrants were Irish Catholics, escaping from the effects of the Famine. Poole's *Bowery Boys* often fought against the *Dead Rabbits*, Irish-Catholic immigrants and supporters of the Democrats.[22] If these gang names sound familiar, you have probably come across them in Martin Scorsese's film, *Gangs of New York*. Scorsese used the gang names but took more than a few liberties with history.

The No-Nothings died out in the late 1850s, its members drifting into the Republican Party, where its influence can still be seen.[23] The recent nomination of Donald Trump as the Republican candidate, and his subsequent election to the Presidency, shows how pervasive this influence is. It is anti-immigrant and 'Nativist', with a healthy dollop of anti-Catholicism, and hatred against the new enemy, Islam, thrown in for good measure.[24]

The Democratic Party has not escaped this insidious bigotry. While the Democrats were moving in a left-ward, more liberal direction in the northern states, in the south it was still, well into the Twentieth Century, the party of the racial and sectarian bigot. In fact, the Democratic Party in the south was inextricably linked to the Klan; the two organisations often indistinguishable.[25] When John F Kennedy stood for the Presidency in 1960, he had to bring on board a 'good old boy' from Texas, Lyndon B Johnson, as his running mate. Had he not done so, it is doubtful that he would have been elected. There is still evidence of anti-Catholic bigotry within the Democratic Party, which showed its ugly face in 2014 during the Washington State senatorial campaign.[26]

Of course, it is not only Catholics that suffer from this bigotry, as the presidential campaign of Mitt Romney in 2012 proved. Romney is a member of the Church of Jesus Christ of Latter-Day Saints; a Mormon. Many Americans view Mormonism as a cult, rather than a religion[27] and it was quite a surprise when Romney won the Republican nomination. Many liberals were outraged and Romney's Mormonism was brought up quite often during the campaign; even by members of his own party.

The problem was that the LDS Church, up until 1978, barred black men from holding the priesthood. Black people were welcome to join the church, become baptised and take the sacrament but it was believed that God had made them black to distinguish them as descendants of Cain and to indicate that they were, as a consequence, prevented from being ordained to the priesthood. In fact, there was a bit more to it than that, as church authorities made clear that black people were inferior and that God intended for them to serve white folk, even in the afterlife.[28] Such beliefs are no longer part of the church's tenets, but that did not stop them being continually thrown at Romney.

There is no escaping the fact that the Mormons *did* believe in this racial prejudice; some breakaway sects still do. It is a bit hypocritical, however, to use the historical beliefs of the Mormons as a stick with which to beat them. After all, during the time that the Mormons held such beliefs, so did the rest of American society. Viewing black people as inferior was pretty common right up until the 1970s, and even beyond; it was hardly a peculiarly Mormon trait.

If liberals are prepared to revile Mormons for their past racist doctrines, conservatives dislike them for a different reason entirely. Although Mormons see nothing wrong with making money and being involved in the capitalist system, they also believe in social responsibility. The church sees it as everyone's duty to look after each other; not only spiritually, but seeing to the physical and psychological well-being of members and ex-members too. This is touchingly illustrated in the story of Arthur Kane, of seminal rock band *The New York Dolls*, whom the LDS Church helped to get back his life and self-respect.[29] And it is not just members and ex-members that the church wants to help.

Mormons believe that there is some great catastrophe coming our way, but they do not know when; it could be in ten years, it could be in a hundred. Everyone is supposed to be prepared for this and stock up on non-perishable food. Unlike redneck survivalists, however, this food is intended to be shared with others, whether church members or not. The church even has plans to organise distribution centres and to work with authorities to get supplies to those that need it. This altruism is not just for some unspecified future; the Mormons are closely involved in aid provision in developing countries and charities closer to home.

Such beliefs no doubt played their part during Mitt Romney's tenure as Governor of Massachusetts between 2003 and 2007. In an unusual move for a Republican, Romney introduced a health-care law that was a precursor to, and possibly an inspiration for, Obamacare. This law was known, rather obviously, as Romneycare.[30] This health-care law was, predictably, praised and condemned in equal measure but nobody ever seems to have made a connection, either positive or negative, between Romneycare and Mormonism.

It seems that connections between religious faith and politics are usually only made when a Catholic is involved. Yes, there were accusations made against Obama that he was influenced by Islam,[31] but the right-wing expounders of such nonsense know that it is a pack of lies just as much as the rest of us do. In reality, this religious aspect of the hatred for Obama is just a mask for old-fashioned racism; something that is, quite rightly, no longer tolerated. Catholics, however, are fair game.

Whenever contraception or abortion appears on the agenda, you can be sure that Catholicism will crop up somewhere in the discussion. Even though most aggressive pro-life protestors are actually Protestants, nobody ever mentions their religion. They might be vilified as right-wing nutters or conservative extremists, but their churches are not deemed worthy of consideration. As soon as a Catholic is involved, however, even in a legislative capacity, you can be sure that they will be accused of taking orders from Rome. It is easily shown, though, that such accusations are well wide of the mark.

Conservative Catholic groups are often concerned that Catholic politicians are *not* being influenced by their faith when making decisions.[32] That this is the case proves that, when it comes to political decisions, Catholics are no different from anyone else and can be found on both sides of the argument. Those that claim Catholics always follow the dictates of their church, then, are wrong and clearly inspired by their own bigotry.

Perhaps the most prevalent accusation against the Catholic Church is illustrated again in James Martin's article. A commentator on a news show, who advocated compulsory DNA testing for potential criminals, identified the following groups as being at risk of offending: 'teenagers, homeless people, Catholic priests'.[33] So widespread has this particular accusation become that it is not even necessary to say what crime Catholic priests might be at risk of committing. In fact, it has become so steeped in the public consciousness worldwide that it needs a chapter of its own to discuss it.

14
Paedophile Priests: A Purely Catholic Scandal

The UK has a long and ignoble history of child sexual abuse. In mid-Nineteenth-Century London, foreign visitors were often shocked at the number of child prostitutes openly plying their trade in busy streets. Such was the demand for little girls that teenage prostitutes took to trying to look younger to get more custom. And this demand was not just fuelled by perverts. Rather disturbingly, it was a common belief that having sex with a virgin was a cure for venereal diseases.[1] The younger the sexual partner, the more chance there was of her really being a virgin.

The Criminal Law Amendment Act of 1885 raised the age of consent for women to sixteen, while other, stringent measures were put in place to protect girls and young women. Unfortunately, an infamous addition was made to the Bill just before it was passed, effectively outlawing homosexuality. Previously, homosexuals could only be prosecuted under laws prohibiting sodomy. This was obviously a difficult thing to prove and the penalties were so severe (death until 1861; life imprisonment thereafter) that juries were reluctant to return a 'guilty' verdict. The new law allowed for prosecutions under the charge of 'gross indecency', a term that could mean almost anything.

There was no suggestion at the time that homosexuality was in any way connected with child sex abuse; the amendment was added without proper discussion, advantage being taken of the fact that everyone wanted the bill passed quickly. Later events, however, would make this amendment much more significant than it actually was.

After 1885 it seems to have been assumed that child sexual abuse no longer existed. It was something that was never discussed and prosecutions were extremely rare. It is only fairly recently that the extent of child abuse in Britain during the 20th Century has been exposed. Many children were even abused when they were evacuated to the countryside during the Second World War; something that nobody wanted to know. In fact, even when abusers were discovered at the time, it was far more common for them to be beaten half to death and then driven from the neighbourhood than it was for anyone to report them to the police. It was in the 1960s that everything changed.

Everyone has heard of Myra Hindley and Ian Brady; details of their crimes have been replayed over and over by the press and television. What is hard to convey in a TV documentary, however, is the sheer terror inspired in many parents by what they were reading in the newspapers. Almost overnight, the admonition 'not to talk to strangers' took on a real and frightening dimension. I remember, as a five-year-old in 1966, receiving a battering from my mother because I had taken a sweet from a young couple that had been speaking to me over the garden fence. Small children, like myself, had no real conception of what it was all about but learned to run a mile if a stranger even looked at us.

While all this was going on, middle- and upper-class intellectuals were looking at things in a rather incongruous, different light. This was the time of hippies, flower-power, free love and the counter-culture. While young Americans demonstrated against the Vietnam War and campaigned for equal rights for black Americans and young people in Europe rioted in the streets, or even joined terrorist groups, in their anger at the crimes of their parents' generation in the 1930s and 1940s, Oxbridge students and ex-students sat around, smoking dope and telling each other how clever they were.

Much of the British counter-culture music of the period is full of references to gnomes and fairies, showing the influence of Tolkien rather than Marx, Lenin or Trotsky. Counter-culture magazines, like *Oz*, had pictures of naked women on the cover, making them not much different from the *Sun*, or *Playboy*. Even Germaine Greer's, at the time, ground-breaking book, *The Female Eunuch*, now seems like nothing more than a snooty, thinly-veiled attack on working-class women. The whole 'movement' was not counter-culture at all; it was simply a bunch of privileged, young people playing at being rebels, not much different from their ancestors in the 1920s.

Remarkably, this bunch were actually quite influential in the early 1970s, which, for the most part, was harmless since their attitudes, beliefs and pronouncements could be quite ridiculous. For example, Germaine Greer, the great feminist, would gripe about exploitation of women, while posing for pornographic photographs. She could hardly argue that they were not pornographic; she was well aware that she was contributing to male masturbatory fantasies just as much as any 'Page Three Bird' in the *Sun*.[2] Other influences by this 'counterculture' group were far more worrying.

The trial, in 1971, of the editors of *Oz* magazine over the infamous *Schoolkids Edition* was a great cause célèbre at the time; nowadays, it is extremely doubtful that so many celebrities would be clamouring to justify the magazine's publication. Perhaps the most shocking part of the magazine, to modern eyes, is the *Rupert the Bear* cartoon, put together by a fifteen-year-old boy.[3] That a young person would consider the rape of an unconscious woman as somehow normal is deeply disturbing. There was, however, worse to come.

Even before liberal attitudes came into vogue in the 1960s, anyone with any intelligence had begun to realise that beliefs about homosexuality were wrong. It could hardly be a lifestyle choice since nobody with any sense would voluntarily open themselves up to vilification, ostracism and blackmail. Equally, attempts to 'cure' homosexuals using psychotherapy, drugs, hormones, aversion therapy etc. had all failed miserably. Instead of eradicating homosexuality, all these procedures managed was to produce homosexuals with severe psychological problems. Perhaps homosexuality was a natural thing. Besides, what harm were they doing?

To society at large, homosexuals were predatory monsters, ready to pounce on young men, or even young boys. Public Information Films in America warned of the dangers of homosexuals and attitudes were exactly the same in the UK.[4] And, of course, everyone could feel that they were perfectly correct in their prejudice; after all, were homosexuals not lumped together with kiddie-fiddlers as far as the law was concerned? Unfortunately, counter-culture liberals took the same view.

As we saw earlier, the law allowing for the prosecution of homosexuals had been tacked onto the Criminal Law Amendment Act of 1885. Instead of just concentrating on the addition, however, the thought among many liberals was that the whole legislation was flawed. Modern psychology had shown that children were sexual beings, so maybe there should be no such thing as an age of consent.

While it is true that children *do* have a sexuality, it is not the same as that of adults. As a male primary teacher, it is something that I had to be acutely aware of. At college and at various courses, you are taught to watch for signs that children are being sexually abused, as well as making sure that your own actions cannot be construed as inappropriate. You learn to differentiate between normal, child sexual behaviour and indicators that something is not right. You also learn how to deal with child sexuality in an appropriate, non-judgmental way.

For example, five- and six-year-olds are notorious for unselfconsciously fumbling with themselves, oblivious to those around them. I had one Primary 1 girl that decided going to the TV room, where the children sat on a carpet, was a good opportunity for a poke about. I soon put a stop to this embarrassing performance by giving her the 'important' job of holding the register for me. Eventually, she would learn that, while there was nothing intrinsically wrong with what she was doing, it was not something the rest of us wanted to see.

Older girls can be quite flirtatious, in their own, inimitable fashion. It is quite common for girls, between the ages of nine and eleven, to stand in front of their male teacher, trying vainly to look coquettish. They especially like to do this at PE time, when they will often wear their tee-shirt outside their shorts, letting it sit like a mini-dress. It is cute and comical in equal measure. It is enough for them for you to laugh at their presumption, while telling them to get in line with everybody else. That, as far as the girls are concerned, should be as far as it goes. They certainly do not want some grubby grown-up slobbering all over them; their first, and main, concern in their teacher's presence is that they feel totally safe.

This difference in child sexuality was either not understood or ignored by many liberals in the late 1960s and early 1970s. A new, rather inappropriate, word appeared: paedophile – a lover of children. In fact, love had very little to do with it; it was just sexual deviants taking advantage of the confusion between liberalism and libertarianism.

In the 1970s it was possible for paedophiles to be quite open about their desire to abolish the age of consent for sexual intercourse. An organisation, called the Paedophile Information Exchange, started up and quickly became affiliated with the National Council for Civil Liberties.[5] The NCCL argued that there was a huge difference between condoning sexual activity with children and allowing those that did to put their case forward. Some people still argue that those advocating sex with children should be allowed a platform in the name of free speech.[6]

An anomaly in the law also opened the door for paedophiles to affiliate themselves with gay rights groups, much to the shock and disgust of many gay people.[7] The age of consent for heterosexual sex was sixteen, while that for homosexuals was twenty-one. (Homosexuality was still totally illegal in Scotland until 1981.) Obviously gay rights campaigners wanted parity with heterosexuals, which meant lowering the age of consent. Paedophiles saw their chance and managed to tack on calls for the abolition of the age of consent altogether; a move much like what had happened in 1885.

Officials of the Paedophile Information Exchange ended up in prison for sexual offences against children and the organisation was disbanded in 1984.[8] It left us with two legacies: the word 'paedophile' itself and a burning suspicion that paedophile activities have been covered up at the highest levels in the UK.[9] More than a few respectable, Establishment figures have been identified as members of PIE and as being involved in the abuse of children.[10] In fact, there are allegations that Thatcher's Government gave money to PIE and that Special Branch infiltrated it in order to gather information for blackmail purposes.[11]

Although calls for enquiries surface now and again in newspapers, the consensus appears to be that everyone should just forget about what happened in the 1970s and 1980s. It has almost become a tit-for-tat game, with left-wing media wanting Establishment paedophiles investigated and the right-wing press hitting back with stories about liberals and Labour Party members supporting PIE back in the day. Meanwhile, many websites that accuse the Establishment of child abuse are so full of esoteric, mystical nonsense[12] that if there has been, and is, a cover-up, then these sites are probably part of a deflection operation.

Reports and comments on paedophilia and paedophiles, meanwhile, show some remarkable hypocrisy. When the news broke about Gary Glitter's arrest, Richard Madeley and Judy Finnigan spoke about their disgust on *This Morning*. Glitter had been on the programme quite recently and Finnigan said that it 'made her feel sick' to think of him sitting next to her. They then, as they usually did, detailed what was going to be coming up on the show. Highlights included the next round of an under-sixteen modelling competition. That was bad enough but I remember sitting, open-mouthed, as they announced that one of the judges was Bill Wyman of the *Rolling Stones*!

In the late 1980s, Wyman had been all over the tabloid press for having sex with a fourteen-year-old girl.[13] Strangely, though, the word 'paedophile' has never been applied to him. Not so lucky in this respect has been Jonathan King, who used his position in the music industry to entice young men into bed.[14] Essentially, the only difference between King and Wyman was that King preferred men; this, apparently, makes a huge difference as to whether or not you get labelled a 'paedophile'. Probably the most notorious example of this hypocrisy is the film director, Roman Polanski, who is still wanted in the USA for having sex with a twelve-year-old girl. Again, though, he seems to have avoided condemnation and the label 'paedophile'. Hypocrisy, however, cannot even begin to describe the aftermath of the revelations that emerged when Jimmy Savile died.

Savile, it has been discovered, was possibly the worst abuser of children in UK history and that is only based on the offences we know about. Shockingly, Savile's abuse was facilitated, and covered up, by people in the BBC, the music industry, the police, parliament and, possibly, even royalty. He was a frequent visitor to Chequers when Thatcher was Prime Minister and there are many photographs of him with members of the Royal Family, especially Prince Charles. This, understandably, has led to speculation about top people in the UK being involved in child abuse.

For decades, there have been stories about Kincora Boys' Home in Belfast; MI5 apparently ran it as a brothel, blackmailing the clientele into acting as double agents. Establishment figures also visited the home, or had boys taken to nearby hotels; some boys are even alleged to have been shipped over to London to be abused by perverts there.[15]

In London, itself, there have been scandalous stories regarding activities at the Elm Guest House and flats at Dolphin Square. Unbelievably, most Westminster commentators, including reporters, MPs and even current and ex-ministers, profess to know nothing and claim to have been surprised when stories surfaced about Cyril Smith.[16] Nobody, it seems, is prepared to accept that there was ever any kind of Establishment paedophile ring. But the rumours will not go away.

And organised child abuse was, and is, not restricted to London. We have already noted the Kincora Boys' Home, but there are also rumours about many other institutions, including the Haut de la Garenne Children's Home in Jersey, where, allegedly, torture and even murders were carried out.[17] Meanwhile, allegations of sexual abuse also emerged about the Queen Victoria school for the children of armed forces personnel.[18] These allegations were made all the more sinister when Thomas Hamilton was revealed as having links with the school.[19] Hamilton was the perpetrator of the Dunblane Massacre, many details of which have been officially suppressed,[20] fuelling even more speculation about the involvement of the top echelons of society in child abuse.

As always, the best way to deflect attention is to direct it onto someone else. And, just as in Tudor and Stuart times, the scapegoat was obvious. The media, of course, were only too happy to oblige. Much was made of Cardinal Keith O'Brien's 'close friendship' with Jimmy Savile,[21] while the even closer relationship between Savile and the Royal Family was all but ignored. Articles about Myra Hindley make sure that we are always told that she converted to Catholicism,[22] while Lord Longford, who campaigned for Hindley's release, had reference made to his Catholic faith whenever the subject came up.[23] Even Wikipedia deems it worth highlighting the fact that even though Paul Gadd, aka Gary Glitter, was 'a Protestant, he was educated at a Roman Catholic school'.[24]

Also, just as in Tudor and Stuart times, however, the Catholic Church practically offered itself up as a target. Even if only a small part of the allegations against Catholic clergy are true, it is still a damning indictment. It has been a worldwide scandal; one which the church is still trying to resolve.[25] It appears that there were many thousands of cases, which the church dealt with in-house, resulting in nothing more than a cover-up. Unfortunately, many have been only too keen to leap on this scandal to divert attention from other such occurrences.

In early 2016, the movie *Spotlight* was released in the UK. The film had already won critical acclaim in America and did quite well at the box office. It was all about the newspaper, the *Boston Globe*, which had investigated the cover-up in the city, by church officials, politicians, the judiciary and the police, of sex offences against children carried out by Catholic clergy.[26] We had heard all this before, of course, but this was an exposé for which the *Globe's* reporters had won a Pulitzer Prize.

As practically all critics pointed out, this was a story that had to be told. In the UK, the film was welcomed with open arms by certain people. As the Guardian put it in its review, 'Catholic Church called to account over child abuse'.[27] The article's author, Peter Bradshaw, also made the observation that 'the abuse stretches back decades or even centuries'.[28] The comments section was even more damning.

> The catholic church is a criminal organisation, and should be treated as such.
> It should be shut down, and it's (sic) assets seized and sold to pay for their crimes.'

> ...for anyone to imagine that this abuse has not always been an integral part of the life of the Catholic Church, and will continue to be so, is burying their head in the sand. It is sewn into the very fabric of their being.'[29]

According to these observations, that is the movie's whole theme; that the Catholic Church is, and always has been, guilty of child sexual abuse. More than that; child sexual abuse is a predominantly Catholic problem. The Telegraph, rather surprisingly, took a different slant on the message of the film:

> There's no tidy moral to take away here, which is, I think, entirely right: a story like this shouldn't end in comfort. Instead, it leaves your skin prickling – both at the despicable business of secret-keeping, and the courage and resourcefulness that rivetingly overturns it.[30]

This is an aspect of the movie that nobody in the UK wants to recognise; politicians, judiciary and police covering up child abuse. We have been learning, in a piecemeal fashion, that politicians, the judiciary and other public figures have actually been directly involved in the abuse itself, not just the cover-up. It is hardly surprising that the UK media prefers to concentrate on the Catholic Church rather than rock the Establishment boat.

In America, too, the emphasis is on the Catholic Church, rather on the issue of child abuse. For example, *Spotlight* won Best Picture at the Oscars in 2016. This surprised some people, since it was not a great or particularly entertaining film. It seems that the movie's worthiness was the deciding factor. Strangely, though, the worthiness of the topic of child abuse has not always been recognised.

The 1996 movie *Sleepers* dealt with the sexual abuse of young boys in the American penal system. It was claimed to be based on a true story.[31] With a stellar cast, engaging characters and a thrilling plot, as well as a worthy theme, the movie would be expected to do well when it came to the Academy Awards. In fact, the film was only nominated for one Oscar, Best Dramatic Score, losing out to *The English Patient*.[32] The problem with *Sleepers*, as far as a lot of people were concerned, was the questions that hung over the story's veracity.[33] No such question marks, however, hung over *The English Patient*, which won nine Oscars, including Best Picture, even though that film took many liberties with the truth.

There were no such difficulties with the truth when it came to 2010's *The Whistleblower*.[34] The protagonist, Kathryn Bolkovac, was a real person, whose story had been corroborated and proven in a court of law. The story was a harrowing one, detailing Bolkovac's experiences as part of the UN peacekeeping force in Bosnia. She discovered that the soldiers were involved in the trafficking of children and young women, whom they used as sex slaves. The private company running the peacekeeping force, and high-ranking officials of the UN itself, were turning a blind eye and even protecting the criminals from prosecution. It was a shocking story and, just like *Spotlight*, it was one that needed to be told.

The movie was pretty horrific but the truth was even more so; the director left some of the more stomach-turning details out of the film.[35] Watching the film makes one run a gamut of emotions; it is even thrilling in parts, since Bolkovac's own life was in danger. When the movie is over, all you can feel is anger. It is an extremely powerful film.

The Whistleblower was completely ignored at the Academy Awards; it was not nominated in a single category. The winner of the Best

Picture Oscar was the anodyne *The King's Speech*;[36] not exactly a memorable cinema experience. It seemed, yet again, that the worthiness of a movie could be overlooked if the story did not fit with particular agendas. The private company that had been running the peacekeeping operation in Bosnia, DynCorp, was an American one; one that was still being used by the U.S. Government in Iraq and Afghanistan.[37]

So, what made *Spotlight*, which was not exactly edge-of-the-seat stuff, more worthy of an Oscar than *The Whistleblower*? The answer is fairly obvious and is as shocking as the facts revealed in the two movies; the American Establishment wants all attention focused on the Catholic Church just as much as that of the UK. Essentially, nobody gives a damn about what has happened to children around the world, but they need to be seen to care. Blaming the Catholic Church for everything is an easy solution.

Not everyone likes to display their bigotry for all to see, so they hide behind rationalities. One such rationality is blaming the celibacy of Catholic priests for child abuse. The argument is that priests will obviously be sexually frustrated and this frustration will end up being channelled into perverted sexual activity.[38] It is a completely nonsensical argument. If it were true, then far more priests would have been involved in child abuse. It is, however, true that the majority of child abuse cases are *not* carried out by priests; often such abuse is perpetrated by married men, sometimes on their own children. But, still, people are quite prepared to believe that celibacy in men leads to child abuse.

> It's not difficult to work out why there is no protestant child abuse crisis - they are largely happily married men leading normal sexual lives.[39]

One person that would completely disagree with that is Boz Tchividjian, the grandson of famous evangelist Billy Graham and founder of GRACE (Godly Response to Abuse in the Christian Environment). Tchividjian has been running a mission to make Protestants proactive in dealing with child abusers in their own congregations and not wait until they are forced to act, as the Catholic Church was.[40]

Tchividjian's organisation includes lawyers, pastors and therapists;

all ready to help any Protestant church, school or college that needs them. And, if Tchividjian is right, then they most definitely need the help of GRACE. Tchividjian believes that child abuse has been much more of a problem in Protestant churches than in the Catholic Church.[41] Whether or not that is true, Tchividjian sees child abuse as a *Christian* problem, not a Catholic one.

Officials of all Christian churches have been hidebound by their faith in the essential goodness of their fellow man. Even fundamentalist Protestants, who view mankind as fatally flawed, will still deem their own church members as trustworthy. It is pretty much part-and-parcel of being a Christian that the man sitting along from you at church services is a good, moral, trustworthy individual. And Christ Himself taught that if you think otherwise, then the fault is with you, not the other person. Unfortunately, this has opened up huge opportunities for predatory child abusers.

Churches, however, are not alone in being used in this sinister way. Schools, hospitals, youth organisations; in fact, anywhere you find children is a target for these perverts. Even that great American institution, the summer camp, has not been immune.[42] Not that you would know any of this if you relied on national and international media for your news. Boz Tchividjian's crusade has not been widely broadcast, nor has the fact that child abusers have cropped up in practically every organisation.

Both in the USA and in the UK, stories of child sexual abuse are usually reported as individual, stand-alone crimes. Nobody wants to make any links or join any dots to investigate possible cover-ups or even if the abuse was the organised work of more than one person. That is, of course, unless the abuse happens to have been carried out by a Catholic priest, then the headline screams about the Catholic Church being hit with 'yet another scandal'. The implication is always there that it is the Catholic Church itself that is responsible for the abuse.

In the USA, the Jehovah's Witnesses have come under investigation as well for covering up child abuse in their congregations.[43] Jehovah's Witnesses, however, have never really been accepted as a proper religion in America; they are viewed as being more of a cult.[44] As such, it seems perfectly reasonable to expect them to be guilty of perpetrating and covering up child abuse.

The Jehovah's Witnesses are viewed somewhat differently in the

UK, especially in Scotland. I, personally, have known Jehovah's Witnesses that were members of the Freemasons and the Orange Order. Quite how they managed the latter is a bit of a mystery, since the Orange Order claims to only accept Trinitarians. It showed, however, that not only are the Jehovah's Witnesses seen as a mainstream religion in Scotland, but that they are accepted as Protestants. This, perhaps, explains why the media over here have failed to mention the child abuse scandal affecting the Jehovah's Witnesses in America. They want everyone to keep believing that it is a 'Catholic thing'.

Of course, in Scotland, this automatically means that football is involved; and not just Rangers supporters. In 2010 the Scottish Football Association's Head of Referee Development, Hugh Dallas, was sacked for sending an e-mail with a joke urging parents and children to be cautious because the Pope was visiting Scotland.[45] The meaning behind this was obvious and, since it had been sent via a company e-mail account, the SFA had no option but to get rid of Dallas.

There were plenty of people ready to stick up for Dallas, not just in Scotland but throughout the UK. The revolting Richard Dawkins was quickly on the case, urging his disciples to flood the Scottish Catholic Media Office with vile jokes about the Catholic Church and child abuse.[46] We have already seen how Dawkins encourages anti-Catholic bigotry under the guise of secularism; this was just one more example of his hatred.

Orangemen, as you would expect, have gleefully accepted the narrative of child abuse being the preserve of Catholics and the Catholic Church; they somehow felt that their centuries of hatred had finally been vindicated.[47] It has become quite common to hear Rangers supporters singing, 'Jimmy Savile, he's one of your own' and other clubs' supporters have started to use this filthy song when their team is playing Celtic. It is inspired by the fact that Savile was a Catholic, while Celtic is viewed as a 'Catholic' club. The media never report on this little ditty being sung, showing that they tacitly condone it. This, however, is not the only reference to child abuse when it comes to Celtic.

Everybody already knows the story of James Torbett, a successful businessman, starting up Celtic Boys' Club and using his position to abuse teenage players.[48] For such a high-profile offender, whom the

Scottish media like to remind us of periodically, details about Torbett are remarkably thin on the ground. We know he ran a trophy-making business and that he founded and ran Celtic Boys' Club; beyond that there is nothing. His time at Celtic Boys' Club has been investigated with a forensic thoroughness, but nobody has been interested in what went on before. It makes one wonder why.

Rumours have been doing the rounds for years that Torbett worked at Rangers before founding Celtic Boys' Club; nobody, however, has bothered to investigate this claim. The story goes that he was thrown out when it was discovered what sort of person he was, but was given a positive reference when contacted by Celtic. Whether this is true or not is impossible to determine because Torbett's earlier days are shrouded in mystery; a bit like those of Thomas Hamilton. It seems that we are supposed to believe that being involved with Celtic somehow led to Torbett becoming a child abuser; as if that is what happens when you get mixed up with Catholics!

It is certainly shocking when you consider that Torbett was allowed back to work with Celtic Boys' Club after Jock Stein supposedly threw him out. The board members that let him back, though, are the same folk that ran Celtic into the ground, leading to the club almost disappearing in 1994. Rather hypocritically, the standard view is that Celtic, as a club, is tainted by Torbett's crimes, rather than the individuals involved. When it comes to the financial irregularities at Rangers, however, it is the other way around; it is the *individuals* to blame.

As for the slurs aimed at Jock Stein, who, apparently, gave Torbett a beating and threw him out the door; as I have already mentioned, this was the standard way of dealing with such people in those days. Complaints to the police were extremely rare, even after the Moors Murders; the usual way of dealing with this type of individual was to beat hell out of the 'dirty bastard' and send him on his way. And yet, Stein is to be vilified for doing what everybody else did.

As I write this, a new scandal is beginning to emerge in British football. There are allegations that there was a paedophile ring operating in English football clubs for many years; a fact that was covered up by the clubs concerned.[49] There are even claims that such abuse is still going on.[50] Investigations are only just beginning but the NSPCC has already had many calls to its dedicated hotline and expects to receive a lot more.[51]

So, how has Scotland reacted to this news? Is there to be an investigation into youth football here, or a dedicated hotline for victims? The reaction of some sections of the population can be gauged from this tweet by Jack McConnell, once Scotland's Labour First Minister, and now sitting in the House of Lords:

> Very strange that none of the reports on football abuse today seem to mention the Celtic Boys Club scandal. 20 years ago.[52]

In fact, as might be expected, TV reports *did* mention Celtic Boys Club. When this was pointed out to McConnell, he replied:

> I know, thanks. But not in endless coverage all day on UK news. Story presented as 'new' when the trial raised this 20 yrs ago.[53]

As usual, the bigots in Scotland are not interested in justice or protecting children; all they are concerned about is that fingers are firmly pointed in Celtic's, and the Catholic Church's, direction. As more names emerge in this new footballing scandal, expect the internet to crash as frantic searches are made to discover what schools the abusers went to.

As for the chants of Jimmy Savile being 'one of your own', which the Scottish media tacitly condone, they are nothing more than a deflection. Pictures of Savile with Catholic figures and people connected with Celtic are eagerly sought out by bigots to 'prove' that Catholicism is the common denominator when it comes to child abuse.[54] Much more worrying, however, should be the easily-proven links Savile had with top people in UK society, including prime ministers, businessmen and the Royal Family. They are the ones that facilitated, and, perhaps, were even involved in, the abuse perpetrated by Savile. Again, though, nobody seems willing, or able, to investigate this.

Despite the vast cover-up of Savile's crimes, the media still appear to insist that he acted alone, which is unlikely. The concealment of crimes on the scale of Savile's would take some organising and it is impossible that he could have done it on his own. In fact, the concealment of Cyril Smith's crimes by Special Branch and MI5 show that the cover-up *was* organised.[55]

How many others had their crimes hidden by this organised cover-up? Allegations have been made against Leon Brittan, Edward Heath, Nicholas Fairbairn and others; if true, then it means that this organised cover-up was wide-ranging. And yet, even suggesting that there was a paedophile ring at Westminster can have one branded a lunatic conspiracy theorist.[56] Actually, it would appear that the paedophile ring stretches far beyond the Elm Row Guest House and Dolphin Square. The stories involving the Kincora Boys' Home and Haut de la Garenne suggest some kind of nationwide organisation of child abusers.

Such a scenario was being investigated by social workers in the early 1990s when, rather conveniently, the Orkney Abuse Case cast serious doubt on their work and that of medical professionals. I still believe that this was a deliberate operation, planned to achieve the results that it did and to stop investigations into organised child abuse in the UK. I used this scenario in my novel, *Catalyst*.

Another scenario I used in this novel was that of a child-abusing organisation influencing politics in the background by the use of blackmail. It is quite possible that this happened in the past and is still happening. As late as 2013, the BBC was still being accused of left-wing bias, as it had been for decades.[57] Since then, the BBC has become noticeably more right-wing.[58] Is it a coincidence that this change came about during the Yewtree investigations?

Meanwhile, the deflection continues. A new scapegoat to blame for all child abuse has emerged in England: Muslims.[59] It seems that child abuse is no longer just a Catholic thing; it is a Muslim thing as well. Scotland has not quite caught up with this new aspect of scapegoating, but it will not be long in coming. There is no denying that there were Muslims and Catholic priests involved in abusing children and young teenagers; they are not, however, responsible for all abuse, much though the bigoted media would have us believe. There is, moreover, a different common denominator in many abuse cases.

Child abuse cases, not just those involving Catholic priests, appear to be mostly prevalent in the USA, Australia and the UK; at least as far as the reportage in our media is concerned. Let us also bring Ireland into the equation and even those Pakistanis that many English people want to blame for the abuse of children. What do all these places have in common? They have all had the misfortune to have been colonised by England!

15
Irish Slaves:
A Political Conundrum

I spent the three years between 1979 and 1982 on the dole. I got lots of reading done in that time and, since I was not much of a drinker, I had enough for the necessities of life: Irn Bru and fags. After giving 'keep' money to my da, there was even enough for buying records now and again. This was at a time when it was only £2.50 for an LP and fags had recently gone up to 63p for twenty. You could live not too badly on the dole, without any need to be overly frugal.

It was in 1980 that I started to get hassled. I would go down to Rutherglen with everybody else, hand over my UB40, sign my name and then get told that I had to go upstairs to speak with somebody at the DHSS. The others could go off home, while I had to sit and be harangued by some civil servant for not having a job.

After this happening a few times, I pointed out to the DHSS guy that there were 4 million people unemployed in Britain; what made me any different? His reply was that not all those 4 million were sitting with five Highers, as I was. He then proceeded to show me six, tall filing cabinets, which he said held the details of just about all the area's unemployed. Next to them was a small cabinet, about half the size of the others. The folk in the large cabinets, he explained, were not expected to find jobs any time soon; whereas those in the small one had no excuse for being out of work. I, unfortunately, was one of the ones in the small cabinet.

Basically, though, he was right. As it turned out, I went to college, back to university and then into teaching. The others that I used to sign on with either stayed on the dole for decades or were forced into some crappy job. I had been unemployed, just as they were, but my experience could hardly be compared to theirs.

The same thing can be said about the experience of indentured servants compared to that of African slaves between the 17th and

18th Centuries. Essentially an indentured servant was a slave in all but name. This is a point, however, which many historians dispute.

Many indentured servants volunteered for the positions; it was the only way they could afford to get to America. You would sign yourself over, for a set period, to an employer, who would then pay for your passage to America. Once there, however, you found that you belonged to that employer for maybe ten years or more. Not only did you have to work for him but he controlled every aspect of your life. For example, one servant in Virginia was 'publicly scourged for four days with his ears nailed to the post. He had been flirting with a servant girl.'[1]

An indentured servant could not move to another employer unless, of course, his current employer sold him. You received no pay, since you were working to pay off the debt incurred when your employer paid your traveling expenses. You would need your employer's permission to see someone of the opposite sex or to marry. What else could you call such a person but a slave?

As some historians are quick to point out, there were fundamental differences between slavery and indentured servitude. Whether indentured labourers were volunteers or criminals, sentenced to such a fate by English courts, their servitude was only for a set period. Most importantly, they were treated in law as white people, as opposed to negro slaves.[2] It is interesting to see, however, how black people reacted to indentured servitude in the Caribbean when slavery was abolished.

With the modern vogue for revisionist history, it was inevitable that slavery would come under the spotlight. One historian, Pieter C. Emmer, points out that Caribbean plantations were labour-intensive, meaning that the abolition of slavery caused no end of economic problems for the planters.[3] According to his thesis, it was the end of slavery that caused the decline of the Caribbean colonies. As is usual with right-wing, revisionist historians, Emmer is, apparently, quite selective in his use of sources and figures, which makes his conclusions rather suspect, as another historian, Michael J Craton, points out.[4]

There is, however, an important element within Emmer's paper; albeit one he does not highlight, since it is irrelevant to his purely economic discourse. When slaves were given their freedom, they refused point-blank to sign up as indentured labourers. They were prepared to work for wages when it suited them or grow their own crops on readily-available land, rather than work full-time and live on the plantations. This meant that they were actually worse-off financially than they would have been as indentured labourers.[5] This baffled observers at the time; and, indeed, is baffling for historians since we have no way of discerning how the ex-slaves thought or felt.

It is possible, however, to postulate the reason why the ex-slaves did not sign up as indentured labourers. As already stated, they were quite prepared to work in the fields as they had always done, but only when it suited them. Many of them, though, still wanted to live in the slave quarters on the plantations, even when they no longer worked there.[6] Since the ex-slaves obviously had no problem with labouring on the plantations, and seemed quite content with the living arrangements on the plantations, why, then, did they not become indentured labourers? The only possible conclusion is that they prized their freedom and saw indentured labour as just slavery under a different name.

It is unlikely that the Caribbean ex-slaves were consulting dictionaries and sitting around having philosophical arguments about semantics, as modern historians are doing. Their apprehension about signing up as indentured labourers was based on experience; and experience had obviously taught them that indentured labour was just the same as slavery.

This, of course, gives the lie to historians' arguments that indentured servitude and slavery were fundamentally and perceptively different. The anecdotal evidence given by one group of historians about an 'Irishman who was likely an overseer on a larger plantation', and who maltreated a negro slave,[7] is a rather disingenuous presentation and proves nothing. Black overseers, slaves themselves, were not uncommon and might abuse the plantation workers just as much as any white man.[8]

On the other hand, there is the question of why it was felt necessary to call white slaves 'indentured servants' at all. This is not just a phrase invented by historians; it was used at the time. The answer as to why this term was employed is simple: racism; black people were slaves but white people were indentured servants. It might seem ridiculous but such distinctions have always mattered when deciding one's position in society. Middle-class, white-collar workers always earned a 'salary' and would take it as a personal affront if you used the word 'wages' to describe their remuneration. Even nowadays, to suggest in an office or at a course for teachers that it is time for a 'tea break' rather than a 'coffee break' will elicit some unfavourable reactions.

Indentured servants themselves, then, would use the term to describe their circumstances and would have been none too happy to be classed as slaves. In their minds, they were completely different from African slaves, whom they would view as being no better than animals. The fact that their masters, throughout North America and the Caribbean, used the phrase as well showed that they were just as sensitive to these nuances of language.

Such distinctions were even evident in the 1980s among the unemployed. One of the worst things you could be called back then was 'one of the long-term unemployed'. This implied that you were a 'no-hoper'; somebody that was destined to spend his life on the dole unless thing in the country improved. Effectively, it meant that you had no control whatsoever over your life and were subject to the vagaries of the economy. Even if it were obvious that you *were* one of the long-term unemployed, it was hardly something that you wanted to be reminded of. Most people preferred to say that they were out of work 'just now'.

There was, however, one group of people in the 17th Century for whom semantic games would mean nothing whatsoever.

When Cromwell emerged triumphant in Ireland, he did something that, even in those days, was rather old-fashioned. It was a long-accepted principle in war that 'to the victor belong the spoils' and part of those spoils had been the vanquished people themselves, to be used or sold as slaves. Cromwell's men rounded up several thousands of Irish Catholics and sold them to plantation owners in the Caribbean, to work in perpetuity for their masters.[9] Many of these slaves were the destitute widows and orphaned children of men killed during the war in Ireland.[10]

The circumstances of these poor wretches were markedly different from the experience of indentured servants in the Caribbean, both before and after. Not that their working or living conditions were any better or worse; it was the fact that they were slaves for life that made them different. This fact cannot be stressed enough. As we have already noted, most indentured servants might have been slaves in all but name; but only for a set period. Unfortunately, this difference has become blurred and has become a source of vitriolic argument.

For decades now, there have been calls from black Americans for some kind of reparation to be made for what happened to their ancestors due to slavery and the slave trade. There is a precedent for this; European companies had been forced to compensate families for the use of Jewish slave labour under the Nazis.[11] It is a contentious issue and one that has had white racist groups foaming at the mouth.

The days when American rednecks could dress up in bedsheets and hang or burn to death 'uppity niggers' are long gone; nowadays they have to employ arguments, even ridiculous ones. The fate of those perhaps 10 or 12 thousand Irish people in the 17th Century is conflated with the experience of all indentured servants right up until the 19th Century. In this way, racist whites in the USA try to counter the arguments of African Americans that their ancestors' suffering was in any way unique. White people were slaves too, is the war cry.

Although white indentured servants *were*, effectively, slaves, their experience was nothing like that of African Americans. Most indentured servants were either volunteers or exiled prisoners, condemned to servitude for a set time. Their life of slavery would come to an end and then they were free to work for wages, start a business or get themselves a plot of land. The black slave, meanwhile, was in an entirely different situation; he was a slave for life, as were his children and his children's children.

Like most right-wing groups revising history, these racists avoid using evidence that is too specific. Instead, great, sweeping statements are employed, which imply that white people were slaves for nearly three hundred years. A simple word is all that is needed in this respect; for example, saying '*from* the early 17th century' instead of '*in* the early 17th century'.[12] In this way, it is made to look as if those Irish that were forced into slavery by Cromwell were just the beginning of a huge flood of white slaves being transported to the Americas.

Of course, the simple answer to this nonsense is to ask another question; with such a ready supply of slaves to hand, why the hell would anybody bother going to Africa? In fact, most of these supposed histories claim that African slaves were treated better than white indentured servants because they were more expensive to obtain.[13] Again, this begs the question as to why anybody would bother buying African slaves.

A sure sign that a historical theory or narrative is wrong is when the historian resorts to employing complete lies, as Michael Hoffman does. In 1846 David Wilmot introduced his famous Proviso to the US House of Representatives, looking to ban slavery in the new territories won during the Mexican-American War. He said, 'neither slavery nor involuntary servitude shall ever exist' in these territories.[14] Wilmot's idea was that free, white men should not face competition from slave labour.[15] Hoffman twists Wilmot's intentions to suit his own agenda.

Hoffman quotes further from Wilmot, showing that the Congressman wanted the new lands to belong to 'the sons of toil, my own race and color'.[16] He also widens the scope of Wilmot's vision to the whole American West and claims, erroneously, that Wilmot specifically referred to *black* slaves.[17] To Hoffman, this allowed for *white* slavery and, indeed, he implies that 'the sons of toil' meant just that; white slaves. In fact, Wilmot was no doubt referring to the Protestant Work Ethic and the mythical building of the United States by the toil of free, white Americans. Hoffman is being completely disingenuous in this respect.

Also disingenuous, and almost laughable, is the way Hoffman, a right-wing Holocaust denier,[18] uses a left-wing, almost Marxist, view of history to further his agenda. He talks of British workers in the 19th Century as 'slaves', especially child workers. He contrasts the could-not-care-less attitude of the British Parliament to these workers with their abolition of slavery in the British Empire in 1833.[19]

This, of course, is a specious argument. A Victorian ragamuffin running away from his employer, whether that be a factory owner or a chimney sweep, would not have the authorities chasing after him. A runaway slave in the USA, on the other hand, would have the full weight of the law against him and would be a fugitive for the rest of his life. As for adult employees in Britain, they were free to walk out of the mine or factory whenever they chose. They might find it difficult to get another job but, and it is a big but, they would not be dragged back to their employer in chains to be tied to a post and whipped. Even the most rabid Marxist would hardly compare the lot of a Nineteenth-Century British workman to that of an African-American slave.

Some proponents of white slavery are even more desperate in their arguments, going all the way back to Roman times and the Dark Ages to show that white people were slaves as well.[20] Rather more sinister are the stories of white people being sold as slaves by Muslims, especially in the way that one author puts it: 'The filthy Muslims captured hundreds of thousands of our White women over the years, raping them and selling them as prostitutes.'[21] A picture accompanies this rather telling outburst, showing what must be a shocking sight for your average racist: black hands all over naked, white, female flesh.

As you would expect, all this rubbish does not go unchallenged. The Southern Poverty Law Center is an organisation that promotes equality and fights against bigotry and racism.[22] It runs a campaign, called *Hatewatch*, which monitors hate groups, especially on the extreme right, and reports their activities to the public and to law-enforcement agencies.[23] Of course, all the stuff about white slaves, peddled by racist extremists in America, was pretty quickly picked up.[24] Unfortunately, that is where problems start to arise.

To refute the arguments of Hoffman and the rest, the Southern Property Law Center approached an Irish historian, Liam Hogan. Hogan has published online a point-by-point negation of everything one finds in 'white slavery' literature.[25] He also has another site where he debunks the images used in such literature, most, if not all, of which comes from sources completely detached from what the 'white slavery' advocates argue.[26]

The problem is that, in debunking all this right-wing claptrap, Hogan also dismisses any claim that those Irish people shipped to the Caribbean by Cromwell were just as much slaves as any black person forcibly uprooted from Africa. He touches on this himself in one article, coming close to admitting that those individuals present a different case from all the other indentured servants.[27] It seems, however, that to admit even this exception is to be viewed as playing into the hands of right-wing racists.

Another issue to consider is what Hogan's agenda might be. Yes, his fight against right-wing, extremist appropriation of history is to be applauded but there is another aspect to his debunking of 'myths'. As he states himself, the narrative of Irish slavery 'whitewashes history' not only in the 'service' of 'white supremacist causes' but also in the 'service of Irish nationalist' causes as well.[28] One cannot help but wonder which 'causes' Hogan finds more objectionable.

A possible clue to Hogan's agenda is given in an article he wrote about Irish Nationalist hero John Mitchel.[29] In it he points out that Mitchel was a racist exponent of slavery and a supporter of the Confederacy during the American Civil War. Fair enough, you might say since it is true. But Mitchel was not the only such individual in the 19th Century and it is unfair to judge him by modern standards. Hogan argues that there were plenty of people that opposed slavery at the time, including most Irish Nationalists, so, even by contemporary standards, Mitchel can be condemned. This, however, is a disingenuous argument.

There are plenty of websites presenting evidence that Abraham Lincoln himself was a racist. It is hardly fair, though, to hold that against him. The 19th Century was full of pseudo-scientific explanations for almost everything and racism and slavery were no exceptions.[30] Would anyone condemn Lincoln just because they found evidence that he had contemporaries that were not racist? Even in modern times there are folk that are racist without even thinking about it, such as bigoted, old boor Prince Philip. And, by God, don't we get some excuses for his behaviour!

> You cannot expect the older generation to be aligned with today's right-on pc attitude to all things, and thank the lord for that.[31]

> My God, he's 94 he comes from a different age. An age when the 'N' word was commonly used for example. Its very challenging for the elderly to adapt to the modern PC culture, my 86 year old (sic) mother in law still uses the 'pa*i' word.[32]

> The blokes (sic) ninety four (sic) years old for goodness sake and from a totally different era. Instead of taking offence, just ignore him. I do wish the intolerant Guardian Thought Police would give it a rest sometimes.[33]

Would Liam Hogan condemn Prince Philip for his bigotry, or would he be one of the ones making excuses? Certainly, if he is anything like some other Irish historians, he would be firmly in the camp that supports anything English, including the Royal Family. This has been a trend for quite a while now; painting the English as not so bad after all, while condemning anything that smacks of Irish nationalism. If he is one of this group, and his article about Mitchel would suggest that he is, it casts his dismissal of Irish slavery as a myth in an entirely different light.

No need for any such guesswork when it comes to the execrable Ruth Dudley Edwards. At a Confederate flag rally in Mississippi in August 2015, somebody told a reporter, 'Even the Irish, we were slaves. At some point, you just have to get over it.'[34] Compare this with what Edwards said in the Belfast Telegraph, 'Yes, so Ireland was occupied - get over it'.[35] Obviously, Edwards has the same, right-wing viewpoint as those racists in America, which reveals the dichotomy at the heart of the debate about Irish slaves.

In America, the debunking of the stories about Irish slaves has a left-wing/liberal agenda; it is all about the admission that African Americans are right to feel aggrieved about what happened to their ancestors not all that long ago. In the UK and Ireland, however, the opposite is the case. Here the dismissal of such stories is part of a right-wing agenda against Irish nationalism, which, in turn, is inspired by anti-Catholicism. No wonder the whole issue gets confusing!

A huge part of the confusion is the co-opting of Irish grievances against the English by American bigots, who, traditionally, hate Catholics just as much as they hate blacks. This is recognised by some of them and they are at pains to point out that there were *Protestant* slaves as well.[36] They are not, however, too sure of their ground in this respect, which is why they feel the need to include British working-class labourers as white slaves.

A more interesting conundrum is why there are those of Irish descent in America going along with this right-wing agenda. The answer is a simple one; it is in order to be accepted. In fact, it is more than that; it is to deflect discrimination away from themselves. This type of behaviour can be observed in any school where a bullied child will join in, or even instigate, the bullying of another to direct the focus away from himself. It is an easily- observable phenomenon between groups of people as well. Historian Noel Ignatiev's book, *How the Irish Became White*, pursues this idea and is an intensive study of how Irish-Americans assimilated by participating in discrimination against, and even persecution of, blacks.[37]

The difference between left-wing, Catholic Irish people and Irish Americans was brought into sharp focus when Bernadette Devlin visited the USA in 1969. She was shocked at the racist attitudes she encountered and could not understand how the Irish Americans did not recognise the similarities between how blacks were treated in the US and the way Catholics were treated in Northern Ireland.[38]

It is clear from this that many in the Irish Nationalist movement had to compromise their beliefs to raise funds in America. When it comes to the arguments about white slavery, it seems that this compromise is still in place as I have been unable to find any condemnation of this right-wing idea by any Irish Nationalist.

And so, we have the insane situation where Irish Nationalist grievance against English imperialism, exemplified in those miserable wretches that were sent to be slaves in the Caribbean, is inadvertently aiding racist, right-wing agendas in America. Equally, left-wing and liberal arguments in America are helping to justify anti-Irish and anti-Catholic agendas in Britain and Ireland; something that would probably horrify them.

According to some commentators, the Irish sent out to the Caribbean to be slaves were freed by Charles II after the Restoration.[39] If true, this would appear to be a massive game-changer and prove that Liam Hogan is completely correct in his assessment. None of these commentators, however, gives any source to explain where they got their information and I have been unable to find any such source myself. There is no real evidence, then, that the Irish slaves were ever set free, meaning that the argument that they were slaves for life still stands.

But, then, even if anyone out there finds such a source, and proves that those Irish slaves were set free in 1680, it really makes no difference to the argument. An African-American slave born on a Virginian plantation in the 1840s was going to be freed before he reached the age of thirty, but he would hardly be aware of that. Before the Civil War, his lot was exactly the same as that of his forefathers. The same goes for those Irish slaves in the Caribbean; even if they were freed in 1680, they did not know about it beforehand. Their experience was completely different from that of indentured servants and more akin to the slaves transported from Africa.

Not that any of this makes the slightest difference to the bigots on either side of the Atlantic. The American bigots will continue to hate blacks, while our homegrown versions will continue to hate Catholics. And the likes of Ruth Dudley Edwards will continue to pour scorn on any attempt to liken the experience of Catholics in Northern Ireland with that of African Americans.

16
Most Oppressed People Ever: The Revisionist Historians

Back in the mid-1980s I was at Stirling University, which, as you might know, is a campus university. There were various facilities available, including a campus radio station; all staffed by student volunteers. One of these facilities was a sort of counselling service, where volunteers would work in shifts to give anyone with problems somebody to talk to. There was training available so that the volunteer counsellors could point anyone that turned up towards any professional help they might need.

A girl I knew decided that she was going to volunteer, claiming that she already knew how to deal with someone that was down or depressed. 'I would just explain to them that there are a lot of people worse off than them in the World. There are people out there starving to death, being tortured, being blown to pieces in wars and battling against natural disasters.'

She could not understand why the rest of us were laughing and we had to explain that, rather than make anyone feel better, she would cause a plague of suicides on campus. She eventually realised her error and decided that being a volunteer counsellor was maybe not for her after all.

Liam Kennedy, Professor of Economic History at Queen's University in Belfast, tried the exact same technique as that girl was advocating in his 2016 book, *Unhappy the Land*. In what appears to be a political polemic, rather than a work of history, Kennedy rails against the idea that the Irish are the *Most Oppressed People Ever*, a phrase that he uses as a subtitle for his book. His method for undermining the sense of victimhood among the Irish is to point out that there are a lot of victims in the World. The Irish are nothing special in this respect.[1]

As well as being rather insulting in the same way as that girl at Stirling's counselling sessions would have been, Kennedy's thesis is reminiscent of the 'white slavery' argument. The right-wing bigots of America want to undermine the genuine grievances of African Americans by arguing that their experiences were only a small part of a greater whole. Kennedy uses the exact same methodology to undermine genuine Irish grievances against England. As the old saying goes, if you fly with the crows, you get shot with the crows; Kennedy proves himself to be as much of a right-wing bigot as any American redneck.

That subtitle to Kennedy's book, *Most Oppressed People Ever*, is a well-known phrase among right-wingers in Ireland and Britain. It is often abbreviated to the acronym MOPE and is meant as a slur against Irish Nationalists. The idea is that Irish Nationalists cannot see outside their own little bubble and believe that they are the only people ever to have been oppressed. In fact, it is difficult to find a statement of this sort, or even an allusion to it, by any Irish Nationalist. It seems to have been invented by revisionists and Loyalists, who have pretended since that it is the belief of Irish Nationalists. This makes their arguments against this belief almost a tautology.

Strangely, while broadcasting this MOPE nonsense, the same revisionists condemn Irish Nationalists for viewing their fight as the same as people's in other countries. For example, while Nelson Mandela was languishing in prison and the British Government was helping to support the South African Apartheid regime, Sinn Fein and the IRA made links with the ANC and Umkhonto we Sizwe.[2] Apparently, the IRA trained MK members and even took part in the bombing of an oil refinery in South Africa.[3]

When Mandela died, everyone was falling over themselves to praise the man; even those that had previously branded him nothing more than a terrorist. And, yet, the vile Ruth Dudley Edwards accused Sinn Fein of 'using the late African leader for propaganda purposes'.[4] Meanwhile, she deemed all the mealy-mouthed world leaders, especially the British, who had stood by and done nothing against Apartheid but were now mourning Mandela, as not worthy of comment.

It is a constant theme of Edwards to condemn any attempt to liken the lot of the Irish to any other subjugated peoples. For example, when Gerry Adams made his, rather ill-thought-out, tweet after watching the movie *Django Unchained*,[5] Edwards was straight on the attack. She quoted Alex Kane, a right-wing columnist for the *Irish News*:

> Nationalists in Northern Ireland were never the property of unionists. They were never kept on plantations. They were never denied an education. They were never used as slave labour. There was never a law which permitted them to be chained, hobbled and shot on sight. There was never an 'underground' which assisted nationalists to escape from the 'owners' and take them to a place of safety.[6]

Looking at things that way, you might say that Adams's critics have a point; although Kane's argument is as over-the-top as Adams's own. Edwards, however, decides to take things further:

> Gerry Adams isn't prejudiced about skin colour, yet his love of victimhood is such that he can't bear to admit that, for instance, African Americans or black South Africans have had a worse time than the Irish.[7]

The implication there is that, even after slavery was abolished in America, Irish Catholics in Northern Ireland never had it as tough as African Americans. After all, Catholic civil-rights marches were not attacked by rednecks as the police stood by and watched, or even joined in, were they? Peaceful civil-rights demonstrators were never shot at by troops. Catholics were not discriminated against when it came to jobs and housing, were they? Nor was there vote-rigging to make sure that Catholic voices did not count. And ordinary Catholics were never murdered just because they happened to be Catholics. Oh, wait…

In fact, the experience of Catholics in Northern Ireland was very much like that of African Americans, especially in the 1960s. Why the hell does Edwards think that Bernadette Devlin went to America? No doubt Edwards and her clique would have us believe that Devlin was in the USA to raise funds for the IRA. In reality, she went there to learn how to fight for civil rights from black Americans and succeeded in linking the Catholic Irish struggle with theirs.[8] Irish revisionist historians, like the Ulster Unionists they fawn over, like to ignore these facts.

Not only was ridicule and scorn poured on Adams for his tweet but everyone was quick to condemn his use of the word 'nigger', even though he explained why he used it. Perhaps these people forget some of the old names used for Irish Catholics: *green niggers*, *potato niggers*, *shamrock niggers*, *spudniggers*, *white niggers*.[9] In fact, the phrase *white nigger* was still being used to refer to Irish Catholics in the 1970s, especially in Northern Ireland.[10] The term *bogwogs* was much used in the 1970s and can still be found on Rangers supporters'[11] forums. Maybe the ones that criticised Adams could explain the reasoning behind these epithets.

Incidentally, one of the ones condemning Adams for using the 'N-word', albeit ironically, was Bernice Harrison,[12] who just happens to be a columnist for the *Irish Times*.[13] One of her articles concerned her disgust for black pudding, which she argued should be named more appropriately, with the word 'blood' used. On Twitter, she saw fit to re-tweet a comment, which said, 'Call a spade a spade, it's blood pudding says @BerniceHarrison'.[14] In case anyone is unaware, this expression about plain speaking does not refer to a gardening implement. Hypocrisy? I shall leave you to decide.

It seemed that Irish Nationalists could not win. If they compared the experience of Irish Catholics to that of anyone else, they were castigated and ridiculed. Meanwhile, they were accused of wallowing in victimhood and claiming that they were the 'Most Oppressed People Ever'. There had to be a reason for all this vilification; it was obvious that some kind of agenda was behind it.

An historian by the name of Philip Ferguson offers an answer.[15] Revisionist history seems to have begun in the 1930s as a reaction to the accepted narrative of Irish history. It was a rather elitist academic movement, started among historians in Dublin. They viewed traditional Irish history as too agenda-ridden, which was true, but instead of a more rigorous examination of the facts, they simply replaced one agenda with another.

Dublin had always been an English city and it appeared that professional elites there saw it that way even after independence. The English-speaking professional classes had more of an affinity with London than they had with all those peasants and Gaelic-speakers 'beyond the Pale'. This, of course, influenced their attitudes toward

Ireland and the Irish.

Revisionist history would have remained the preserve of an elite clique if it had not been for what happened in Northern Ireland in the late 1960s. The war by the Provisional IRA against the British forces threw the Dublin Establishment into a state of utter confusion. How could they celebrate the heroes of 1916 while condemning the IRA in Northern Ireland as 'terrorists'? Surely it was the same fight?

Rather than face up to the situation, the Dublin Establishment decided to just change its view of history. Commemoration of the Easter Rising were quietly dropped, while the media were not allowed to interview anyone from Sinn Fein or to appear to side with the Nationalists in Northern Ireland. Effectively, this meant that much of Irish history was out of bounds as well, since the PIRA claimed to be the modern part of the long struggle. Newspaper articles or TV programmes putting a positive slant on Connolly, Pearse or Collins could fall foul of anti-IRA legislation. Not wanting to tempt fate, the media obligingly fell into line.

This meant that the revisionists were the only historical voices heard and, even though most ordinary Irish people would cling to their traditional history, this led to revisionist Irish history being viewed as the *real* history. This, of course, encouraged those that considered themselves more intelligent than the uneducated masses to accept that revisionist Irish history was, in fact, the truth.

In the 1960s a more scientific approach was brought to bear on History as an academic discipline, meaning that inconsistent facts should not be ignored but analysed and explained. It was felt, rightly, that many traditional versions of history were not telling the whole truth. Revisionist historians claim to be using these modern ways of working but they most manifestly are not. Rather than reanalysing history, all they were concerned about was destroying it. Just like traditional history, they were working to an agenda, which blinded them to many facts.

Traditional histories have evolved over long periods and, even though they might be wrong in some respects, in others they contain the truth. Revisionist histories, by contrast, start with an agenda and everything is geared towards confirming that agenda, meaning that many facts are completely ignored, leading to some rather strange conclusions.

For example, Ruth Dudley Edwards claims that 'It was the IRA that wrecked the civil rights movement (in Northern Ireland) by resorting to arms.'[16] This flies in the face of all the known facts and is quite a breathtakingly unhistorical statement. It would be interesting to see by what circuitous route Edwards arrived at this conclusion. This statement certainly shows one thing: agenda-driven History is not, in fact, History at all.

If the agenda of Edwards and her ilk is driven by a snooty elitism, that of Liam Kennedy is easier to determine. In 1986, he published a book called *Two Ulsters: A Case for Repartition*. This addressed a great worry around a word; a word that still strikes fear into every Loyalist heart. That word is 'demographics'.

It is quite laughable to see Ulster Unionists bemoan the 'undemocratic' nature of power-sharing in Northern Ireland. They argue that majority rule should trump all other considerations.[17] But it was precisely to avoid majority rule that Northern Ireland was set up in the first place. Ulster was to stay a little enclave of empire and, just to make sure, three of the nine counties were jettisoned to ensure a Protestant majority there.

The big concern, however, was that things might not always stay that way. The stories of Catholics always having big families[18] served to frighten the Unionists in Northern Ireland; what if the Protestants became a minority? Short of instituting some sort of breeding programme, there was not a lot they could do about it. Liam Kennedy, however, had the answer.

Instead of worrying over Catholic majorities, he reasoned, why not just do what had been done before and cede two or three counties, which were mostly Catholic, to the Irish Republic? Quite what he had in mind for the Catholics left behind in this 'rump' Northern Ireland cannot be easily discovered. His book seems to be extremely difficult, if not impossible, to get hold of and any other papers or articles he might have published on the subject are not on the internet. Perhaps he envisioned a mass exodus of Catholics, all bound for the 'Promised Land'.

At any rate, it was clear what Kennedy's main concern was: maintaining the Protestant Ascendancy. Reportedly, Kennedy was unhappy when the UDA took his idea to its logical, and rather frightening conclusion.[19] This probably explains why his book is no longer in publication and why there is no evidence of Kennedy's idea from the man himself on the internet.

The UDA came up with their 'Doomsday Plan' in 1994, looking forward to a time when the British might withdraw from Northern Ireland.[20] Like Kennedy's blueprint, the idea was to abandon mainly Catholic counties and create an 'ethnic Protestant homeland'.[21] The most sinister aspect of the plan, however, involved those Catholics that would be stranded in this Protestant Paradise. The options of how to deal with these Catholics were: 'expulsion, internment, or nullification'.[22] 'Nullification' was a euphemism that any dictatorial regime would be proud of. Furthermore, those Catholics that were 'interned' were to be used as hostages; 'bargaining chips' in any negotiations.[23] There was a distinct smell of the gas chamber around the whole thing; and yet Ruth Dudley Edwards and her ilk still insist that the IRA were the Nazis!

It was hardly surprising that Liam Kennedy quickly dissociated himself from these ideas, even though they were his ideas in the first place. What was surprising was that Kennedy did not realise the full implications of his 1986 book. It was a bit like Hitler denying responsibility for the extermination of Europe's Jews since he did not explicitly mention this 'Final Solution' in *Mein Kampf*. Inadvertently, Kennedy had exposed one of the main driving forces behind revisionist Irish history: anti-Catholicism.

There is no questioning the massive influence the Catholic Church had in the Irish Republic from its very inception. Even after the Church's 'special position' was abolished in 1973,[24] it was still a dominant force. In 1980, Bob Geldof's band could still release a song, called *Banana Republic*, decrying the domination of Ireland by the Catholic Church.[25]

Dublin's intellectual and academic elite mostly agreed with Geldof's assertion. They compared the freedom enjoyed by other western democracies to that of Ireland, where one could not get a divorce or even buy a condom. Any argument, however, that the aims of the heroes of 1916 had been betrayed was to walk on dangerous ground; it would put them on the same side as Republican Nationalists in Northern Ireland. It was a much easier proposition to condemn the Republicans themselves; Sinn Fein and the IRA. After all, most, if not all, the rebels of 1916 were Catholics.

This, of course, ignored the fact that it was those supporting the Free State that won the Civil War, not the Republicans. The Dublin elite, however, had an ace up their sleeve: Éamon de Valera. There was no doubting de Valera's credentials; he was one of the leaders in the Easter Rising and narrowly escaped being executed and it was he that was responsible for making the final break with Britain.[26] He was the architect of modern Ireland, with all its faults and foibles; unfortunately, that meant that he was also responsible for the dominance of the Catholic Church.[27]

Of course, there is a distinct line between not wanting to be under the dominance of the Catholic Church and expressing sectarian hatred for that Church and its members. That line, however, can easily become blurred, making it too easy to end up on the wrong side of it. Such a thing, though, did not happen with the Dublin elite; the decision to cross that particular line was a deliberate one.

The new narrative put forward by revisionist historians was that the Irish Nationalist movement had been taken over by Catholic bigots, who were intent on founding a Catholic state. The failure of Protestant leaders, like Parnell, to achieve Home Rule led to more extreme elements taking up the reins; elements that wanted a complete break from the UK and the elimination of Protestantism from Ireland.

The greatest exponent of this idea was Canadian historian, and I use the term loosely, Peter Hart. Hart researched for his PhD at Trinity College, Dublin, submitting a thesis, and receiving his doctorate, in 1993.[28] His thesis, later expanded into a book, *The IRA and Its Enemies: Violence and Community in Cork, 1916-1923*, argued that the IRA, during the Irish War of Independence, was engaged in a sectarian campaign against Protestants. His 1998 book immediately became a bible for revisionist historians in Ireland and beyond.

Other historians were not quite so enthusiastic about Hart's book. It appeared that Hart, like other revisionists, was not averse to ignoring evidence that did not agree with his thesis. He made mistakes over details and even used anonymous sources.[29] This poses serious questions about History as an academic discipline in Dublin. Why was Hart granted a doctorate while using details that would not even be accepted in a First-Year university essay?

Some commentators claim that Hart's work needs to be looked at in total, instead of concentrating 'on a few micro episodes'.[30] This view, however, shows a complete misunderstanding of what History, as an academic discipline, is all about. An historian is supposed to amass evidence and then reach a conclusion; not the other way around. Anyone starting with an agenda will find historical research a rather frustrating occupation. The only way to make it work is to ignore some of the evidence staring you in the face. This, it seems, is what Hart did.

Niall Meehan, a lecturer in Journalism and Media Communications at Griffith College, Dublin, states that Hart corrected some of the errors in his PhD thesis when it came to writing his book. He did not bother, however, to change the conclusions that he had made from the mistakes. As Meehan says, 'It appeared that for Hart conclusions came first.'[31]

A history book, article, thesis or even an essay lives or dies by the details that back up the conclusions and Hart's details were markedly not up to the task. Apart from using anonymous sources, which belong more in the realm of sensationalist journalism, he also claimed to have interviewed people that were already dead or incapable of even speaking coherently. Meanwhile, when it came to his named sources, he only reported pieces of what they had said or written, leaving out the bits that contradicted his conclusions.[32] By any academic standards, Hart was not an historian; so how did he manage to be awarded a PhD?

By the time Hart's PhD thesis was submitted, the anti-Catholic, revisionist agenda was already well-established among Dublin's academic elite. Conor Cruise O'Brien, for example, went from being an admirer of the early Republicans to one of their fiercest critics; all in the space of a few years.[33] But O'Brien was not only an historian; he was a politician as well. He was, therefore, caught up in Dublin's efforts to distance itself from the conflict in Northern Ireland; indeed, it was he that introduced the censorship legislation, which banned Sinn Fein and the IRA from the media.[34] His perceptions of the past became coloured by his prejudices against the IRA in Northern Ireland; and he was most certainly prejudiced.

O'Brien's assessment of the IRA in Northern Ireland can be summarised by the following statement he made, 'During the hunger strikes when men died, you wouldn't have seen too many volumes of Das Kapital around, but you saw the missal, the rosary beads, the holy water, all the paraphernalia of Roman Catholicism.'[35] This, of course, put O'Brien firmly in the same camp as the Ulster Unionists and it is interesting to note that he got involved in politics in

Northern Ireland in 1996 on the Unionist side.[36] This came not long after the publication of his book, *On the Eve of the Millennium: The Future of Democracy Through an Age of Unreason*, in which he ranted against the Catholic Church and Pope John Paul II.[37] In essence, he comes across as nothing more than an anti-Catholic bigot.

This bigotry was projected back into history and used as a stick with which to beat Irish Nationalists. In the 1970s, Ruth Dudley Edwards was decrying Patrick Pearse as being 'deranged' and a possible paedophile.[38] She later did the same hatchet job on James Connolly and recently published another book, turning her bile onto all the Nationalist protagonists of the Easter Rising. Even the Protestant Wolfe Tone has not escaped the attentions of the revisionists, with one Marianne Elliott performing the demonising.[39] Obviously Tone's crime was that he supported a united Ireland, including Catholics. In fact, the only figures in Irish history to escape censure are the Home Rule advocates, like Parnell, who wanted Ireland to stay in the UK, albeit with a devolved parliament.

Since the beginning of the new millennium, it seems that historians, and others, are, at last, starting to question the revisionist agenda. The usual dismissal of such criticism as coming from blinkered Nationalists is not working anymore. The rude behaviour of Ruth Dudley Edwards, at the launch of the republication of her book about Patrick Pearse, shows how unused she is to such criticism. She spent most of her speech railing about a critical journalist and then refused to answer a reasonable question about her view of history.[40]

So accepted and ingrained have these revisionist histories become that, for decades, nobody questioned them at all in Ireland and certainly not in the media. The journalist that Edwards was complaining about, Jack Lane, quoted a piece by a fellow journalist, John Waters, which is worth looking at in full.

> Many of us were convinced by the need to pull the historical rug from under the Provos, and were therefore acquiescent in the rewriting of the past; and yet we were at the same time secretly traumatised by the loss of our inherited sense of where we had come from. The revisionist project succeeded because of the urgency of shutting down the Provos, and for no other reason…This idea will strike some people as morally dubious pragmatism…,

Although most of us have sullenly or silently acquiesced in the rewriting of the record, very many of us do not hold in our hearts the views we feel obliged to venture in the public realm.[41]

It looked as if Philip Ferguson was right when he said that 'being actively republican in the south became dangerous; in fact, it became the equivalent of being a communist or having communist friends during the McCarthy period in the United States.'[42] No wonder everyone in the media was championing the revisionists. Of course, O'Brien's censorship laws did not help either.

With power-sharing and a ceasefire in force in Northern Ireland and Sinn Fein making political inroads in the Irish Republic,[43] revisionist history is beginning to look irrelevant. In fact, it is worse than that for the revisionists; they are an embarrassment and are becoming nothing more than an anachronism.

To Ruth Dudley Edwards, flaunting her Unionist credentials now comes before being a professional historian. She wrote what amounts to a hagiography of the Orange Order, *The Faithful Tribe: An Intimate Portrait of the Loyal Institutions*, which paints the Order as it wants to be seen and argues that it has been unfairly maligned. Of course, she ignores any evidence that the Orange Order is a bigoted organisation or that it has been involved in violence.[44] She has also been to speak at an Orange rally in Northern Ireland.[45] Then there was her complete acceptance of one person's version of what happened at Hampden at the end of the Scottish Cup Final in 2016. She was shocked, she said, at 'the extent and depth of the demonisation of loyalists' that the incident showed.[46]

Her colours were nailed to the mast as long ago as the 1990s, when she changed her mind about Oliver Cromwell, about whom she still, apparently, carried some 'Irish Catholic baggage'.[47] The book that changed her mind was by an amateur historian from Drogheda, called Tom Reilly. Reilly, in true revisionist style, had reassessed Cromwell's image in *Cromwell – An Honourable Enemy: The Untold Story of the Cromwellian Invasion of Ireland*, blaming 'Restoration propaganda' and 'anti-British sentiment from the pens of Irish nationalists' for the man's tainted reputation.[48]

If Reilly's paper in *History Today* is anything to go by, it seemed that he, just like other revisionists, started off with set conclusions before looking at the evidence. He argues that 'not one person in either town (Drogheda and Wexford) left written details of the deaths of even one unarmed civilian'.[49] An easy answer to this is that there was nobody left to do so; or at least, nobody that could write. But, then, he could contend with the argument that in 'Drogheda's municipal records of 1649...I read about the activities of hundreds of Drogheda people who went about their daily business in the days immediately after Cromwell's visit'.[50] The obvious question there is: who wrote those records?

His trump card seems to be that it was not possible that a man 'with such lofty moral ethics could engage in the senseless slaughter of Ireland's innocents'.[51] Was Reilly talking about the same Cromwell that, as we saw earlier, reneged on promises to Scottish Presbyterians and did not even bother to consult his allies before committing regicide? In any reasonably disinterested assessment of Cromwell, he would come across as a man not to be trusted, rather than one of 'lofty moral ethics'. In any event, even Cromwell's own officers confirmed that civilians were indiscriminately slaughtered at Drogheda.[52]

Edwards, as one might expect, was ready to swallow this revisionism whole. She was even more convinced when her friend, David Trimble, leader of the Ulster Unionist Party and, at that time, First Minister at Stormont, compared the siege of Drogheda favourably with 'the sack of Magdeburg where tens of thousands of Protestants were murdered by a Catholic army; it put the two events in perspective.'[53]

It seemed that Edwards was prepared to accept not only Reilly's theory, but the idea that history can be argued in a tit-for-tat way; that Drogheda can be discounted because more people were killed at Magdeburg. This also appears to be an acceptance of the version of European history as a long struggle between Protestants and Catholics. We encountered this nonsense before when we saw how William of Orange is portrayed as the saviour of Protestantism from the evil clutches of the 'Catholic' James II/VII, while Louis XIV of France was apparently trying to re-establish Catholicism as the dominant force in Europe. Edwards had obviously been spending too much time with that 'Faithful tribe'. And this woman calls herself an historian! She obviously, rather conveniently, forgot that not only Catholics were killed at Drogheda and Wexford.

All that the revisionist historians and their supporters among Dublin's elite have managed to do is to put a veneer of historical respectability on anti-Catholic bigotry. They have also helped to bolster the resolve of many Unionists in Northern Ireland, at a time when cooler heads need to prevail to make the peace process and power-sharing work. Those involved in violent demonstrations over city-hall flags, arrogant demands for Orange parades to march wherever they like and dire threats if anyone tries to put a stop to those huge conflagrations on 11th July each year can all feel secure in the knowledge that Ruth Dudley Edwards and her cronies are right behind them.

The way things look in Northern Ireland, if there is to be any resurgence of violence it will probably come from the Loyalist side. Not everyone in the Unionist community is happy with power-sharing, especially among those that still cling to the idea of the Protestant Ascendancy. So enmeshed in Unionist politics have the revisionists and their supporters become that it would be virtually impossible for them to backtrack if the Unionists become the 'terrorists' instead of the Provos.

In the Republic itself, things might come full-circle and traditional Irish history could be in vogue yet again. We might yet see a film, based on *Django Unchained*, where the Irish are the ones being oppressed. Let me be the first to recommend Ruth Dudley Edwards for the Samuel L Jackson role!

Still, Edwards can content herself with the knowledge that she will always have at least one man on her side. When the day comes when Catholics outnumber Protestants in Northern Ireland, there might well be a referendum called to decide whether to leave the UK. Ruth can be sure that erstwhile arch anti-establishment figure, 'Sir' Bob Geldof, will be in Trafalgar Square, waving a Union Flag and telling Northern Ireland to 'stay with us'![54]

17
Bigotry is Dead – Long Live Bigotry: Continuing Anti-Catholicism

It is a continuing scandal in the USA that black people are disproportionately represented in the prison population; vastly so.[1] The reasons for this are twofold: racism in the system, from the beat cop to the judiciary,[2] and the fact that black people still tend to live in poor, segregated neighbourhoods.[3] It is something that is of serious concern to organisations campaigning for social justice and state and federal governments.

The exact same problems exist in England and Wales, although, obviously to a lesser, numerical extent. The disproportionate number of black people in prison is due to the same reasons that exist in America; poverty and racial discrimination within the system. The consensus appears to be that if we all ignore it, it will go away and the issue is only rarely raised in the media. With black people routinely subjected to racism and ghettoised almost as soon as they started to arrive here after WWII, it was inevitable that we would go down the same road as the US. As one professor of criminal justice puts it, 'We are reaping the effects of criminalising a community in the 1970s'.[4]

Whenever anyone does highlight the disparity, there are plenty of white people ready to proclaim that crime was never as bad in England until the blacks arrived.[5] One commenter, called Mark Steven Conway, showing remarkable common-sense, points out that crime was always an issue in poor, urban, working-class neighbourhoods; it just so happens that those neighbourhoods are now predominantly black.[6] This is something that many white people will not accept, still talking about the old days when you could leave your door open and everyone pulling together, showing the 'Dunkirk Spirit'. In fact, crime increased substantially during WWII, including looting of bombed houses, theft of all kinds, armed robberies and even rapes and murders.[7] And most UK cities were plagued with gang violence both before and after WWII. People, however, tend to view the past through rose-tinted glasses.

Scotland is no different from America and England in facing problems inherited from the past, from a time when bigoted attitudes were much more open and acceptable. What is different is that that it was not black people that were the victims of bigotry in Scotland; there are relatively few black people in Scotland[8] and there is no such thing as a black community like in Brixton or Toxteth. The victims of bigotry in Scotland, for nearly two centuries, have always been Roman Catholics, especially of the Irish variety.

We have already seen how much hatred there is for any idea that the experiences of Irish Catholics are in any way comparable to those of African Americans; the same is true about Catholics in Scotland, especially since most of them are of Irish extraction. The facts, however, speak for themselves.

I have been unable to find more up-to-date figures but in 2011 there was a disproportionate number of Catholics in Scottish prisons;[9] there is no reason to believe that five years have made any difference. In fact, not only were there proportionately more Catholics in prison, but Catholics seemed to be sentenced to longer terms in prison as well.[10] As usual, this kind of article attracts a dismissive comment: 'It's all the Judges, politicians, Scots etc. fault. Yawn!! The important fact is guilty or not guilty not whether the offender is Catholic or not.'[11] That, unfortunately, sums up the attitude of Scottish society in general.

Who decides if someone is guilty or not guilty? That is either a judge or a jury, who bring with them all their prejudices, even if they claim to have none. Obviously, there are no records to show how Catholic defendants fare against Protestant judges or juries mostly comprised of Protestants, but there have been recent examples of blatant prejudice in Scottish courts.

On 11th May 2011, television audiences were stunned when they saw a Hearts supporter get onto the touchline at Tynecastle, make his way to the Celtic technical area and punch Celtic manager, Neil Lennon. Those around the area heard the man, John Wilson, call Lennon a 'Fenian bastard', including Tynecastle security manager, Peter Croy.[12] The jury, however, preferred the evidence of Wilson, who had admitted to downing 'half a bottle of Buckfast and two cans' on top of painkillers before the match.[13] The sectarian assault case against Wilson was found 'not proven'; he was simply found guilty of a breach of the peace and was jailed for eight months.[14]

And then we had the ones that sent bombs through the post to Neil Lennon and others. Lennon and his family had to live through months of terror, with twenty-four-hour police protection. Eventually, the scum responsible were caught but, again, the sentences hardly reflected the distress they had caused and the intent behind sending the bombs. Trevor Muirhead and Neil McKenzie got five years apiece, with McKenzie being handed an extra eighteen months for sending a hoax bomb to Lennon at Celtic Park.[15]

Every report about the sentencing described the packages the men sent in the same, precise, way, saying that they were devices that 'they believed were capable of exploding and causing injury'.[16] No inverted commas were used, but it is obvious that this phrase must have been delivered by the judge. Unbelievably, the judge went on to say that it was 'obvious' that he was not dealing with 'acts of terrorism'.[17] Somebody needs to get that man a dictionary; how else could you describe what those two did?

Compare how this pair was treated with what happened to the ones that were convicted of plotting to murder ex-UDA kingpin, Johnny 'Mad Dog' Adair and his 'right-hand man', Sam McCrory. The three men were also convicted of terrorism charges and received hefty sentences. Antoin Duffy, described as 'instigator and driving force', went down for seventeen years.[18]

So, how did this criminal mastermind, Duffy, go about trying to obtain the weapons he and his fellow conspirators required? He walked into the crowded *Brazen Head* pub, in Glasgow, and asked Celtic player, Anthony Stokes, if there was any chance his father could get a hold of some guns.[19] If Duffy was the 'Republican terrorist' with all the connections he supposedly had, why the hell would he do such a thing?

Duffy and his little band came across as nothing more than fantasists, especially when you consider the evidence that Duffy was addicted to powerful painkiller Tramadol.[20] But these three were considered dangerous terrorists, while the ones that sent what they believed to be viable, explosive devices, intended to maim or kill, were painted as ridiculous, irrational clowns.

While Neil Lennon's would-be killers were portrayed as a comedy act, Lennon himself was continually made to look, in the media, as if he was a vicious, violent beast.[21] The newspapers always had a picture of him snarling and looking as if he was ready to take on all comers. It was little wonder, then, that the myth developed of Lennon 'bringing it on himself'.[22] These media portraits no doubt influenced the juries at the two court cases mentioned above.

Lennon was not the only one connected to Celtic to receive the negative attention of the media. In 2014, Anthony Stokes was pictured singing with what was called a 'pro-IRA' band in a bar on the Falls Road in Belfast.[23] By way of contrast, the media were pretty circumspect about Andy Goram's links with Loyalist terrorists and certainly nobody bothered to investigate. In fact, such things were barely mentioned; and, certainly, not until Goram had left Rangers.[24] Nobody at the time questioned that infamous black armband, supposedly worn to commemorate his Aunt Lily, who had died four months previously.

Rangers never punished, or even castigated, Goram for his frequent appearances with Loyalist terrorists, and nobody in the media called for this to happen. All we heard were tales of 'The Goalie' and how marvellous it was when he was signed by Manchester United. It was a completely different story when Anthony Stokes, ill-advisedly, attended a memorial for his friend Alan Ryan, who was a leading member of the Real IRA.[25] He was castigated publicly by Celtic and was punished for bringing the club into disrepute.[26] That, however, was not enough as far as the media were concerned; he should have been sacked immediately.[27] Maybe Stokes's best bet would have been to turn up with some chicken, a can of lager and a fishing rod![28]

Back to the courts, and, even when the cases involve neither football nor Ireland, sectarian bigotry can play its part. Driving under the influence of alcohol or drugs is, quite rightly, not tolerated these days. An individual, wrecked on booze or drugs, is a danger to everybody on the road, whether other road users or pedestrians. Heavy sentences are the norm in such cases but there can be glaring exceptions.

Defence lawyers usually plead for leniency, often offering as mitigating evidence the fact that the accused is a hopeless alcoholic or drug addict. Such pleas, however, do not wash with the courts, whether judge or jury; if you are an addict, you should not be driving, simple as that. Certainly, there is never any suggestion that it is the drink or drugs to blame, rather than the individual on trial.

In February 2016, one Andrew McNeill appeared in court for driving while one-and-a-half times the legal limit. To compound the charge, McNeill was already banned from driving when he got behind the wheel. As the judge said:

> You are already on a Community Payback Order and a Restriction of Liberty Order, you were banned for drink-driving and then you chose to drive with alcohol in your system again - while disqualified.
> An alternative to custody is really not available to me today and that means a sentence of imprisonment.[29]

Well, that seemed straightforward enough; except it was not. The judge continued:

> However, I have decided I'm not going to do that and, instead, I'm going to defer sentence for eight weeks.
> By then you should have carried out the rest of your unpaid hours of work from your Community Payback Order.
> I'm going to defer sentence to see if you can finish the Community Payback Order and complying with the terms of your Restriction of Liberty Order.
> If I get a report saying you have not complied with the order, then my decision will be fairly straightforward and you will get a significant period of imprisonment for these offences.[30]

Effectively, McNeill was being allowed to walk free for what is generally considered to be a serious crime. As usual, McNeill's lawyer had cited his client's alcoholism as a mitigating factor. This time, however, it worked. What appeared to swing the judge was that McNeill was addicted to no ordinary drink; he was addicted to *Buckfast Tonic Wine*, to the tune of between five and ten bottles a day![31]

Another lucky character, who used the *Buckfast* defence, was Callum Anderson, who was accused, with another, of beating up a young boy and smashing a bottle over his head. The judge said, when passing sentence:

> The normal penalty for assaulting someone by striking them on the head with a bottle, even for a first offender, is around 18 months' custody.
> With considerable hesitation, I'm stepping away from that[32]

Instead, Anderson was sentenced to a one year's supervision order, 225 hours of unpaid work and to pay £250 compensation to the victim, as well as an electronic tag, with a curfew between 7pm and 7am.[33] The reason for such leniency was explained by the judge:

> Someone who drinks two-and-a-half bottles of Buckfast (as Anderson claimed to have done) is drinking something which is often seen as a feature of cases involving violence...
> There is in my professional experience a very definite association between Buckfast and violence.[34]

There have long been calls to ban *Buckfast*, with politicians citing studies that conclude that it is the high caffeine content, combined with alcohol, that is the problem.[35] It is claimed that the caffeine masks the perceived effect of the alcohol, making it more likely for the drinker to keep on drinking. This opinion, however, has not been borne out by research.[36]

A far more potent mix is achieved by making a *Jagerbomb*, a popular drink served in pubs all over Europe, combining *Jägermeister* with *Red Bull*. There have been no calls at all for the banning of this particular beverage and any blame for the dangers of drinking it has been directed squarely at the highly-caffeinated, energy drink on its own.[37]

Buckfast is only the latest in a long line of drinks favoured by young people and underage drinkers. There were never any calls to ban *Eldorado*, *Lanliq*, *Four Crowns* or any other of the 'electric soup' brands. Indeed, most newspapers were perfectly happy to carry adverts for these drinks. These were not just the beverages of choice for your discerning jakey; they were equally popular with teenagers. Another favourite with underage drinkers was *Scotsmac*, 'the bam's dram', which, I believe, is still available. And I am sure I am not the only one that remembers the *Mateus Rosé* bottle being passed around before a school disco.

So, what makes *Buckfast* different to all these other low-class drinks? Well, it happens to be made by Benedictine monks at Buckfast

Abbey in Devon.[38] Of course, everyone would deny categorically that sectarian bigotry plays any part in the demonisationn of the drink, but why has no other product attracted so much censure? *Buckfast Tonic Wine* has been around now for well over a hundred years and it is only fairly recently that it has been used for getting inebriated. Many other products, including lighter fuel, glue and cleaning gels have been abused over the years, yet calls for them to be banned are few and far between. In normal circumstances, it is the individual abusing the product that is to blame; *Buckfast*, it seems is the glaring exception.

Although you get the odd trendy individual claiming to enjoy the stuff, *Buckfast* is mainly the drink of choice in deprived council schemes. Poverty and addiction usually go hand-in-hand, with crime invariably linked to both. And, yet again, Catholics in Scotland are overrepresented when it comes to poverty. Figures show that Catholics are more likely to be unemployed, have no qualifications, suffer from long-term illnesses and live in poorer areas.[39] As usual, however, nothing of substance is done to redress this imbalance; it is mostly ignored.

The East End of Glasgow, like many other impoverished areas, has been crying out for regeneration for decades. The area around, and to the west of, the Saltmarket and High Street has long since been cleaned up and marketed as the Merchant City, with snooty bars and bistros and shops where you would need to take out a mortgage to buy a pair of shoes. All this regeneration, if that is what it can be called, has always come to an abrupt halt at the beginnings of the Gallowgate and Duke Street. Beyond that was a no-man's land, an area caught in a time-warp; going there was like walking into a scene from *No Mean City*. The scene northwards was not much better; from Bridgeton, all the way along London Road and into Parkhead, one almost expected to see ragged, barefoot children, suffering from rickets and coughing phlegm from tuberculosis-infested lungs.

Many, if not most, of the residents of Glasgow's East End are the descendants of Irish immigrants. Of course, it would always be denied that this was a factor in deciding whether an area was to be regenerated or not, but the East End always seemed to be at the bottom of the list of places that needed money spent on them. In 2014, it looked like all that was about to change.

It is debatable whether the Commonwealth Games was a good

thing for the East End of Glasgow. Such enterprises usually end up promoting gentrification rather than regeneration and local residents hardly benefit at all. In fact, they can find themselves displaced from their community altogether.[40] What was interesting was the reaction in some quarters to the perception of regeneration.

Those wearing orange-tinted spectacles had a field day, bemoaning that there were other areas more deserving of regeneration.[41] Those staunch defenders of everything Protestant, Vanguard Bears, meanwhile, painted the whole Commonwealth Games as nothing more than an exercise in aggrandisement for Celtic at the expense of the tax payer.[42] The general opinion seemed to be that Glasgow City Council only worked in the interests of Catholics, while the Protestant population was left to rot. As usual, the facts play no part in how these people view the world.

For Scottish Catholics, however, there was good news. Tom Devine, Emeritus Professor of History at Edinburgh University, announced in 2014 that sectarian bigotry against Catholics was dead or, at least, sounding its death rattle.[43] The old, heavy industries of Scotland were gone, replaced by multi-national companies that put profit well before any religious considerations. There has also been a marked secularisation of Scottish society, meaning the death of sectarian bigotry. So, that is that, then. Except, of course, that it is not.

It appears that there is a quite heated argument going on among Scottish historians about discrimination against Catholics. On one side, we have Patricia Wallis and Rory Williams, who argue that anti-Catholic bigotry is still a problem in Scotland.[44] On the other side are Steve Bruce, Tony Glendinning, Iain Paterson and Michael Rosie, who deny that there is any sectarian problem at all in Scotland.[45] Indeed, Steve Bruce and his colleagues go even further than that. In a move certain to gladden the hearts of the Irish revisionist historians, they deny that sectarian bigotry and discrimination has ever been a problem in Scotland.[46]

The debate over this issue is far from over, as Professor Devine himself admits.[47] It is quite a heated argument[48] and, while each camp insists on using different methodologies, no firm conclusions will be reached any time soon. It is, however, possible to reach some conclusions of our own.

One of the main claims made by those denying the existence of anti-Catholic bigotry is that one's perception is not the same as actual evidence. In this argument, the people interviewed by Patricia Wallis and Rory Williams might well have the wrong idea about their experiences or could even be lying. While advancing this claim, Bruce and his colleagues argue that their opponents fail to take account of the media in Scotland.[49] This is a rather disingenuous argument since journalists are just as capable of lying and perceiving things incorrectly as any other individual.

In fact, conscious decisions are made at an editorial level to deliberately skew presentations of matters in newspapers to fit political agendas. The vilification of Liverpool supporters at the Hillsborough Disaster by *The Sun* is a particularly graphic example.[50] Even in the 1880s, when exposing the scandal of children involved in the sex trade in the *Pall Mall Gazette*, journalist WT Stead spared the blushes of his English readers by portraying the prostitution of children as a white-slave trade, perpetrated by Johnny Foreigner.[51]

For decades, the Scottish media virtually ignored the sectarian signing policy adopted by Rangers. If they were capable of doing that, then who could tell what other instances of discrimination they chose to hide. Relying on newspapers rather than the reported experiences of individuals is a method of historical investigation that needs to be treated with caution. Newspapers, by their very nature, have more reason to lie than do individuals.

Bruce and his colleagues also claim that most of the clergy in Scotland preached tolerance and did not support the likes of the Scottish Protestant League and the Protestant Action Society.[52] Again, however, they are being disingenuous. Many of the Protestant clergy in Scotland were members of the Orange Order and account should be taken of that, rather than support for fly-by-night fascist organisations. Unless, of course, Bruce and his colleagues believe in the Ruth-Dudley-Edwards version of the Orange Order!

Speaking of La Edwards, some people have taken a leaf out of her book and try to make it appear as if Irish Catholics were the ones that started all the bigotry. It has even been claimed that Celtic was founded for sectarian reasons, since Brother Walfrid was keen for his fellow Catholics to avoid the *Souperism* inherent in Protestant charity kitchens.[53] The real bigotry, surely, resided in those that would only feed the Catholic poor if there were strings attached. There is, however, no reasoning with a bigot.

Anti-Catholic bigotry has been, and still is, a major problem in Scotland. This has permeated through all levels and all organisations of Scottish society, affecting the lives and prospects of Scottish Catholics. The big question, though, is why. Why did anti-Catholic bigotry become so entrenched in Scotland? It is time to pull together everything we have learned and reach some conclusions.

18
Non-Protestant Protestants Why Scotland?

We have seen how anti-Catholic bigotry was practically non-existent in Scotland after the Reformation and how it was the Union with England that brought such prejudices there. Not only was Scotland infected with English paranoia, but being in a Union with England meant that Scotland was dragged into that morass of bigotry that was Ireland. The 1745 Jacobite Rebellion helped to convince Scottish Protestants that the English had been right all along in their paranoia.

Obviously, the seeds of paranoia did not fall on stony ground, so what made Scotland so susceptible? Why did anti-Catholic bigotry take such a hold there and develop in such a way that it has permeated the whole of Scottish society? We have seen how anti-Catholicism is still an issue in England and America, but it does not affect people's lives as much as it does in Scotland. Even people from Northern Ireland are shocked at some of the bigotry evident in Scotland.[1] What was so special about Scotland? The answer is twofold: democracy and Calvinism.

In England, as we have seen, there was tension between the Protestantism of ordinary people and the High-Church Anglicanism of the upper classes, which appeared to be just Catholicism without the Pope. All the ceremonial, the vestments, the set routine of the service; all of this was anathema to the ordinary Protestant. William of Orange, you will remember, called his coronation ceremony a 'Popish mockery',[2] confirming the idea that there was something rather suspect about High-Church Anglicanism.

As for Catholicism itself, it came to be seen in England as the preserve of upper-class elements, unwilling to give up their old religion. In many instances this was, in fact, the case; it was aristocratic Catholics that kept the religion alive in England.[3] For the most part, such people were tolerated by the Establishment, unless they openly caused trouble, like the Catholic nobles involved in the Rising of the North, whom we met in Chapter 1.

The Catholic Emancipation Act of 1829, therefore, hardly made any difference to the country as far as ordinary people were concerned. Only the well-off could vote and there was not much to choose between upper-class Catholics and upper-class High-Church Anglicans anyway. Ordinary English Protestants might hate Catholics with the best of them, but their main concern, in the late 18th Century and into the 19th, was in getting the vote.

One of the great liberal preoccupations in the 19th Century, along with extending the franchise and free trade, was the disestablishment of the Church of England. This was fuelled by the involvement of many Nonconformists in liberal politics, who viewed an established church as holding back the progress of the country. 'The Tory Party at Prayer' was how the Anglican Church was viewed and the opinion was not far wrong.

In the 1830s, a new phenomenon appeared that raised suspicions about High-Church Anglicanism to new levels; the Oxford Movement. As its name suggests, this started at Oxford University and was about returning the Church to its Catholic roots.[4] Such was the furore caused by this movement that it inspired the founding of the *Protestant Truth Society* to counteract its Catholicising influence.[5] Ultimately, the Oxford Movement was successful in its aims; many modern Church of England services are practically indistinguishable from the Catholic Mass. It must have made many an Orange head practically explode to see Prince William, their future 'King Billy', and his bride bless themselves at their wedding.

Anti-Catholicism in England, therefore, took on a liberal and left-wing, anti-authoritarian flavour. Thus, we get the apparent anomaly presented by the anti-Catholic bigotry displayed by supposed left-wing, humanist and humanitarian figures such as Richard Dawkins and Stephen Fry. This is distinctly not the case in Scotland.

For some strange reason, it is believed that the Reformation somehow turned Scotland into a kind of democracy. We have already encountered the myth of the 'Lad O' Pairts' and the idea that everyone was taught to read in Church of Scotland schools; an idea which is complete nonsense. Throughout society, nothing really changed: the nobility still ruled the land, the rich were still rich and the poor were still poor. Meanwhile, church services might be different but you were still obliged to attend.

Ostensibly, Calvinism, with its Presbyterian form of church government, was a democratic institution and this aspect is certainly played up by apologists for the Church of Scotland.[6] The reality, of course, was somewhat different; church elders, for example, came mostly from the upper and middle classes.[7] And it would be a brave minister indeed that would refuse Communion to the laird, or insist that a local, well-to-do worthy take his turn on the penitent's stool.[8]

Even when it came to Calvinist doctrine, the wealthy had their own way. With Purgatory no longer on the agenda, there was no need for headstones to remind people going in and out of church to pray for your soul. Calvin and Knox themselves were buried in unmarked graves; the whereabouts of Calvin's final resting place is still unknown. That was not good enough for Scotland's wealthy; they wanted to be buried in 'consecrated' ground, with grandiose tombstones to announce how special they were. The Church tacitly condoned such practices; imposing a 'fine' on the family of the deceased.[9]

Essentially, the Church of Scotland was a church for the upper and middle classes, as were the Scottish Episcopal Church and the Free Church of Scotland. Working-class people were made to feel alienated; often deliberately so.[10] In fact, the evidence suggests that poor people only attended church services to benefit from poor relief; when local authorities took over the administration of such relief, church attendances declined accordingly.[11]

So, what, apart from the odd meal, was the benefit of maintaining the *status quo* for ordinary, Scottish people? The answer has to be: not a lot. Indeed, many in Scotland got caught up in the Chartist agitation during the 1830s and 1840s. Chartism in Scotland, however, took on its own, peculiar, character. Chartist churches sprang up, giving the movement a religious, rather than a political flavour. These churches appeared to have a rather brief life[12] and it is generally reckoned that their members drifted into the new Free Church of Scotland. As far as I know, nobody has done an in-depth analysis of the membership of these organisations and how the Church Disruption Crisis affected their existence.[13]

A telling incident took place at the Scottish Chartist Convention in 1842. The English executive council had amended the new petition; calling not only for the Six Points of the Charter to be implemented, but other issues as well. These new issues included the dissolution of the Union between Britain and Ireland; an attempt to gain the support of Irish Nationalists. This caused consternation at the Scottish Convention and the proposal was put forward:

> That this meeting of Scottish delegates, disapprove of the petition proposed by the English executive council, and recommend to the people of Scotland the adoption of a petition for the People's Charter, without embracing any question of detail.[14]

A compromise was suggested, that each local association should decide for itself whether to support the new, English petition or to stick to the original Six Points. This was defeated 'by a considerable majority'.[15] This episode showed how close Scottish and Ulster Protestantism had already become. It also showed that sectarian bigotry was more important than securing support for the implementation of the Charter.

And this was the dichotomy at the heart of Scottish, working-class Protestantism; on the one hand seeking democracy, while, on the other, desperate to exclude Catholics from any extension of the franchise. As we have seen, the Orange Order in Scotland openly boasts of campaigning against any widening of the franchise in the UK.[16] Why were Scottish Protestants so intent on keeping power from Catholics, even to the extent of denying themselves that power as a consequence?

In the movie, *Mississippi Burning*, the Gene Hackman character recounts a story from his childhood. A black neighbour owned a mule; something which sent Hackman's father into paroxysms of fury. It was not just envy that inspired this anger; it was the knowledge that a black man was doing better than he was. He found this impossible to tolerate since nobody likes to be faced with the fact that he is at the bottom of the heap.

Scottish, working-class Protestants felt the same way about Catholics; they, the Protestants, might be at the bottom but they were not as low as Catholics, especially Irish Catholics. This idea of Catholics as *Untermenschen* was essential for the self-respect of working-class Protestants in Scotland. But it went even further than that.

You will remember how, when trying to determine who was among the *Elect*, earthly success became the measure.[17] But what if you were not successful? That would mark you out as one of the *Damned*; not exactly a pleasing prospect. The only way that working-class Protestants could be sure of their own status as part of the *Elect* was to measure their success against that of Catholics. Keeping Catholics out of certain jobs, keeping them poor and denying them a say in the running of society were all necessary to working-class Protestants in Scotland; in fact, their Heavenly salvation depended upon it.

Scottish Catholics had not provided for this need; living in remote, rural communities as they did. They kept their heads down and were practically invisible. It was not until the Union of Parliaments in 1707 that Scotland was dragged into Ireland and Scottish Protestants came across unashamed Catholics for the first time since the Reformation. Here were folk that working-class, Scottish Protestants could join their fellows in Ulster in feeling superior to. Alienated from their own church in their own country, working-class Protestants in Scotland began to define their Protestantism as *non-Catholic*. Their standing in the Church of Scotland no longer mattered; it was not being part of the Catholic herd that marked them out, at least to their own minds, as *Elect*.

This explains the discrimination that Irish Catholics faced when they came to Scotland. It also explains the triumphalism displayed at Orange parades; celebrating their place in Heaven, guaranteed by the plain fact of not being Catholics. It also provides an explanation of how ordinary, Scottish Protestants came to believe that they were part of the Establishment and that their best interests were served by maintaining the *status quo*. What it does not explain, however, is the visceral hatred of Catholics that still exists in Scotland.

The usual reason given is the old *They come over here* excuse; that Irish Catholics were stealing Scottish people's livelihood by undercutting them in the jobs market. This, however, is nonsense since Irish Catholics were only welcome in the filthy, dangerous jobs that nobody else wanted to do. In Glasgow, for example, the major employer of Irish immigrants was the huge St. Rollox Chemical Works. By all accounts, this factory was a living hell[18] and only the truly desperate would consider working there. The nearby Copper Works and Steel Works in Garngad were not much better.

In times of high unemployment, such jobs might seem more

attractive than they actually were but, in the main, most people would avoid them. Glasgow's Protestants were more likely to be working at the nearby St. Rollox Locomotive Works, where RCs needed 'not apply'. Essentially, there was no real competition between Irish Catholics and Scottish Protestants for jobs. Besides, it was not just working-class Protestants that harboured a hatred of Catholics. This suggests something more fundamental.

It is from St. Augustine that we get the phrase, popular among modern Christians, 'Love the sinner, hate the sin.'[19] This maxim is coming to be used less and less, as Christians struggle with separating sin from the sinner,[20] while others realise that it is just a convenient mask for homophobes to hide behind.[21] Traditionally, Calvinism takes a rather different view.

While Calvinists are trying to figure out who the *Elect* are, one thing has always been certain; those recalcitrant Catholics, clinging onto their outdated beliefs were destined for the Big Bad Fire. Calvinist belief was that we were all pre-programmed, away at the beginning of time, to be either saved or damned. God decided, on a mere whim, who his *Elect* were and would practically force them into having faith in Christ; a proper belief in a proper *Calvinist* Jesus. The ones destined for damnation would not be granted Grace and would, therefore, not follow Christ; or, at least, not properly.

It is quite interesting, and often amusing, to encounter a Calvinist trying to equate the God of Love of the New Testament with the monster that created people just to condemn the majority to eternal damnation.[22] It is also notable that most of the criticism of Calvinism comes not from Catholics, but from other Protestants.[23] And it is not just that Calvinism denies free will and possibly makes God responsible for sin; it is the fact that Calvinism often promotes hatred, rather than love.[24]

Bill Murray, in his book, *The Old Firm*, suggested that many Scottish Protestants hated Catholics because they envied them; they could drink and enjoy themselves without anyone looking over their shoulders. There might be an element of truth in this but, essentially, Irish Catholics were seen as a latter-day *Sodom and Gomorrah*, ready to drag everyone down with them. As the infamous Church of Scotland report of 1923, *The Menace of the Irish Race to our Scottish Nationality*, put it:

> They (Irish Catholics) have had an unfortunate influence in modifying the Scottish habit of thrift and independence. An Irishman never hesitates to seek relief from charity organisations and local authorities, and Scotsmen do not see why they should not get help when Irishmen receive it. Indeed, it must be said that the social problem has been complicated and increased by the presence of the Irish population. Generally speaking, they are poor partly through intemperance and improvidence, and they show little inclination to raise themselves in the social scale.[25]

It was another dichotomy within Scottish Protestantism that the very elites that encouraged Irish Catholics to Scotland in order to exploit them in their factories were in the vanguard of expressing hatred for them. The elders in the Church of Scotland were composed of the middle classes, after all.

The Church of Scotland has changed somewhat from the bad, old days and they preach nothing but love and, it would appear, salvation for all.[26] The Church has even apologised for their bigoted report of 1923.[27] The damage, however, was done long before that particular date and the legacy of hatred is still there.

As well as the hatred of Catholics deriving from Calvinist doctrine, there was another element involved. Again, the Church of Scotland's 1923 report gives a clue.

> Even now the Irish population exercise a profound influence on the direction and development of our Scottish civilisation. Their gift of speech, their aptitude for public life, their restless ambition to rule, have given them a prominent place in political, county, municipal, and parochial elections.[28]

So much for those unambitious, drunken layabouts the Church complains about later on the same page! It does, however, show how much the English paranoia about Catholics had infected Scotland. The painful reality that all Catholics over the age of twenty-one now had the vote, along with the realisation that some Catholics were doing quite well for themselves was something that Scottish Protestantism found hard to stomach. With success being the pointer to one's status as one of the *Elect,* obviously, something underhand and suspicious was going on. It was a conspiracy!

In the 21st Century, the English bogeyman is the Muslim. Right-wing claims that Muslims are trying to impose Sharia Law on the rest of us are used as part of an agenda to disenfranchise them.[29] Many English people, and some, it has to be admitted, in Scotland prefer their Muslims frightened and docile. Any attempt by Muslims to fight back against prejudice is painted as them 'trying to take over'. This is the exact same situation as Catholics faced in Scotland in the 20th Century. Scottish Protestantism was used to frightened, docile Catholics and wanted them kept that way.

Now, in 1923, working-class Catholics had the vote, middle-class Catholics were on the rise, Catholic schools were part of the state system and even their football club, Celtic, was dominating Scottish football. This was not the way things were supposed to be. As the Church of Scotland report pointed out, evil conspiracies were afoot. There are many in Scotland that still believe this, despite the Church's apology for, and distancing itself from, that 1923 document.

And therein lies the problem; the Church of Scotland has become an irrelevance to Scottish Protestants. We saw earlier how working-class Protestants felt alienated from the Church in the 19th Century and this continued to be the case, despite the Church's best efforts to reverse the trend at the end of the century and into the 20th.[30] Unfortunately, many Scottish Protestants had found a new church.

This new church came to define how many working-class Protestants, and even some middle-class Protestants, viewed their Protestantism. Bill McMurdo, on his (now deleted) blog, went even further, with many agreeing with him totally. Incredibly, (and I swear I am not making this up) McMurdo claimed that Rangers supporters did not choose to become so, but were chosen. In effect, what he was saying was that, rather than worldly success showing one's status as one of the *Elect*, it was being a Rangers supporter that proved that you were one of God's chosen! This was how Protestantism was being defined throughout the 20th Century and into the 21st; not through membership of a church, but by following a football team.

That this is the case is quite easily proven. Ask anyone that professes to be a Protestant what church he was baptised into and, nine times out of ten, he will have no idea. He will initially claim to be a member of the 'Protestant Church' but will become confused when it is explained that there is no such thing. The only way he can justify his claim to be a Protestant is that he is not a Catholic and that he supports Rangers. It can be quite amusing to taunt such a person with the possibility that he might have been baptised a Catholic without ever knowing. How amusing this is, of course, depends on the size of the individual, his propensity for violence and how much he has had to drink. A much more acceptable prospect is that he is, by the standards of any church, a heathen.

And so, modern-day, anti-Catholic bigotry has become somewhat divorced from its origins. With Protestantism no more than a badge to denote that the person is not a Catholic and that he follows a particular football team, justification for bigotry has to be found in other places than the Church. As we have seen throughout this book, such justification is not hard to find.

With the media, both in the UK and America, promoting anti-Catholic agendas such as child sexual abuse being a purely Catholic problem, and even fictional programmes and films using anti-Catholic images and rhetoric, bigotry in Scotland has plenty out there to keep it fed. The ironic thing is that, although this bigotry in the media originally stems from Protestantism, it is no longer Protestants that are the exponents. Nowadays it is more likely to be atheists and Humanists attacking the Catholic Church; people who would argue that they are not bigoted at all.

But, again, it all depends on your definition of a Protestant. *Real* Protestants have moved on from the days of hatred and bigotry, but the legacy remains. Your average knuckle-dragger in Scotland has grown up with the mantra, straight out of *Animal Farm*, of *Protestant Good, Catholic Bad*. With no idea of what being a Protestant means anymore, all he is left with is the notion that the Catholic Church is evil, Catholic schools are evil and Catholics are evil. Meanwhile, the Orange Order 'defends' Protestantism from imaginary enemies, even though the Protestants doing the 'defending' are not, in fact, Protestants at all!

This is the problem that organisations supposedly fighting to eradicate bigotry from Scotland fail to understand. They see sectarian bigotry as a *Catholic versus Protestant* thing, which it is not. *Proper* Protestants no longer hate Catholics and Catholics no longer hate Protestants. Anti-Catholic bigotry, however, has pervaded Scottish society so completely that it is often not even recognised as such.

Meanwhile, out-and-out, in-your-face, bigotry from the Orange Order and supporters of Rangers is almost completely ignored, or justified on the grounds that 'the other lot is just as bad'. Until Scotland faces up to these facts, then those claiming to want to eradicate sectarian bigotry are wasting their time.

NOTES

Introduction

[1] https://owlcation.com/humanities/The-Habsburg-Jaw-And-Other-Royal Inbreeding-Deformities-and-Disorders
[2] https://sheokhanda.wordpress.com/2012/05/03/king-charles-ii-the-stupid-of-spain-and-inbreeding/
[3] http://reformation500.csl.edu/bio/charles-v/
[4] http://www.christianity.com/church/church-history/timeline/1501-1600/german
-peasant-revolt-11629931.html
[5] ibid
[6] http://wiki.lawguru.com/index.php/Cuius_regio%2C_eius_religio
[7] Diarmaid MacCulloch - Reformation; Europe's House Divided Penguin 2003 pp 457-464
[8] http://www.heraldscotland.com/opinion/letters/13164828.List_of_martyrs_not_
extensive/
[9] ibid
[10] http://ukpopulation2016.com/scotland
[11] http://www.genuki.org.uk/big/sct/population
[12] http://www.localhistories.org/population.html
[13] MacCulloch. Op. Cit. p 379
[14] http://www.bbc.co.uk/scotland/history/articles/scottish_reformation/
[15] http://www.thereformation.info/firstblast.htm
[16] http://archive.churchsociety.org/churchman/documents/Cman_078_4_ Hughes.pdf
[17] MacCulloch. Op. Cit. p 379
[18] http://www.thereformation.info/catholic_church.htm
[19] http://www.staloysius.rcglasgow.org.uk/stjohnogilvie
[20] ibid
[21] https://www.theguardian.com/uk/2006/nov/28/religion.catholicism
[22] http://www.independent.co.uk/news/uk/this-britain/the-big-question-in-2006
-are-catholics-really-being-discriminated-against-in-scotland-417777.html

Chapter 1

[1] https://catholicunderthehood.com/2010/10/17/today-in-catholic-history-henry-
viii-is-declared-the-defender-of-the-faith/
[2] http://anglicanhistory.org/reformation/henry/sixarticles.html

[3] https://en.wikipedia.org/wiki/List_of_Protestant_martyrs_of_the_English_Reformation#Protestants_executed_under_Henry_VIII
[4] http://www.bbc.co.uk/history/historic_figures/edward_vi_king.shtml
[5] http://www.historyextra.com/article/premium/who-hijacked-henry-viiis-will
[6] http://www.tudors.org/undergraduate/protestant-reformation-under-edward-vi-an-agenda/
[7] http://www.luminarium.org/encyclopedia/pilgrimagegrace.htm
[8] Downloadable PDF at www.shs-history.net/Edward VI Rebellions 2.pdf
[9] http://britishheritage.com/mary-tudor-a-most-unhappy-queen/
[10] http://www.catholicherald.co.uk/commentandblogs/2013/10/31/forget-her-bloody-reputation-mary-i-was-loved-in-her-lifetime/
[11] http://britishheritage.com/mary-tudor-a-most-unhappy-queen/
[12] https://www.britannica.com/topic/auto-da-fe
[13] https://www.churchofengland.org/prayer-worship/worship/book-of-common-prayer/articles-of-religion.aspx
[14] http://faculty.history.wisc.edu/sommerville/361/361-14.htm#Regnans
[15] http://www.tudorplace.com.ar/Documents/NorthernRebellion.htm
[16] http://tudorhistory.org/primary/papalbull.html
[17] http://www.foxes-book-of-martyrs.com/history.html
[18] http://www.exclassics.com/foxe/foxintro.htm
[19] http://www.catholic.org/encyclopedia/view.php?id=10308
[20] http://www.exclassics.com/foxe/foxintro.htm
[21] ibid
[22] http://britishheritage.com/francis-walsingham-elizabethan-spymaster/
[23] https://www.ucumberlands.edu/downloads/academics/history/vol2/JackieBorgeson90.htm

Chapter 2

[1] http://www.history.com/news/guy-fawkes-day-a-brief-history
[2] http://www.bonfirenight.net/framed.php
[3] http://justus.anglican.org/resources/bcp/Scotland/james6intro.html
[4] ibid
[5] http://justus.anglican.org/resources/bcp/Scotland/BCP_1637.htm
[6] http://www.englishmonarchs.co.uk/stuart_16.html
[7] http://www.historyofwar.org/articles/people_charlesI.html
[8] ibid
[9] http://www.historytoday.com/sarah-mortimer/civil-wars
[10] https://www.britannica.com/event/Bishops-Wars
[11] http://www.thereformation.info/bishopswars.htm
[12] ibid
[13] http://www.historytoday.com/sarah-mortimer/civil-wars

[14] http://www.undiscoveredscotland.co.uk/usbiography/g/jennygeddes.html
[15] http://www.history.co.uk/biographies/charles-ii
[16] http://bcw-project.org/military/third-civil-war/dunbar
[17] https://www.britannica.com/biography/Charles-II-king-of-Great-Britain-and-Ireland
[18] http://www.thereformation.info/killing_time.htm
[19] http://www.bbc.co.uk/history/british/civil_war_revolution/charlesi_masq_01.shtml i
[20] http://www.historylearningsite.co.uk/stuart-england/titus-oates/
[21] http://www.parliament.uk/about/livingheritage/evolutionofparliament/parliamentaryauthority/revolution/overview/ reignofjames/
[22] ibid
[23] http://www.jacobite.ca/documents/16870212.htm
[24] https://www.geni.com/people/William-III-King-of-England-Ireland-and-Scotland/6000000003285553237
[25] ibid
[26] http://www.britainexpress.com/History/William-III-Becomes-King-of-Scotland.htm

[27] https://www.britannica.com/biography/Titus-Oates

Chapter 3

[1] http://www.historytoday.com/richard-cavendish/flight-earls
[2] http://bcw-project.org/church-and-state/sects-and-factions/covenanters
[3] http://www.thereformation.info/solemnleague.htm
[4] http://bcw-project.org/military/third-civil-war/cromwell-in-ireland/index
[5] http://www.constitution.org/eng/eng_bor.htm
[6] http://www.ulsterancestry.com/ulster-scots.html
[7] http://edinburgh.universitypressscholarship.com/view/10.3366/edinburgh/9780748638871.001.0001/ upso-9780748638871-chapter-7
[8] http://www.irishidentity.com/stories/penai.htm
[9] http://forgedinulster.com/scots-irish-in-the-usa/4548015472
[10] ibid
[11] http://www.historyireland.com/early-modern-history-1500-1700/celtic-contrasts-ireland-scotland/
[12] http://members.pcug.org.au/~ppmay/acts/penal_laws.htm
[13] http://oneillcountryhistoricalsociety.com/history/formation-of-the-orange-order/
[14] ibid
[15] http://www.grandorangelodge.co.uk/history.aspx?id=99485#.V-mS85UVBjo
[16] http://oneillcountryhistoricalsociety.com/history/formation-of-the-orange-

order/
[17] http://flag.blackened.net/revolt/ws99/ws57_order.html
[18] http://www.fsmitha.com/h3/h34-ireland.htm
[19] http://www.wesleyjohnston.com/users/ireland/past/history/17891800.html
[20] http://www.ireland-information.com/articles/wolfetone.htm
[21] http://www.bbc.co.uk/history/british/empire_seapower/irish_reb_01.shtml
[22] ibid
[23] http://www.victorianweb.org/history/ireland1.html
[24] http://www.actofunion.ac.uk/actofunion.htm#union
[25] ibid
[26] Downloadable PDF at http://www.orangeorderscotland.com/page12.html
[27] http://www.victorianweb.org/history/emancipation2.html
[28] Ibid

Chapter 4

[1] http://www.educationscotland.gov.uk/higherscottishhistory/treatyofunion/worseningrelations/ kingwilliam.asp
[2] www.scran.ac.uk/scotland/pdf/SP1_CH4.pdf
[3] ibid
[4] ibid
[5] ibid
[6] http://www.undiscoveredscotland.co.uk/usbiography/monarchs/anne.html
[7] ibid
[8] http://www.disbanded.co.uk/Jacobite_Rebellion.html
[9] ibid
[10] http://www.british-history.ac.uk/no-series/new-history-london/pp325-353#h3-0018 (1744)
[11] http://www.nationalarchives.gov.uk/education/resources/jacobite-1745/catholic-threat-1745/
[12] http://www.undiscoveredscotland.co.uk/usbiography/c/dukeofcumberland.html
[13] ibid
[14] https://simplyscottish.wordpress.com/2013/08/06/where-did-all-the-highlanders-go/
[15] http://www.educationscotland.gov.uk/scotlandshistory/jacobitesenlightenmentclearances/rebelliousscots/ index.asp
[16] http://www.secretscotland.org.uk/index.php/Secrets/NorthBritain
[17] http://www.grandorangelodge.co.uk/history.aspx?id=99485#.V-suiYWcFjp

Chapter 5

1 Bill Naughton - *The Goalkeeper's Revenge* (Heinemann New Windmills, 1967) p 113 (Story: *Maggie's First Reader*)
2 http://www.biography.com/people/max-weber-9526066
3 https://psmag.com/the-protestant-work-ethic-is-real-42740cb3e6d5#.v9ff5lue1
4 This site has the book in various formats: https://archive.org/details/pdfy-8fnkKz0SleumNaIz
5 MacCulloch. Op. Cit. p 143
6 http://workethic.coe.uga.edu/hpro.html
7 http://www.sciencedirect.com/science/article/pii/S0191659903000020
8 http://www.solon-line.de/2010/03/20/with-a-little-help-from-max-weber-the-american-ideology-and-the-puritan-puzzle/
9 https://www.nps.gov/blac/learn/historyculture/index.htm
10 http://archive.boston.com/bostonglobe/ideas/articles/2010/09/26/new_englands_hidden_history/
11 http://www.medfordhistorical.org/medford-history/africa-to-medford/slaves-in-new-england/
12 http://www.history.ac.uk/ihr/Focus/Slavery/articles/sherwood.html
13 http://plato.stanford.edu/entries/weber/
14 http://riseofthewest.com/thinkers/weber03.htm
15 ibid
16 http://www.ruthdudleyedwards.co.uk/journalism16/BTel16_29.html
17 http://www.digplanet.com/wiki/Souperism
18 http://search.aol.co.uk/aol/search?s_it=sb-top&s_chn=hp&v_t=aolukhomePage50.a&q=souperism&s_qt=ac
19 Kellow Chesney – *The Victorian Underworld* (Readers Union Limited, 1970) pp 68-69
20 Samuel Green - *Scotland 100 Years Ago* (Bracken Books, 1994) p 88
21 http://wearenotthepeople.blogspot.co.uk/2008/09/racist-famine-song.html
22 http://www.heraldscotland.com/news/13086699.Famine_myth_warning_by_top_historian/
23 The Menace of the Irish Race to our Scottish Nationality downloadable at http://docslide.us/documents/menace-of-the-irish-race-to-our-scottish-nationality.html
24 ibid
25 Downloadable PDF at http://www.orangeorderscotland.com/page12.html
26 http://www.parliament.uk/about/livingheritage/evolutionofparliament/houseofcommons/reformacts/overview/reformact1832/
27 http://www.nationalarchives.gov.uk/pathways/firstworldwar/aftermath/brit_after_war.htm
28 http://www.parliament.uk/about/livingheritage/transformingsociety/electionsvoting/womenvote/parliamentary-collections/collections-the-vote-

and-after/representation-of-the-people-act-1918/
[29] http://www.digplanet.com/wiki/Scottish_Protestant_League
[30] Chesney. Op. Cit. pp 39-47
[31] http://truthonsectarianism.blogspot.co.uk/2011/05/ira-are-sectarian.html
[32] http://www.telegraph.co.uk/culture/tvandradio/tv-and-radio reviews/10026098/Dave-Allen-Gods-Own-Comedian-BBC2-review.html
[33] http://www.herald.ie/news/ira-didnt-threaten-to-kill-dave-allen-we-were-fans and-watched-in-prison-29259370.html
[34] http://www.dailyrecord.co.uk/news/local-news/anger-ira-graffiti-appears-across2442692

Chapter 6

[1] https://www.amazon.co.uk/Old-Firm-W-H Murray/dp/0859765423/ref=sr_1_1?s=books&ie=UTF8&qid=1476581295&sr=1 1&keywords=the+old+firm
[2] http://www.followfollow.com/eupdates/loadsend.asp?id=160789
[3] http://www.historyhome.co.uk/peel/ireland/gladire.htm
[4] http://www.historylearningsite.co.uk/ireland-1845-to-1922/gladstone-and-ireland/
[5] http://www.thegallantpioneers.co.uk/Sir-John-Ure-Primrose.html
[6] Downloadable Word document at www.math.nus.edu.sg/aslaksen/celtic/Sanders.doc p.10
[7] ibid
[8] JessicaHarland-Jacobsquoted at   https://simonmayers.com/2013/12/28/the masonic-and-orange-orders-fraternal-twins-or-public-misperception-guest-blog/
[9] http://www.victorianweb.org/technology/ir/ir7.html
[10] http://www.bbc.co.uk/history/british/victorians/workshop_of_the_world_01.shtml
[11] http://www.vice.com/en_uk/read/the-far-right-in-scotland-pegida-ukip-liam-turbett
[12] ibid
[13] http://www.belfasttelegraph.co.uk/opinion/news-analysis/rangers-and-unionismits-a-question-of-identity-30451365.html
[14] http://www.orangeorderscotland.com/index.html
[15] Downloadable PDF at http://www.orangeorderscotland.com/page12.html
[16] https://www.geni.com/people/William-III-King-of-England-Ireland-and-Scotland/6000000003285553237
[17] http://nilbymouth.org/history/
[18] http://www.scotzine.com/2012/12/fran-sandaza-interview-opens-up-old-wounds-of-sectarianism/

[19] http://www.dailyrecord.co.uk/news/scottish-news/singing-the-hokey-cokey-could-land-1002751
[20] http://www.scotsman.com/news/catholic-leaders-say-hokey-cokey-is-faith-hate1-1152724
[21] http://www.scotsman.com/news/hokey-cokey-humbug-1-1153191
[22] https://www.youtube.com/watch?v=orz_KQE416w

Chapter 7

[1] http://flag.blackened.net/revolt/cc1913/flag.html
[2] ibid
[3] http://news.bbc.co.uk/hi/english/static/northern_ireland/understanding/events/civil_rights.stm
[4] http://www.csap.cam.ac.uk/network/graham-gudgin/
[5] http://cain.ulst.ac.uk/issues/discrimination/gudgin99.htm
[6] ibid
[7] http://news.bbc.co.uk/hi/english/static/northern_ireland/understanding/events/civil_rights.stm
[8] http://www.divorceinireland.net/divorce-in-ireland/divorce-in-ireland
[9] http://www.history.com/this-day-in-history/ireland-allows-sale-of-contraceptives
[10] https://en.wikipedia.org/wiki/Contraception_in_the_Republic_of_Ireland
[11] http://www.cflp.co.uk/a-brief-history-of-divorce/
[12] http://www.belfasttelegraph.co.uk/news/health/northern-ireland-women-ignoringcontraception-30578590.html
[13] http://www.belfasttelegraph.co.uk/news/uda-chief-tells-orange-order-to-walk away-from-garvaghy-road-28519631.html
[14] http://www.belfasttelegraph.co.uk/news/republic-of-ireland/samesex-marriage-officially-becomes-law-in-the-republic-of-ireland-34155021.html
[15] http://www.belfasttelegraph.co.uk/news/northern-ireland/samesex-marriage-first-minister-arlene-foster-vows-to-continue-blocking-attempts-to-introduce-law-change-in-northern-ireland-35167799.html
[16] http://www.belfasttelegraph.co.uk/news/northern-ireland/surge-in-northern ireland-applications-for-irish-passports-28748830.html
[17] http://www.belfasttelegraph.co.uk/news/northern-ireland/derry-loyalists-flock-to get-irish-passports-28476069.html
[18] http://www.belfasttelegraph.co.uk/news/irish-presidents-husband-helped-uda chief-get-fasttrack-irish-passport-28453062.html

Chapter 8

[1] Downloadable PDF from
www.legislation.gov.uk/asp/2012/1/pdfs/asp_20120001_en.pdf
[2] http://www.dailyrecord.co.uk/news/scottish-news/celtic-fan-accused-singing-ira9022873
[3] http://www.dumbartonreporter.co.uk/news/14498856.Sheriff_slams_flawed_law_as_Rangers_football_fans_cleared_of_singing_songs_in_support_of_terrorist_organisation/

[4] Downloadable PDF from
www.legislation.gov.uk/asp/2012/1/pdfs/asp_20120001_en.pdf
[5] http://www.dailyrecord.co.uk/news/scottish-news/hate-parade-sickening-scotsextremists-6978496
[6] http://www.dailyrecord.co.uk/news/scottish-news/right-wing-scottish-defence league-8101283
[7] http://www.dailyrecord.co.uk/news/scottish-news/hate-parade-sickening-scots
extremists-6978496
[8] http://www.dailyrecord.co.uk/sport/football/isnt-there-enough-to-worry-about-without-beating-991268
[9] I can find no references online, but this practice is explained at the Scottish Mining Museum in Newtongrange.
[10] In my own experience, I worked at Scottish Power next to two sisters, whose mother worked in another section, a trainee manager, whose father was a manager, as well as various husbands and wives and nieces and nephews. My wife worked at Post Office Counters, where different families had three generations working together. Religion never entered into it; it was just nepotism, pure and simple.
[11] http://www.hiddenglasgow.com/forums/viewtopic.php?f=3&t=3023&start=60
[12] http://www.vanguardbears.co.uk/same-city-council-same-old-story.html
[13] http://www.hiddenglasgow.com/forums/viewtopic.php?f=3&t=3023&start=15
[14] http://www.vanguardbears.co.uk/same-city-council-same-old-story.html
[15] http://www.sconews.co.uk/news/18734/is-glasgow-planning-a-u-turn-on-orange
walks/
[16] http://www.dailyrecord.co.uk/news/scottish-news/orangefest-orange-order-event-goes-5833335
[17] http://www.bbc.co.uk/news/uk-scotland-glasgow-west-25658184
[18] http://www.bbc.co.uk/news/uk-scotland-glasgow-west-30045419
[19] http://www.dailyrecord.co.uk/sport/football/football-news/after-rangers-bigges-tever-win-1447935

[20] http://www.vanguardbears.co.uk/article.php?i=2&a=rangers-chomsky-and propaganda
[21] http://www.dailyrecord.co.uk/sport/football/football-news/silent-majority-need
to-rise-up-1512272

Chapter 9

[1] Downloadable PDF at http://www.orangeorderscotland.com/page12.html
[2] https://liamconway.wordpress.com/2013/01/10/catholic-schools-religious discrimination-and-racism/
[3] ibid
[4] http://www.scotsman.com/news/education/creationist-row-headteachers removed-from-school-1-3091562
[5] www.gla.ac.uk/media/media_425530_en.pdf
[6] http://www.ed.ac.uk/education/about-us/maps-estates-history/history/part-one
[7] www.scran.ac.uk/scotland/pdf/SP2_1Education.pdf
[8] http://archive.spectator.co.uk/article/16th-september-1871/8/the-edinburgh hospital-schools
[9] https://www.humanism.scot/what-we-do/education/
[10] http://www.secularsociety.scot/
[11] http://www.scotsman.com/lifestyle/kirsty-wark-interview-the-long-wark-home1-1029824
[12] ibid
[13] http://www.dailymail.co.uk/news/article-3908286/Newsnight-presenter-Kirsty-Wark-signs-saying-s-going-play-national-anthem-shows-God-Save-Queen-Sex-Pistols-instead.html
[14] http://www.heraldscotland.com/news/11908136.Catholic_school_backlash_put_McConnell_on_the_retreat_Bishops_warn_of_election_consequences/
[15] http://www.heraldscotland.com/news/11909453.Conti_attacks_critics_of_Catholic_schools/
[16] http://www.heraldscotland.com/news/12336245.Some_former_pupils_show_the_way/
[17] http://www.heraldscotland.com/news/11909453.Conti_attacks_critics_of_Catholic_schools/

Chapter 10

[1] http://www.grandorangelodge.co.uk/history.aspx?id=99481#.V_GjnuQVBjo
[2] http://struggle.ws/talks/king_billy.html
[3] http://www.bbc.co.uk/history/british/civil_war_revolution/william_iii_01.shtml
[4] https://www.britannica.com/event/Edict-of-Nantes
[5] https://www.geni.com/projects/Nine-Years-War-1688-1697/11816
[6] http://www.prca.org/books/portraits/orange.htm
[7] Downloadable PDF 'Battle of the Boyne' at http://www.orangeorderscotland.com/page12.html
[8] http://faculty.history.wisc.edu/sommerville/123/123%20600%20James%20II.htm
[9] http://forum.followfollow.com/showthread.php?758598-Ceptic-Park-Closed-During-the-War
[10] http://www.redflag.org.uk/frontline/four/04sectar.html#notes
[11] http://churchandstate.org.uk/2016/06/hitler-the-catholic/
[12] http://liberalslikechrist.org/Catholic/Hitlersfaith-1.html
[13] http://catholicarrogance.org/Catholic/Hitlersfaith-3.html
[14] http://www.historylearningsite.co.uk/nazi-germany/the-church-in-nazi-germany/
[15] http://www.bibliotecapleyades.net/vatican/esp_vatican55.htm
[16] http://www.winstonchurchill.org/resources/myths/churchill-knew-about-the-holocaust
[17] http://www.telegraph.co.uk/culture/books/non_fictionreviews/3667859/Winston-Churchill-a-good-friend-to-the-Jews.html
[18] http://www.ewtn.com/library/ISSUES/BLETP12.HTM
[19] http://www.renewamerica.com/columns/abbott/090507
[20] http://archive.adl.org/braun/dim_14_1_role_church.html#.V_IB2JUVBjo
[21] http://www.history.ucsb.edu/faculty/marcuse/classes/33d/projects/church/Church/PiusXIIHolly.htm
[22] http://www.renewamerica.com/columns/abbott/090507
[23] http://www.pbs.org/wgbh/pages/frontline/shows/nazis/readings/sinister.html
[24] ibid
[25] http://www.jewishgen.org/ForgottenCamps/General/TimeEng.html
[26] http://articles.latimes.com/1998/jan/13/news/mn-7822
[27] http://hmd.org.uk/resources/stories/paul-gr%C3%BCninger
[28] http://www.pbs.org/wgbh/pages/frontline/shows/nazis/readings/sinister.html
[29] ibid
[30] http://www.independent.co.uk/news/the-nazis-british-bankers-1275885.html
[31] http://www.nytimes.com/1998/05/31/books/l-defending-the-swiss-072117.html?_r=0

32 https://en.wikipedia.org/wiki/Plan_W
33 http://www.irishcentral.com/news/nazi-plans-to-invade-ireland-revealed 97376329-237361631
34 https://en.wikipedia.org/wiki/Operation_Green_(Ireland)
35 http://victims.org.uk/nazi.html
36 http://www.independent.co.uk/voices/commentators/fisk/robert-fisk-german-u-boats-refuelled-in-ireland-surely-not-2356105.html
37 http://www.jewishireland.org/irish-jewish-history/history/
38 http://www.curragh.info/klines.htm
39 http://www.telegraph.co.uk/culture/books/3665355/The-ties-between-the-Mob-and-the-allies.html
40 http://www.jewishireland.org/irish-jewish-history/history/
41 ibid
42 http://www.history.ac.uk/ihr/Focus/War/reviews/revkellysean.html
43 http://www.museeprotestant.org/en/notice/protestantism-in-switzerland/
44 http://www.politics.ie/forum/history/180381-shatter-ww2-neutrality-moral-bankruptcy.html
45 http://whatishappeninginsouthafrica.blogspot.co.uk/2011/06/ossewabrandwag.html

Chapter 11

1 http://infed.org/mobi/samuel-smiles-and-self-help/
2 'Walk the Walk and Talk the Talk' Downloadable PDF at https://journals.equinoxpub.com/index.php/HSCC/article/view/16922
3 http://www.bbc.co.uk/news/uk-11701269
4 http://talfanzine.com/sectarianism.htm
5 http://stv.tv/news/west-central/1370844-young-rangers-fan-s-shock-after-abhorrent-bottle-attack/
6 ibid
7 http://followfollowfilth.blogspot.co.uk/2008/03/scotsman-15031996-man-was-jailed-for.html
8 http://news.bbc.co.uk/1/hi/scotland/3486456.stm
9 http://discuss.glasgowguide.co.uk/index.php?showtopic=1084&st=30&
10 http://www.heraldscotland.com/news/12516752.Pastor_Jack_Glass/
11 http://discuss.glasgowguide.co.uk/index.php?showtopic=1084&st=30&
12 https://www.theguardian.com/news/2004/feb/28/guardianobituaries.religion
13 http://www.bbc.co.uk/news/uk-scotland-11216562
14 https://en.wikipedia.org/wiki/Glasgow_Hillhead_by-election,_1982
15 https://www.youtube.com/watch?v=2Kh4S_6z0ss
16 http://www.dailyrecord.co.uk/news/politics/jewish-mp-storms-out-partys-8320876

[17] http://www.zionbaptists.org.uk/pdf/spvsummer2014.pdf Page 10
[18] ibid. Pages 7, 9
[19] https://outreachjudaism.org/evangelizing-the-jews/
[20] http://www.gla.ac.uk/stafflist/?action=person&id=4fdde9e48495
[21] http://scottishchristian.com/labour-msp-sang-the-sash-at-rangers-match/
[22] http://www.dailyrecord.co.uk/news/local-news/rev-hits-out-old-firm-2620790
[23] ibid
[24] http://www.lyricsmode.com/lyrics/d/dropkick_murphys/fields_of_athenry.html
[25] https://en.wikipedia.org/wiki/The_Masque_of_Anarchy
[26] http://wearenotthepeople.blogspot.co.uk/2008/09/racist-famine-song.html
[27] http://www.thetimes.co.uk/tto/news/uk/scotland/article2631660.ece
[28] http://www.scotsman.com/lifestyle/insight-glasgow-city-of-culture-25-years-on-1-3899379
[29] http://www.dailyrecord.co.uk/news/local-news/rutherglen-man-who-brought-mandela-2913988
[30] http://www.eveningtimes.co.uk/news/13269123.The_day_Mandela_danced_in_square/
[31] http://www.workerscity.org/keelie/july_1992.html
[32] http://www.dailyrecord.co.uk/news/local-news/rev-hits-out-old-firm-2620790

Chapter 12

[1] http://www.catholicherald.co.uk/commentandblogs/2014/10/31/pope-franciss-comments-on-the-big-bang-are-not-revolutionary-catholic-teaching-has-long-professed-the-likelihood-of-human-evolution/
[2] http://physicsoftheuniverse.com/scientists_lemaitre.html
[3] http://www.intelligentdesign.org/
[4] http://www.genesisexpo.org.uk/
[5] http://www.belfasttelegraph.co.uk/news/politics/caleb-foundation-the-creationist-bible-group-and-its-web-of-influence-at-stormont-28787760.html
[6] http://www.newstatesman.com/blogs/politics/2012/07/creationism-and-political-power-northern-ireland
[7] http://www.express.co.uk/news/uk/611231/Richard-Dawkins-in-extraordinary-blast-at-Muslims-To-hell-with-their-culture
[8] http://www.telegraph.co.uk/education/educationnews/7951358/Richard-Dawkins-faith-schools-should-not-be-allowed-to-opt-out-of-religious-education.html
[9] http://www.dailymail.co.uk/news/article-2251963/Being-raised-Catholic-worse-child-abuse-Latest-incendiary-claim-atheist-professor-Richard-

Dawkins.html
[10] ibid
[11] http://irishsalem.com/individuals/writers-and-journalists/richard-dawkins/index.php
[12] http://www.theatlantic.com/politics/archive/2011/12/a-dumb-persons-idea-of-a-smart-person-whose-line-is-it/249932/
[13] http://www.intelligencesquared.com/events/the-catholic-church-is-a-force-for-good-in-the-world/
[14] http://freethinker.co.uk/2009/10/20/catholic-church-humiliated-by-fry-and-hitchens-in-an-historic-london-debate/
[15] http://www.amindatplay.eu/en/2009/12/02/intelligence%c2%b2-catholic-church-debate-transcript/
[16] https://www.scribd.com/document/227140541/Hume-David-A-Letter
[17] http://www.amindatplay.eu/en/2009/12/02/intelligence%c2%b2-catholic-church-debate-transcript/
[18] https://www.theguardian.com/uk/2005/jun/05/religion.hayfestival2005
[19] https://web.archive.org/web/20051013055101/http://www.amconmag.com/2005/2005_10_10/article3.html
[20] http://www.amindatplay.eu/en/2009/12/02/intelligence%c2%b2-catholic-church-debate-transcript/
[21] William L Shirer - *The Rise and Fall of the Third Reich* (Simon and Schuster, (1990) p 236
[22] http://www.amindatplay.eu/en/2009/12/02/intelligence%c2%b2-catholic-church-debate-transcript/
[23] http://www.indcatholicnews.com/news.php?viewStory=15028
[24] https://www.youtube.com/watch?v=I6sz8D411kE (Comments section)

Chapter 13

[1] https://www.youtube.com/watch?v=SKQkF-j_RnM
[2] http://freethinker.co.uk/2009/12/16/there-will-be-no-sequels-to-the-golden-compass-because-of-catholic-pressure/
[3] http://www.imdb.com/title/tt0385752/board/nest/224568787?ref_=tt_bd_2
[4] http://freethinker.co.uk/2009/12/16/there-will-be-no-sequels-to-the-golden-compass-because-of-catholic-pressure/
[5] ibid
[6] Downloadable PDF at www.wiu.edu/cas/history/wihr/pdfs/Banwart-MoralMajorityVol5.pdf
[7] http://tvseriesfinale.com/tv-show/soap/
[8] http://www.americamagazine.org/issue/281/article/last-acceptable-prejudice
[9] Tom Holland – *Rubicon, The Triumph and Tragedy of the Roman Republic* (Abacus, 2004) pp 210-211

[10] http://www.americamagazine.org/issue/281/article/last-acceptable-prejudice
[11] http://theweek.com/articles/453057/most-bigoted-anticatholic-column-youll-read-year
[12] http://www.cbsnews.com/news/supreme-court-exempts-hobby-lobby-from-obamacare-contraception-mandate/
[13] ibid
[14] http://www.usnews.com/debate-club/do-the-little-sisters-of-the-poor-have-a-case-against-obamacare
[15] http://www.usnews.com/
[16] http://www.usnews.com/opinion/blogs/jamie-stiehm/2014/01/07/the-catholic-supreme-courts-war-on-women
[17] ibid
[18] ibid
[19] http://magazine.nd.edu/news/1155-the-right-of-a-catholic-to-be-president/
[20] http://history1800s.about.com/od/immigration/a/knownothing01.htm
[21] http://www.nypress.com/bill-the-butcher-he-died-a-true-american-but-not-how-you-think/
[22] http://www.history.com/news/history-lists/7-infamous-gangs-of-new-york
[23] https://www.firstthings.com/blogs/firstthoughts/2016/03/know-nothings-and-the-republican-coalition
[24] https://leanleft.com/2015/09/24/is-the-republican-party-becoming-todays-know- nothing-party/
[25] http://newstalk1130.iheart.com/onair/common-sense-central-37717/the-democratic-party-and-the-kkk-11769046/
[26] http://www.catholicleague.org/anti-catholic-political-ad-washington-st-2/
[27] http://www.huffingtonpost.com/matthew-bowman/is-mormonism-a-cult_b_1332204.html
[28] http://www.defendchristians.org/commentary/mitt-romneys-racist-mormon-skeletons/
[29] http://www.imdb.com/title/tt0436629/?ref_=fn_al_tt_1
[30] http://www.factcheck.org/2011/03/romneycare-facts-and-falsehoods/
[31] http://www.americanthinker.com/articles/2011/06/the_un-american_american_president.html
[32] http://catholicism.org/catholics-who-serve-planned-parenthood-in-the-massachusetts-house-of-representatives-naming-names-pulling-no-punches.html
[33] http://www.americamagazine.org/issue/281/article/last-acceptable-prejudice

Chapter 14

[1] Chesney. Op. Cit. pp 325-326
[2] https://www.theguardian.com/commentisfree/2007/jul/16/art.comment See the quote from Ken Tynan used by 'insouciance' in the comments section.

3 http://home.wlv.ac.uk/~fa1871/expagate.gif#
4 https://www.youtube.com/watch?v=otXIaIxkWTI
5 http://www.ibtimes.co.uk/harriet-harman-pie-nccl-controversy-what-was-paedophile-information-exchange-1437862
6 http://www.spiked-online.com/newsite/article/the-nccl-was-right-to-affiliate-with-pie/14718#.WClpZZVvhjo
7 http://www.bbc.co.uk/news/magazine-26352378
8 https://en.wikipedia.org/wiki/Paedophile_Information_Exchange
9 http://www.mirror.co.uk/news/uk-news/paedophile-information-exchange-leon-brittan-5825108
10 https://theukdatabase.com/councillorspolitical-party-affiliated/ westminster-scandal-114-secret-files-on-paedophile-cases-missing/more-than-10-politicians-on-list-held-by-police-investigating-westminster-paedophile-ring/the-civil-servant-in-the-home-offices-pie-funding-inquiry-and-his-academic-articles-on-boy-love/p-i-e/
11 http://www.express.co.uk/news/uk/485529/Special-Branch-funded-Paedophile-Information-Exchange-says-Home-Office-whistleblower
12 http://www.bibliotecapleyades.net/sumer_anunnaki/reptiles/reptiles12.htm
13 http://www.dailymail.co.uk/femail/article-1266664/Mandy-Smith-I-DID-sleep-Bill-Wyman-I-14--man-life-God.html#ixzz0lemZCzQJ
14 https://www.theguardian.com/uk/2001/nov/21/childprotection.society
15 http://www.ibtimes.co.uk/kincora-boys-home-mi5-westminster-paedophile-ring-1512230
16 https://www.theguardian.com/politics/2015/mar/17/westminster-child-abuse-paedophile-ring-failure
17 http://www.telegraph.co.uk/news/uknews/1580284/Secrets-and-terror-of-Jersey-care-home.html
18 http://www.express.co.uk/scotland/588918/Top-Scotland-school-abuse-claims
19 ibid
20 http://www.telegraph.co.uk/news/uknews/1421898/Dunblane-100-year-ban-on-report-may-be-lifted.html
21 http://www.express.co.uk/news/uk/380350/Cardinal-Keith-O-Brien-s-close-friendship-with-Jimmy-Savile-revealed
22 http://news.bbc.co.uk/1/hi/england/452614.stm
23 https://www.theguardian.com/uk/2006/oct/14/ukcrime.weekend7
24 https://en.wikipedia.org/wiki/Gary_Glitter
25 http://www.bbc.co.uk/news/10407559
26 http://www.imdb.com/title/tt1895587/?ref_=nv_sr_1
27 https://www.theguardian.com/film/2016/jan/28/spotlight-review-catholic-church-called-to-account-over-child-abuse
28 ibid
29 ibid
30 http://www.telegraph.co.uk/films/2016/04/14/spotlight-review-skin-

prickling/
[31] http://www.imdb.com/title/tt0117665/
[32] https://en.wikipedia.org/wiki/69th_Academy_Awards
[33] http://www.nytimes.com/1996/10/22/movies/sleepers-debate-renewed-how-true-is-a-true-story.html
[34] http://www.imdb.com/title/tt0896872/
[35] https://www.theguardian.com/world/2012/jan/15/bosnia-sex-trafficking-whistleblower
[36] https://en.wikipedia.org/wiki/83rd_Academy_Awards
[37] http://www.rogerebert.com/reviews/the-whistleblower-2011
[38] https://gotquestions.org/Catholic-abuse.html
[39] https://www.theguardian.com/commentisfree/andrewbrown/2010/mar/19/religion-catholicism-celibacy-ireland VoxAC30, Comments section page 1
[40] http://prospect.org/article/next-christian-sex-abuse-scandal
[41] ibid
[42] http://www.houstonpress.com/news/parents-never-dreamed-sending-their-kid-to-camp-la-junta-would-turn-into-a-sexual-abuse-nightmare-6357754
[43] https://www.revealnews.org/blog/jehovahs-witnesses-sex-abuse-scandal-is-a-lot-like-catholic-churchs/
[44] http://www.cultwatch.com/jw.html
[45] http://news.bbc.co.uk/sport1/hi/football/scot_prem/9230531.stm
[46] http://www.telegraph.co.uk/sport/football/competitions/scottish-premier/8171463/Leading-scientist-Richard-Dawkins-slams-Scottish-Football-Association-over-sacking-of-Hugh-Dallas.html
[47] http://www.vanguardbears.co.uk/article.php?i=31&a=celtic-and-child-abuse-inextricably-linked-
[48] http://www.heraldscotland.com/news/12364258.Celtic_Boys_apos__Club_founder_guilty_of_shameless_indecency_Anger_over_allegations_suggesting_that_Jock_Stein_was_involved_in_20_year_cover_up/
[49] http://www.dailyrecord.co.uk/news/uk-world-news/football-paedophile-ring-covered-up-9333193
[50] http://www.dailyrecord.co.uk/news/uk-world-news/former-scotland-star-pat-nevin-9329786
[51] http://www.dailyrecord.co.uk/news/uk-world-news/nspcc-launches-dedicated-football-hotline-9320641
[52] https://twitter.com/LordMcConnell/status/802235035193524224?lang=en-gb
[53] ibid
[54] https://themanthebheastscanttame.wordpress.com/2012/11/12/the-celtic-sex-case-2/
[55] http://www.dailystar.co.uk/news/latest-news/432102/Special-Branch-covered-up-Cyril-Smith-crimes-seven-times
[56] http://www.breitbart.com/london/2014/07/08/calling-all-tin-foil-hat-wearing-internet-conspiracy-theorists/

[57] http://www.telegraph.co.uk/culture/tvandradio/bbc/10235967/BBC-is-biased-toward-the-left-study-finds.html
[58] http://www.independent.co.uk/news/uk/politics/bbc-accused-of-political-bias-on-the-right-not-the-left-9129639.html
[59] https://theukdatabase.com/uk-child-abusers-named-and-shamed/muslim-paedo-rings-in-the-uk-why-how/

Chapter 15

1 http://www.telegraph.co.uk/culture/books/3664862/The-forgotten-history-of-Britains-white-slaves.html
[2] http://www.thejournal.ie/readme/irish-slaves-myth-2369653-Oct2015/
[3] http://www.history.ac.uk/ihr/Focus/Slavery/articles/emmer.html
[4] Downloadable-PDF-at https://www.researchgate.net/publication/41125777_Response_to_Pieter_C_Emmer%27s_%27Reconsideration%27
[5] http://www.history.ac.uk/ihr/Focus/Slavery/articles/emmer.html
[6] ibid
[7] http://www.thejournal.ie/readme/irish-slaves-myth-2369653-Oct2015/
[8] http://nationalhumanitiescenter.org/tserve/freedom/1609-1865/essays/slavelabor.htm
[9] http://www.historyireland.com/early-modern-history-1500-1700/shipped-for-the-barbadoes-cromwell-and-irish-migration-to-the-caribbean/
[10] ibid
[11] http://news.bbc.co.uk/1/hi/world/americas/1523669.stm
[12] http://revisionisthistory.org/page1/page3/page3.html
13 http://www.africaresource.com/rasta/sesostris-the-great-the-egyptian-hercules/the-irish-slave-trade-forgotten-white-slaves/
[14] http://www.ushistory.org/us/30a.asp
[15] ibid
[16] http://revisionisthistory.org/page1/page3/page3.html
[17] ibid
[18] http://www.realjewnews.com/?p=375
[19] http://revisionisthistory.org/page1/page3/page3.html
[20] http://www.electricscotland.com/history/other/white_slavery.htm
[21] http://www.dailystormer.com/the-history-of-white-slavery/
[22] https://www.splcenter.org/
[23] https://www.splcenter.org/hatewatch
24 https://www.splcenter.org/hatewatch/2016/04/19/how-myth-irish-slaves-became-favorite-meme-racists-online
[25] ibid
26 https://medium.com/@Limerick1914/the-imagery-of-the-irish-slaves-myth-

dissected-143e70aa6e74#.dugyl3ycm
[27] https://www.opendemocracy.net/beyondslavery/liam-hogan/%e2%80%98irish-slaves%e2%80%99-convenient-myth
[28] ibid
[29] http://www.thejournal.ie/readme/john-mitchel-was-hailed-as-a-totem-for-irish-liberty-but-he-was-a-white-supremacist-1266182-Jan2014/
[30] http://talkingpointsmemo.com/edblog/was-lincoln-a-racist
[31] https://www.theguardian.com/commentisfree/2015/jul/17/prince-philip-who-you-sponge-off Comments section, page 2
[32] ibid
[33] ibid page 4
[34] http://www.thejournal.ie/readme/irish-slaves-myth-2369653-Oct2015/
[35] http://www.belfasttelegraph.co.uk/opinion/columnists/ruth-dudley-edwards/yes-so-ireland-was-occupied-get-over-it-and-look-at-how-the-invaders-spared-us-a-worse-fate-34814536.html
[36] http://www.dailystormer.com/the-history-of-white-slavery/
[37] http://obrag.org/?p=34626
[38] http://www.historyireland.com/20th-century-contemporary-history/fidel-castro-in-a-miniskirt-bernadette-devlins-first-us-tour/
[39] http://www.historyireland.com/early-modern-history-1500-1700/shipped-for-the-barbadoes-cromwell-and-irish-migration-to-the-caribbean/

Chapter 16

[1] http://www.irishtimes.com/culture/books/unhappy-the-land-by-liam-kennedy-review-sceptic-debunks-irish-history-as-hysteria-1.2538462
[2] https://ansionnachfionn.com/2011/08/29/black-provos-the-anc-and-the-ira/
[3] http://www.independent.co.uk/voices/comment/time-to-remember-nelson-mandela-s-soft-touch-with-the-ira-9029511.html
[4] http://www.ruthdudleyedwards.co.uk/journalism13/IrInd13_49.html
[5] http://www.express.co.uk/news/politics/666284/Gerry-Adams-sparks-outrage-when-using-N-word-talk-about-slavery-movie-Django-Unchained
[6] http://www.ruthdudleyedwards.co.uk/journalism16/IrInd16_12.html
[7] ibid
[8] http://www.dailykos.com/story/2015/3/22/1371801/-Bernadette-Devlin-McAliskey-an-Irish-heroine
[9] http://www.rsdb.org/search?q=Irish
[10] http://streetcarnage.com/blog/one-less-white-nigger/
[11] http://www.lrb.co.uk/v12/n08/paul-foot/bogwogs
[12] http://www.express.co.uk/news/politics/666284/Gerry-Adams-sparks-outrage-when-using-N-word-talk-about-slavery-movie-Django-Unchained

[13] http://www.irishtimes.com/profile/bernice-harrison-7.1010641
[14] https://twitter.com/mcdigby/status/801413031729233920
[15] https://theirishrevolution.wordpress.com/2011/08/01/politics-and-the-rise-of-revisionism/
[16] http://www.ruthdudleyedwards.co.uk/journalism13/IrInd13_49.html
[17] http://cain.ulst.ac.uk/issues/discrimination/gudgin99.htm
[18] ibid
[19] http://ulstersdoomed.blogspot.co.uk/2009/06/partition-and-repartition-part-4-udas.html
[20] http://www.heraldscotland.com/news/12701362.UDA__apos_has_drawn_up_Doomsday_plan_apos_/
[21] ibid
[22] ibid
[23] http://ulstersdoomed.blogspot.co.uk/2009/06/partition-and-repartition-part-4-udas.html
[24] http://www.irishexaminer.com/ireland/de-valera-and-the-churchs-special-position-218651.html
[25] http://www.metrolyrics.com/banana-republic-lyrics-boomtown-rats.html
[26] http://www.historylearningsite.co.uk/ireland-1845-to-1922/eamonn-de-valera/
[27] http://www.independent.ie/entertainment/books/de-valera-and-the-one-true-church-26420375.html
[28] https://www.academia.edu/8348624/Examining_Peter_Hart
[29] Niall Meehan - *Distorting Irish History, the stubborn facts of Kilmichael: Peter Hart and Irish Historiography* Downloadable PDF at
http://jeffdudgeon.com/download/Irish%20political%20controversies/Peter%20Hart%20-%20'Distorting%20Irish%20History'%20article%20by%20Niall%20Meehan%20in%20Spiwatch%202010.doc
[30] http://www.theirishstory.com/2010/08/09/peter-hart-a-legacy/#.WED1--Rvhjp
[31] https://www.academia.edu/8348624/Examining_Peter_Hart
[32] Niall Meehan. Op. Cit.
http://jeffdudgeon.com/download/Irish%20political%20controversies/Peter%20Hart%20-%20'Distorting%20Irish%20History'%20article Meehan%20in%20Spinwatch%202010.doc
[33] https://theirishrevolution.wordpress.com/2011/08/01/politics-and-the-rise-of-revisionism/
[34] ibid
[35] http://www.bbc.co.uk/blogs/ni/2008/12/conor_cruise_obrien_a_life_in_1.html
[36] http://www.irishcentral.com/news/death-of-conor-cruise-obrien-3696-237609261
[37] https://www.foreignaffairs.com/reviews/capsule-review/1996-03-01/eve-millennium-future-democracy-through-age-unreason

[38] https://theirishrevolution.wordpress.com/2011/08/01/politics-and-the-rise-of-revisionism/#_ftn25
[39] https://ansionnachfionn.com/stair-history/wolfe-tone-prophet-of-irish-independence/
[40] http://www.indymedia.ie/article/76386
[41] http://www.indymedia.ie/attachments/jun2006/ipr_may_2006p3.gif
[42] https://theirishrevolution.wordpress.com/2011/08/01/politics-and-the-rise-of-revisionism/
[43] http://www.belfasttelegraph.co.uk/news/republic-of-ireland/gerry-adams-sinn-fein-as-well-as-we-could-in-irish-general-election-34494133.html
[44] http://www.historyireland.com/20th-century-contemporary-history/orangeism-the-making-of-a-tradition-kevin-haddick-flynn-wolfhound-press-30-isbn-0863276598-the-faithful-tribe-an-intimate-portrait-of-the-loyal-institutions-ruth-dudley-edwards-harper-colli/
[45] http://www.judecollins.com/2014/07/ruthie-faithful-tribe/
[46] http://www.belfasttelegraph.co.uk/opinion/columnists/ruth-dudley-edwards/success-on-the-pitch-would-be-the-perfect-way-for-resurgent-rangers-to-confound-those-who-choose-to-demonise-club-34774268.html
[47] http://www.ruthdudleyedwards.co.uk/nonfiction/RDE-writingTribe.html
[48] http://www.historytoday.com/tom-reilly/cromwell-irish-question
[49] ibid
[50] ibid
[51] ibid
[52] http://www.libraryireland.com/HistoryIreland/Massacre-Drogheda.php
[53] http://www.ruthdudleyedwards.co.uk/nonfiction/RDE-writingTribe.html
[54] http://www.telegraph.co.uk/news/uknews/scottish-independence/11099326/Bob-Geldof-and-Eddie-Izzard-at-pro-union-rally-in-London.html

Chapter 17

[1] http://www.voice-online.co.uk/article/black-people-still-over-represented-prison-system
[2] http://www.boulderweekly.com/news/black-men-still-overrepresented-in-prison/
[3] http://www.bbc.co.uk/news/world-us-canada-35255835
[4] https://www.theguardian.com/society/2010/oct/11/black-prison-population-increase-england
[5] Look at the Comments Section on this article:
http://www.thecommentator.com/article/4024/uk_church_asks_british_pm_why_so_many_blacks_are_in_jail
[6] ibid

[7] http://spartacus-educational.com/2WWcrime.htm
[8] http://www.gov.scot/Topics/People/Equality/Equalities/DataGrid/Ethnicity/EthPopMig
[9] http://scottishlaw.blogspot.co.uk/2011/10/sectarian-scotland-reports-on-prison.html
[10] ibid
[11] ibid
[12] http://www.bbc.co.uk/news/uk-scotland-edinburgh-east-fife-14718038
[13] ibid
[14] https://www.theguardian.com/football/2011/sep/30/neil-lennon-hearts-fan
[15] https://www.theguardian.com/football/2012/apr/27/neil-lennon-bomb-plotters-jailed
[16] http://www.bbc.co.uk/news/uk-scotland-glasgow-west-17561849
[17] https://www.theguardian.com/football/2012/apr/27/neil-lennon-bomb-plotters-jailed
[18] https://www.eveningexpress.co.uk/pipe/news/scotland/trio-jailed-for-johnny-mad-dog-adair-murder-plot/
[19] http://www.dailyrecord.co.uk/news/scottish-news/mad-dog-murder-plot-accused-5730276
[20] http://www.eveningtimes.co.uk/news/13308250.Adair_accused_described_as__fantasist_/
[21] Downloadable PDF at :
https://dspace.stir.ac.uk/bitstream/1893/1763/1/An%20outsider%20in%20our%2midst.pdf
[22] http://www.dailyrecord.co.uk/news/scottish-news/former-celtic-manager-neil-lennon-6862305 Have a look at the Comments Section, where one idiot claims the picture showing Lennon being attacked was 'photoshopped', even though everyone had seen the incident on television.
[23] http://www.dailyrecord.co.uk/incoming/celtic-star-anthony-stokes-caught-3480659
[24] http://www.scotsman.com/sport/tom-english-the-self-pitying-goram-still-sees-himself-as-the-victim-1-1362600
[25] http://www.scotsman.com/sport/football/teams/celtic/celtic-punish-anthony-stokes-for-attending-real-ira-linked-function-1-2686483
[26] ibid
[27] http://www.hibs.net/showthread.php?251689-Tom-English-on-Anthony-Stokes
[28] http://www.telegraph.co.uk/news/uknews/crime/7882762/Raoul-Moat-Gazza-arrives-in-Rothbury-to-offer-his-support.html
[29] http://www.dailyrecord.co.uk/news/crime/drink-driver-25000-year-buckfast-7359462
[30] ibid
[31] ibid

[32] http://www.dailyrecord.co.uk/news/scottish-news/buckfast-breeds-violence-sheriff-blasts-9403289#rlabs=2%20rt$sitewide%20p$10
[33] ibid
[34] ibid
[35] http://www.express.co.uk/news/uk/177475/Labour-call-for-ban-on-Buckfast-in-fight-against-drink-abuse
[36] http://www.sciencedirect.com/science/article/pii/S0149763414001729
[37] http://www.dailymail.co.uk/news/article-2574594/Teenager-18-downed-ten-Jagerbombs-nightclub-two-one-offer-three-heart-attacks-DIED-brought-lifedefibrillator.html
[38] http://www.buckfast.com/history
[39] http://scottishchristian.com/catholics-in-scotland-more-likely-to-struggle/
[40] https://glasgowguardian.co.uk/2013/11/15/the-real-losers-of-glasgow-2014/
[41] http://paddyontherailway12.blogspot.co.uk/2014/07/close-seasons-greetin.html
[42] http://www.vanguardbears.co.uk/the-commonwealth-con.html
[43] http://www.glasgowsociology.com/eminent-scottish-history-professor-tom-devine-attacks-anti-sectarianism-industry-and-calls-for-qualitative-research-to-inform-policy/
[44] http://www.tandfonline.com/doi/abs/10.1080/0141987032000087343?journalCode=rers20
[45] http://www.tandfonline.com/doi/full/10.1080/0141987042000280058?src=recsys
[46] http://www.gov.scot/Publications/2005/01/20553/50500
[47] http://www.glasgowsociology.com/eminent-scottish-history-professor-tom-devine-attacks-anti-sectarianism-industry-and-calls-for-qualitative-research-to-inform-policy/
[48] http://www.tandfonline.com/doi/full/10.1080/01419870500092977?src=recsys
[49] http://www.gov.scot/Publications/2005/01/20553/50500 Paragraph 3.4
[50] http://www.bbc.co.uk/news/uk-england-south-yorkshire-19507065
[51] Chesney. Op. Cit. p.344
[52] http://www.gov.scot/Publications/2005/01/20553/50500 Paragraph 3.6
[53] http://ifyouknowtheirhistory.blogspot.co.uk/2009/03/evil-beyond-belief.html

Chapter 18

[1] I base this on my own experience. People I have met from Northern Ireland cannot believe that such a place as Larkhall exists. They have heard of it but think it is some kind of urban myth.
[2] https://www.geni.com/people/William-III-King-of-England-Ireland-and-Scotland/6000000003285553237

[3] http://www.nybooks.com/articles/1977/02/03/the-true-history-of-the-catholics-in-england/
[4] http://www.puseyhouse.org.uk/what-was-the-oxford-movement.html
[5] http://protestanttruth.com/history/
[6] http://christianity.about.com/od/Christians-In-History/a/JZ-John-Knox.htm
[7] Downloadable-PDF-at
http://www.scran.ac.uk/scotland/pdf/SP2_8religion.pdf
[8] http://www.discoveryourancestors.co.uk/sitting-on-the-penitents-stool/#
[9] http://www.sacred-texts.com/etc/fcod/fcod11.htm
[10] Downloadable-PDF-at
http://www.scran.ac.uk/scotland/pdf/SP2_8religion.pdf - Section 3
[11] ibid
[12] http://www.chartists.net/chartist-varieties-and-rivals/christian-chartists/
[13] This was to be the theme of my own PhD thesis. Unfortunately, I could not get funding; the Scottish Grants Committee claimed that it came under the remit of the Economic and Social Research Council, since it was Social History, while the ESRC claimed that it was History and nothing to do with them. There were grants available from charities, but living expenses were not included. I gave up after that. Still, I am sure the World will manage to go on without the information I would have gleaned!
[14] http://www.chartists.net/conferences_and_conventions/scottish-convention-1842/
[15] ibid
[16] Downloadable PDF at
http://www.orangeorderscotland.com/History%20of%20the%20Orange%20Order.pdf
[17] http://workethic.coe.uga.edu/hpro.html
[18] http://www.glasgowwestend.co.uk/garngad-heaven-hell-ian-r-mitchell/
[19] http://www.catholic.com/quickquestions/who-said-love-the-sinner-hate-the-sin
[20] http://rickthomas.net/why-hate-the-sin-love-the-sinner-can-be-dangerous-theology-2/
[21] http://johnpavlovitz.com/2015/08/13/3-reasons-love-the-sinner-hate-the-sin-is-an-abomination/
[22] https://www.gotquestions.org/elect-of-God.html
[23] https://expreacherman.com/2013/09/14/notes-on-calvinism-calvinism-a-rigged-carnival-game/
[24] http://calvinandcalvinism.com/?cat=10
[25] Downloadable PDF at http://docslide.us/documents/menace-of-the-irish-race-to-our-scottish-nationality.html p758
[26] http://www.churchofscotland.org.uk/about_us/our_faith
[27] http://news.bbc.co.uk/1/hi/scotland/2014961.stm
[28] Downloadable PDF at http://docslide.us/documents/menace-of-the-irish-race-to-our-scottish-nationality.html p758

[29] http://www.dailymail.co.uk/news/article-2587215/Sharia-Law-enshrined-British-legal-lawyers-guidelines-drawing-documents-according-Islamic-rules.html
[30] Downloadable PDF at
http://www.scran.ac.uk/scotland/pdf/SP2_8religion.pdf
Section 4